World Music Pedagogy, Volume IV

World Music Pedagogy, Volume IV: Instrumental Music Education provides the perspectives and resources to help music educators craft world-inclusive instrumental music programs in their teaching practices. Given that school instrumental music programs—concert bands, symphony orchestras, and related ensembles—have borne musical traditions that broadly reflect Western art music and military bands, instructors are often educated within the European conservatory framework. Yet a culturally diverse and inclusive music pedagogy can enrich, expand, and transform these instrumental music programs to great effect.

Drawing from years of experience as practicing music educators and band and orchestra leaders, the authors present a vision characterized by both real-world applicability and a great depth of perspective. Lesson plans, rehearsal strategies, and vignettes from practicing teachers constitute valuable resources. With carefully tuned ears to intellectual currents throughout the broader music education community, *World Music Pedagogy, Volume IV* provides readers with practical approaches and strategies for creating world-inclusive instrumental music programs.

Listening Episode music examples can be accessed on the eResource site from the Routledge catalog page.

Mark Montemayor is Professor of Music and Head of Music Education at the University of Northern Colorado.

William J. Coppola is Assistant Professor of Music Education at the University of North Texas and a Smithsonian Folkways World Music Pedagogy certified music educator.

Christopher Mena is a Smithsonian Folkways World Music Pedagogy certified music educator.

Routledge World Music Pedagogy Series

Series Editor: Patricia Shehan Campbell, University of Washington

The **Routledge World Music Pedagogy Series** encompasses principal cross-disciplinary issues in music, education, and culture in six volumes, detailing theoretical and practical aspects of World Music Pedagogy in ways that contribute to the diversification of repertoire and instructional approaches. With the growth of cultural diversity in schools and communities and the rise of an enveloping global network, there is both confusion and a clamoring by teachers for music that speaks to the multiple heritages of their students, as well as to the spectrum of expressive practices in the world that constitute the human need to sing, play, dance, and engage in the rhythms and inflections of poetry, drama, and ritual.

Volume I: Early Childhood Education
Sarah H. Watts

Volume II: Elementary Music Education
J. Christopher Roberts and Amy C. Beegle

Volume III: Secondary School Innovations
Karen Howard and Jamey Kelley

Volume IV: Instrumental Music Education
Mark Montemayor, William J. Coppola, and Christopher Mena

Volume V: Choral Music Education
Sarah J. Bartolome

Volume VI: School-Community Intersections
Patricia Shehan Campbell and Chee-Hoo Lum

World Music Pedagogy

Instrumental Music Education

Volume IV

Mark Montemayor
University of Northern Colorado

William J. Coppola
University of North Texas

Christopher Mena
University of Washington

Routledge
Taylor & Francis Group

NEW YORK AND LONDON

First published 2018
by Routledge
711 Third Avenue, New York, NY 10017

and by Routledge
2 Park Square, Milton Park, Abingdon, Oxon, OX14 4RN

Routledge is an imprint of the Taylor & Francis Group, an informa business

Library of Congress Cataloging-in-Publication Data
The Library of Congress has cataloged the combined volume edition as follows:
Names: Roberts, J. Christopher, author. | Beegle, Amy C., author.
Title: World music pedagogy.
Description: New York ; London : Routledge, 2018– | Includes bibliographical
    references and index.
Identifiers: LCCN 2017050640 (print) | LCCN 2017054487 (ebook) |
    ISBN 9781315167589 () | ISBN 9781138052727 |
    ISBN 9781138052727q(v.2 : hardback) | ISBN 9781138052796q(v.2 : pbk.)
Subjects: LCSH: Music—Instruction and study.
Classification: LCC MT1 (ebook) | LCC MT1. W92 2018 (print) |
    DDC 780.71—dc23
LC record available at https://lccn.loc.gov/2017050640

ISBN: 978-1-138-04120-2 (hbk)
ISBN: 978-1-138-04122-6 (pbk)
ISBN: 978-1-315-17460-0 (ebk)

Typeset in Times New Roman
by Apex CoVantage, LLC

Visit the eResource: www.routledge.com/9781138041226

Contents

             Awakenings   22

             Listening   23
             Recordings in Instrumental World Music
                  Pedagogy   24
             Questions, Tasks, Activities, and Goals   25
             Where to Begin?   28
             Examples for Attentive Listening   31
             Teacher Feature: John Brindle on Offering Diverse
                  Musical Practices in Band   43
             Now, Press "Play"   45

Chapter 3   Participatory Musicking   48

             Techniques of Engaged Listening   51
             From Engaged to Enactive Listening   56
             Practical Considerations of Participatory
                  Musicking   73
             From Participatory Musicking to Immersive
                  Performance   76

Chapter 4   Performing World Music   78

             World Music Pedagogy and Performance   79
             The Process of Developing WMP Performances   81
             Addressing the Details of Performance:
                  Musical Nuance   82
             From the Classroom to the Concert Stage
                  (or Community Center)   89
             Collaborating With Culture Bearers for
                  WMP Performances   94
             Connecting With Musical Cultures Through
                  Community-Based Learning   95
             Performer Feature: Indonesian Culture at
                  Canyon Crest Academy   97
             The World Music Pedagogy Process Through
                  the Performance of Published Works   97
             The Potential of Performing the World's
                  Musical Cultures   102

Chapter 5   Creating World Music   108

Chapter 6   Integrating World Music   137

Chapter 7   Surmountable Challenges and Worthy Outcomes   164

Series foreword

Turning and turning in the widening gyre
The falcon cannot hear the falconer;
Things fall apart; the centre cannot hold;
Mere anarchy is loosed upon the world . . .

(from "The Second Coming," W. B. Yeats)

There is a foreboding tone to the stanza above, which at first may seem out of sync
with a book on the pedagogy of world music. After all, music education is an intact
phenomenon, arguably innocent and pure, that envelops teachers and their students in
the acts of singing, playing, and dancing, and this field is decidedly not about falcons.
Instead, music education conjures up long-standing images of spirited high school
bands, choirs, orchestras, of young adolescents at work in guitar and keyboard classes,
of fourth grade xylophone and recorder players, of first grade rhythm bands, and of
toddlers accompanied by parents playing small drums and shakers. At a time of demographic diversity, with a wide spectrum of students of various shapes, sizes, and hues
laid wide open, music education can press further, as the field has the potential to hold
court in a child's holistic development as a core avenue for the discovery of human
cultural heritage and the celebration of multiple identities based upon race, ethnicity,
gender, religion, and socioeconomic circumstance.

Yet there is a correspondence of the stanza, and the disquiet that Yeats communicates, with this book and with the book series, the Routledge *World Music Pedagogy
Series*. I refer the reader to the start of the third line, and also to the title of a novel

x   Series Foreword

by Nigerian author Chinua Achebe. A landmark in the world's great literature, *Things Fall Apart* has been very much in mind through the conception of this project, its design and development by a team of authors, and its thematic weave in these tempestuous times. Achebe's writing of cultural misunderstanding, of the arrogance and insensitivity of Western colonizers in village Africa, of competing cultural systems, is relevant.

We raise questions relative to music teaching and learning: Do things fall apart, or prove ineffective, when they do not reflect demographic change, do not respond to cultural variation, and do not reasonably reform to meet the needs of a new era? Can music education remain relevant and useful through the full-scale continuation of conventional practices, or is there something prophetic in the statement that things fall apart, particularly in music education, if there are insufficient efforts to revise and adapt to societal evolution? There is hard-core documentation of sparkling success stories in generations of efforts to musically educate children. Yet there is also evidence of frayed, flailing, and failing programs that are the result of restrictive music selections and exclusive pedagogical decisions that leave out students, remain unlinked to local communities, and ignore a panorama of global expressions. There is the sinking feeling that music education programs exclusively rooted in Western art styles are insensitive and unethical for 21st century schools and students, and that choices of featured music are statements on people we choose to include and exclude from our world.

Consider many school programs for their long-standing means of musically educating students within a Western framework, featuring Western school-based music, following Western literate traditions of notation, Western teacher-directed modes of learning, and Western-fixed rather than flexible and spontaneously inventive musicking potentials. All are good for particular times and places, and yet arguably unethical in the exclusion of music and music-makers in the world. Certainly, all practices deserve regular review, upgrades, even overhauls. Today's broad population mix of students from everywhere in the world press on diversifying the curriculum, and the discoveries of "new" music-culture potentials are noteworthy and necessary in making for a more inclusive music education.

So, the Nigerian author selected the Irish poet's phrase as meaningful to his seminal work, much as we might reflect upon its meaning so to muster a response to the societal disruption and contestation across the land, and in the world. The practice of musically educating children, youth, and adults may not at first appear to be the full solution to the challenges of local schools and societies, nor essential to meeting mandates in cultural and multicultural understanding. But music is as powerful as it is pan-human, musicking is musical involvement in what is humanly necessary, and the musical education of children and youth benefit their thoughts, feelings, and behaviors. When things fall apart, or seem to be on the brink of breaking up, serving fewer students and to a lesser degree than they might be served, we look to ways in which the music of many cultures and communities can serve to grow the musicianship of our students as well as their understanding of heritage and humanity, of people and places. Thus, from cynicism springs hope, and from darkness comes light, as this book and book series rises up as a reasoned response to making music relevant and multiply useful in the lives of learners in schools and communities.

THE SERIES

Each of the six volumes in the **World Music Pedagogy Series** provides a sweep of teaching/learning encounters that lead to the development of skills, understandings, and values that are inherent within a diversity of the world's musical cultures. Written for professionally active teachers as well as students in undergraduate and certification programs on their way to becoming teachers, these volumes encompass the application of the World Music Pedagogy (WMP) process from infancy and toddlerhood through late adolescence and into the community.

The books are unified by conceptualizations and format, and of course by the Series aim of providing theoretical frameworks for and practical pedagogical experiences in teaching the world's musical cultures. Individual WMP volumes are organized by music education context (or class type) and age/grade level.

For every volume in the World Music Pedagogy Series, there are common elements that are intended to communicate with coherence the means by which learners can become more broadly musical and culturally sensitive to people close by and across the world. All volumes include seven chapters that proceed from an introduction of the particular music education context (and type), to the play-out of the five dimensions, to the reflective closing of how World Music Pedagogy contributes to meeting various musical and cultural goals, including those of social justice through music as well as issues of diversity, equity, and inclusion.

There are scatterings of music notations across each volume, mostly meant to assist the teacher who is preparing the orally-based lessons rather than to suggest their use with students. Many of the chapters launch from vignettes, real-life scenarios of teachers and students at work in the WMP process, while chapters frequently close on interviews with practicing music educators and teaching musicians who are devoting their efforts to effecting meaningful experiences for students in the world's musical cultures. Authors of several of the volumes provide commentaries on published works for school music ensembles, noting what is available of notated scores of selected World Music works, whether transcribed or arranged, and how they can be useful alongside the adventures in learning by listening.

LISTENING EPISODES FOR THE SERIES

Of central significance are the listening episodes for recordings that are featured in teaching-learning episodes. These episodes are lesson-like sequences that run from 3 minutes to 30 minutes, depending upon the interest and inclination of the teacher, which pay tribute to occasions for brief or extended listening experiences that may be repeated over a number of class sessions. The listening episodes are noted in the episode descriptions as well as at each chapter's end, and users can connect directly to the recordings (audio as well as video recordings) through the Routledge eResource site for each of the Series' volumes, linked to the catalog page of each volume through www.routledge.com/Routledge-World-Music-Pedagogy-Series/book-series/WMP.

All volumes recommend approximately 20 listening episodes, and Chapters 2–6 in each volume provide illustrations of the ways in which these listening selections can develop into experiences in the five WMP dimensions. From the larger set of recommended listening tracks, three selections continue to appear across the chapters as keystone selections which are intended to show the complete pathways of how these three recordings can be featured through the five dimensions. These Learning Pathways are noted in full in Appendix 1, so that the user can see in one fell swoop the flow of teaching-learning from Attentive Listening to Engaged Listening, Enactive Listening, Creating World Music, and Integrating World Music. A second Appendix (2) provides recommended resources for further reading, listening, viewing, and development of the ways of World Music Pedagogy.

***

As a collective of authors, and joined by many of our colleagues in the professional work of music teachers and teaching musicians, we reject the hateful ideologies that blatantly surface in society. We are vigilant of the destructive choices that can be made in the business of schooling young people, and which may result from racism, bigotry, and prejudice. Hate has no place in society or its schools, and we assert that music is a route to peace, love, and understanding. We reject social exclusion, anti-Semitism, white supremacy, and homophobia (and other insensitive, unfeeling, or unbalanced perspectives). We oppose the ignorance or intentional avoidance of the potentials for diversity, equity, and inclusion in curricular practice. We support civility and "the culture of kindness," and hold a deep and abiding respect of people across the broad spectrum of our society. We are seeking to develop curricular threads that allow school music to be a place where all are welcome, celebrated, and safe, where every student is heard, and where cultural sensitivity can lead to love.

ACKNOWLEDGEMENTS

This collective of authors is grateful to those who have paved the way to teaching music with diversity, equity, and inclusion in mind. I am personally indebted to the work of my graduate school mentors, William M. Anderson, Terry Lee Kuhn, and Terry M. Miller, and to Halim El-Dabh and Virginia H. Mead, all who committed themselves to the study of music as a worldwide phenomenon, and who paved the way for me and many others to perform, study, and teach music with multicultural, intercultural, and global aims very much in mind. I am eternally grateful to Barbara Reeder Lundquist for her *joie de vivre* in the act of teaching music and in life itself. This work bears the mark of treasured University of Washington colleagues, then and now, who have helped to lessen the distance between the fields of ethnomusicology and music education, especially Steven J. Morrison, Shannon Dudley, and Christina Sunardi. Many thanks to the fine authors of the books in this Series: Sarah J. Bartolome, Amy Beegle, William J. Coppola, Karen Howard, Jamey Kelley, Chee-Hoo Lum, Christopher Mena, Mark Montemayor, J. Christopher Roberts, and Sarah J. Watts. They are "the collective" who shaped the course of the Series, and who toiled to fit the principles of World Music Pedagogy into their various specialized realms of music education. We are grateful to Constance Ditzel, music editor at Routledge, who caught the idea of the Series and enthusiastically encouraged us to write these volumes, and to her colleague, Peter Sheehy, who carried it through to its conclusion.

As in any of these exciting though arduous writing projects, I reserve my unending gratitude for my husband, Charlie, who leaves me "speechless in Seattle" in his support of my efforts. Once again, he gave me the time it takes to imagine a project, to write, read, edit, and write some more. It could not have been done without the time and space that he spared me, busying himself with theories behind "the adsorption of deuterated molecular benzene" while I helped to shape, with the author-team, these ideas on World Music Pedagogy.

Patricia Shehan Campbell
December 2017

Acknowledgements

We would like to express our sincerest gratitude to those who have contributed to the development of this volume. The perspectives, dialogues, and anecdotes shared among our fellow colleagues working "deep in the trenches" of instrumental music education have continually refined and challenged our thinking. Specifically, we would like to thank Madolyn Accola, Elia Bojorquez, John Brindle, Nicholas Catino, Giuliana Conti, Kaity Cassio Igari, Socrates Garcia, Jake Larçqua, Mario Yuzo Nieto, Katie Noonan, Huib Schippers, Solmaz Shakerifad, Amanda Soto, and Amy Villanova. We would also like to thank our fellow authors of the Routledge series, including Amy Beegle, Sarah J. Bartolome, Karen Howard, Jamey Kelley, Chee-Hoo Lum, Christopher Roberts, and Sarah Watts for their collaborative energies and support throughout this process.

We extend our sincere thanks to our editor at Routledge, Constance Ditzel, for her tireless efforts throughout the development of the WMP project, and to Holly González Smithson and her colleagues at Apex CoVantage for their superb work in the production of this volume. Finally, we are extremely grateful to Patricia Shehan Campbell for her visionary perspectives and unfaltering commitment towards cultural diversity in music education, which have fundamentally shaped the progress of our profession toward more global and equitable ends.

Episodes

Listening Episode music examples can be accessed on the eResource site from the Routledge catalog page.

1
Teaching and Learning in Context

Over recent decades, conversations about cultural diversity seem to have taken the field of music education by storm, provoking dialogues that are undeniably relevant to instrumental music teachers in elementary, middle, and high school programs everywhere. Today, there is less a question of *if* cultural diversity is important in instrumental music classrooms, and more of *how* it might take shape. Books, articles, and workshops nationwide have attempted to address such questions, providing educators with a practical and philosophical foothold on which to build a music classroom that is truly globally minded. As it turns out, however, these resources have been overwhelmingly intended for non-performance-based music curricula, seen primarily in K–12 general music and music appreciation courses. Sadly, a scarcity of resources currently exist that provide an avenue for teachers of instrumental ensembles to implement non-Western traditions into their classrooms, despite a resounding call for them. The result is a body of literature that permits the profession of music education to globally advance, but in doing so perhaps leaves instrumental music ensembles behind. And with local and national communities that are consistently growing in cultural diversity year after year, how can the profession of music education truly progress if some school music traditions—especially those which are arguably central to school life and culture— struggle to remain relevant in an increasingly globalized society?

As school music programs exist today, a large proportion of students who choose to participate do so only through some sort of ensemble participation (i.e., wind band, orchestra, choir), usually exempting them from the classroom music courses where global traditions are more commonly taught.[1] What arguably results is an overwhelmingly large body of young musicians attaining a level of so-called musical excellence, but perhaps without a sense of what that means on a global scale. Indeed, these students become musically defined chiefly by the traditions included in their performance repertoire— which, as it happens, tends to be music of predominantly European origin.

And little can we immediately blame educators for following this well-paved path of Eurocentric musical performance. To attempt anything different would mean making a steeper climb out of what is already an uphill battle of teaching instrumental music. In addition to the scarcity of resources for developing culturally diverse instrumental programs, conversations regarding their importance and method of implementation are either somewhat contentious or non-existent within the classrooms and boardrooms that determine best practices for the profession at-large. For example, the National Association for Music Education (NAfME)—the flagship school music organization within the United States—is committed to diversity as one of its core values, but it has yet to either actively pursue or endorse a culture-rich curriculum specifically for instrumental music education. Moreover, it could be argued that existing school music organizations innocuously reward the continued performance of Anglo-American musical expressions through festivals and competitions. Receiving a "gold" or "gold with distinction" rating on an All-State performance is the coveted reward that many band directors and students actively seek above any other, and a necessary requirement for performing music "suitable" for adjudication at such festivals is that the repertoire must be selected from a narrowly scoped and significantly Eurocentric curated list of pieces deemed "important" to the art form. In effect, there is no tangible reward to performing diverse musical practices in instrumental ensembles, at least not insofar as awards and recognitions go. When instrumental directors desperately seek quantifiable measures of success in today's high-stakes, assessment-based educational climate, the path that is inevitably pursued is one in which the worth of a program can be tangibly demonstrated.

Understandably, whether a music teacher is new to the teaching profession or a seasoned professional, the task of implementing a globally conscious curriculum into any instrumental classroom might be met with trepidation. How might the practical needs of an instrumental ensemble (including concert preparation, performance, and competition) be negotiated within the larger musical desires of a culture-rich music curriculum? What might an instrumental classroom which is committed to representing a diversity of musical cultures look like to begin with? Is it a matter of performing more diverse musical genres, a matter of creating an assortment of new "world music" ensembles, or some mixture of both? Do students need to trade in their saxophones and violins for *erhus* and *ouds*? And perhaps most provocative: If the wind band tradition is historically American, and the orchestra historically European, should these instrumental ensembles be the laboratory for exploring world music cultures in the first place? For many of these legitimate questions and concerns, this book seeks to provide some long-awaited practical avenues for teachers to not only implement solutions into their classrooms, but also to capably express these worthwhile goals to administrators and stakeholders. However, many issues will prove quite difficult to digest within the boundaries of a single text. These are the larger philosophical issues with which teachers will likely grapple throughout this book, and indeed, should continue to grapple with throughout their careers.

The most pressing issue, it seems, is that conversations around cultural diversity in music education have remained largely theoretical, and teacher-practitioners have perhaps become so strapped for time with their already jam-packed professional responsibilities that reimagining a fresh and new culturally conscious instrumental curriculum is beyond the realm of realistic possibility. Thus, there is a theory-to-practice rift within the context of instrumental music education,[2] and it is possibly this very chasm which hinders a great deal of advancement in education at-large. One essential solution lies in developing high-quality and fully accessible resources that directly answer the outspoken call for globally minded teaching approaches within ensemble-based classrooms. Therefore, this volume on instrumental ensembles intends to provide teachers with a resource that is rooted in theory but steeped in practice. A resource that directly responds to instrumental teachers' desires for mindfully and creatively implemented global music experiences in their classrooms.

With all this in mind, however, it is important to note that the purpose of this book is not to "sell" the importance of cultural diversity in instrumental music education. Plentiful literature within the fields of music education, general education, sociology, ethnic studies, area studies, gender studies, and so on have advocated for the importance of global awareness in both education and society, and the authors of this book have been significantly inspired by these writings (see Appendix 2 for a sampling of such resources). Instead, the primary purpose of this book is to focus on the *how* over the *why*: To help practitioners understand how to develop more culturally conscious practices and approaches for teaching instrumental ensembles, and to encourage them to question their everyday responsibilities as teachers and conductors in an increasingly globalized society.

Where Am I? Understanding the Classroom in Context

With student populations that increasingly represent cultures and ethnicities of non-European descent, the question of *what* music to teach has become an issue of utmost importance. In cities all over America, large and small, rural and urban, populations do not necessarily reflect the Anglo-American majority around which Western musical traditions were initially established. Moreover, every community and school district in America is demographically distinct, further challenging the possibility of a singular approach towards achieving cultural responsiveness.

Within this book, the authors argue that there are two simultaneously operating forces at play when it comes to approaching culturally diverse musical practices. On the one hand is *locality*—that is, any culturally responsive music classroom should consider first and foremost the cultures that are represented within it. A commitment to locality allows for previously silenced and disenfranchised voices to once again "earn a seat at table," so to speak. On the other hand, however, is what one could comparatively call *"globality"*—that is, the equally crucial understanding that any musical practice from around the world is worthy of serious study simply because it represents the active celebration of a pan-human phenomenon—one which, gifted by the multiplicity of human life, compels people to come together toward the shared desire of creating provocative and meaningful art. Certainly, musical interchanges inspired from celebration and conflict alike will motivate the globally minded music educator to embark upon these diverse musical excursions. Whether stirred by the Olympics or a global crisis, motivated by a new student or a new blockbuster film, or driven by the teacher's goals or the students' own interests, musical choices reflecting a commitment to both "locality" and "globality" will not only be immensely more meaningful for musical learners, but equally captivating, compelling, and intriguing as they embark upon uniquely curated musical journeys.

Before embarking, it is essential for the reader to take stock of what is already in existence within his or her school community—including what is already being done in addition to what more could possibly be undertaken. Throughout this book, the reader is encouraged to continually consider their positionality as the teacher within the given community. To start, it is essential for the teacher to examine his or her cultural background in relation to that of the students. If the teacher's cultural identity is not reflected in the student body, he or she should think critically and introspectively about the biases, assumptions, and privileges that this positionality might have over his or her students. This requires humility, honesty with oneself, and an openness to considering opposing worldviews with which the educator may not particularly align.

Next, beyond examining themselves, teachers should examine their music room. What cultures are represented within the four walls of the rehearsal space or classroom? Do these musical styles represent the student body in any way? To what instruments do students have access? If there are instruments from other cultures, do the students know what they are called, in what musical style(s) they are used, and how to play them? How often are they given opportunities to explore, experiment with, and play them? Are there posters or other types of artwork posted around the room that refer to other musical expressions beyond those of the Western elites (e.g., Mozart, Beethoven, Sousa, Stravinsky)? Might students also come in meaningful contact with the musical greats of other traditions—Wynton Marsalis with jazz, Andy Statman with Klezmer and bluegrass, Ala Farka Touré with intersected blues and Malian music, and Anoushka Shankar in Indian sitar music, for example? In short, of which musical traditions does the music room seem to demonstrate value?

Next, the teacher ought to look beyond the immediate classroom. What musics have the instrumental ensemble(s) featured in performances over the past few years? Have students played any music of non-Western styles recently? If so, were these pieces written by Anglo-American arrangers and composers attempting to fulfill a particular style (e.g., Leonard Bernstein's "America") or by composers who are well-versed or perhaps native to that particular culture's music (e.g., H. Owen Reed's "La Fiesta Mexicana")?[3]

Beyond the classroom, teachers should continue to examine their position as the instrumental music teacher within their particular community. Consider the neighborhood in which the school is located. What cultures are represented within that neighborhood? Note that the cultural makeup of a particular neighborhood may not necessarily reflect that of the students in the music classroom; in fact, highly diverse communities are often found to have problematically monocultural music programs. Perhaps unsurprisingly, this has often been found to be the result of music programs that fail to provide a voice and identity for the students not represented by the ensemble's repertoire—not to mention issues of inaccessibility to musical instruments and lessons among marginalized populations.

Zooming out further, teachers should continue to look past the neighborhood and begin to consider the uses of music within society at-large. Think about the ways in which people interact through music, and how it may be used to bring people together. Do certain cultures seem to value singing? Listening? Dancing? Is there a specific time and place for making music? Does it accompany mealtime, prayer, play, or sleep? Is music created by anyone and everyone within the community, or is it reserved for those deemed to be professionals? An understanding of the larger socio-musical purposes of different traditions provides a more holistic expression of how music functions within various societies, which in turn may inform the musical values that may contribute to a sense of identity and ownership among students of diverse backgrounds. After all, these musical values may be different from those facilitated within the wind band and orchestra traditions.

Doing Fieldwork: Putting on Your Ethnomusicologist Hat

You may have realized that in order to have a stronger grasp on some of these questions, it is necessary to physically enter into these communities to enrich your understanding of how musical participation occurs within them. That is, you might need to conduct your own small-scale fieldwork. While this certainly does not need to take on the fully immersive exploration that a professional ethnomusicologist might conduct, it may require more than just Internet research and reading. Understanding an unfamiliar musical tradition begs for observations, as well as conversations, asking meaningful questions, and perhaps—even if only for a short time—participating directly in the musical practice.

Make an effort to attend community festivals, parades, and celebrations, which may feature music from several different cultural groups within the community. Don't be afraid to talk to people, young and old, and ask them about the meaning and significance of the occasion—including the music, the dancing, and even the food and drink. If invited to participate, do not hesitate to dance, sing, or play along and experience the music as a full-on participant. An informal conversation with the right person may turn into the development of a larger musical relationship, with this person becoming a "culture bearer" (Campbell, 2004). This insider can provide guidance, resources (including high-quality recordings), and instruction to you and/or the students.

Nonetheless, understanding how to conduct fieldwork responsibly and ethically is important to consider, and some resources which discuss these matters are listed here. However, don't become overwhelmed by the complicated task of data collection. Since your research aims foremost to inform your teaching practice (and not to be used in scholarly writing), data collection is not as important as the questions you ask and the activities in which you participate or observe.

Selected Resources

- Barz, G. F., & Cooley, T. J. (Eds.). (2008). *Shadows in the field: New perspectives for fieldwork in ethnomusicology*. New York, NY: Oxford University Press.
- Emerson, R. M., Fretz, R. I., & Shaw, L. L. (2011). *Writing ethnographic fieldnotes*. Chicago, IL: University of Chicago Press.
- Titon, J., & Cooley, T. J. (2009). Discovering and documenting a world of music. In *Worlds of music: An introduction to the music of the world's peoples* (5th ed., pp. 533–559). Belmont, CA: Schirmer Cengage Learning.
- Wade, B. C. (2009). Thinking about fieldwork. In *Thinking musically: Experiencing music, expressing culture* (pp. 195–204). New York, NY: Oxford University Press.

After reflecting upon the ways in which people around the world engage and interact with music, a stark wanting of global perspectives may suddenly become evident within the existing curriculum. Nonetheless, many would argue that there already exists within Western instrumental ensembles a rich and vibrant culture all its own, and global perspectives toward instrumental practices should certainly not mean an outright rejection of the significance of the Western canon. Truly, the desire to celebrate the paradigms of the Western classical orchestra and the American wind band is not diametrically opposed to the desire to incorporate a culture-rich approach to teaching instrumental music. Instead, a holistic approach which celebrates *all* forms of musical participation and chooses to view the act of instrumental performance as globally dynamic and pan-musical is one which places no judgments of value or worth on any musical culture over another. Because of these desires to incorporate global approaches while continually celebrating the rich histories of Western instrumental music, one of the immediate challenges this book will face is how to negotiate the historical and traditional roles of Western ensembles with the increasingly outspoken call for more cultural representation in students' musical engagements.

While the importance of engaging in diverse musical cultures should stem from both a commitment to locality as well as the globalistic and humanistic desire to celebrate the various ways of making music *for its own sake*, more must first be said about the apparent absence of thinking on "local" terms when it comes to developing music curricula in such a globalized society. Such a brief discussion is deemed necessary because it appears as if articulating the importance of locality may be less straightforward for many teachers than rationalizing the desire to pursue music "for its own sake." That is, while it may be logical to most musicians that exploring diverse musical expressions is important for the all-around wealth of musical learning to which students could and should be subjected, acknowledging that these students' home identities are an important starting point may be either less apparent or more contentious for some.

To illustrate the meaningfulness of thinking about the locality of a given teaching context, consider the demographic makeup of the United States' largest school district. In New York City, Latino students represented the largest ethnic group during the 2015–2016 school year with approximately 41% of the population, compared to about 27% Black/African American, 16% Asian, and 15% White minorities.[4] However, within each borough of New York City, this picture differs quite dramatically. In Brooklyn, African American students represent the majority, while Latino students are represented in greater proportions in Queens and Manhattan. Consequently, the subject matter presented in Brooklyn classrooms ought to look reasonably different than the matter presented in classrooms throughout Queens and Manhattan. Zooming in further, within each neighborhood of Brooklyn student demographics will look continually different. For example, the neighborhood of Crown Heights, Brooklyn, has a large West Indian population, while a highway splits that neighborhood from one of the densest populations of Hasidic Jews in the borough.

Viewing the demographics of any society can be likened to Matryoshka Russian nesting dolls, in which multiple and unique layers of society reveal themselves as one digs deeper and examines each more closely. Viewing a particular region broadly, school demographics may appear one way, but will reveal quite different pictures as more distinct neighborhoods, boroughs, and districts are examined.

In contrast to New York City, another urban school system such as Seattle Public Schools claims a 56% majority of White students, with minorities represented by merely 22% Hispanic/Latino, 7% Asian, and 4% Black/African American students.[5] Again, within each of these distinct environments, schooling ought to look quite different. Yet currently available resources for teaching music typically attempt to establish a "one-size-fits-all" approach, essentially removing student backgrounds from consideration altogether. In the New York City Department of Education for example, White students comprise just 15% of the overall student population, yet the musics that are performed by musical ensembles within these school districts are represented by an overwhelming proportion of White composers and arrangers. This drives home the crucial point: What is effectively created is a music curriculum in which student bodies are distilled down to a common—although not connecting—denominator.

Considering the diversity of American schools on national, regional, and local levels reveals that there is truly no such thing as a "one-size-fits-all" curriculum, method of teaching, or standard set of repertoire. Instead, the music teacher need look no further than his or her own classroom for a starting point. In other words, perhaps the most inclusive approach toward instrumental music education would start with the individual students within the classroom, and branch outwards from there—thus working directly to value and promote the cultural identities of the students within the music program.

Avoiding Othering, Tokenizing, and Essentializing

Whether instrumental teachers are grappling with issues of locality (by selecting particular musical traditions with a student's home culture in mind) or addressing concepts of globality (by selecting a sweeping assortment of cultures for students to musically study), a critical issue necessarily presents itself. In the process of homing in on students' cultural identities, how does one know if they are *othering*, *tokenizing*, or *essentializing* that student's culture? For example, if a teacher decides to include Syrian music in his or her classroom because there is a single Syrian child in the class, could one surmise that such an act serves only to demonstrate how that child is different from other students in the class? Or, in the process of incorporating Syrian music, how does the teacher know that he or she is not essentializing that culture by implying that the selected musical tradition—simply by being from Syria—is the music with which the student identifies?

Concerns of othering, tokenizing, and essentializing are pervasive when embarking on journeys of global musical learning and must be thoroughly considered by the teacher in order to avoid falling into this potential pitfall. "Othering" results when a so-called outsider (such as a teacher who is not a member of a particular culture group) brings attention to another group by demonstrating the ways in which members or practices of that culture are different from the dominant majority. An example of othering in music would be to use differentiating words such as "their" music versus "our" music, which suggests possession and perhaps implies preference of one musical culture over another. "Tokenizing" occurs when a feeble attempt is made to represent certain cultural groups by seeking surface-level inclusion. For example, a teacher might tokenize students by actively seeking participation from minority groups in order to establish the appearance of diversity within an ensemble, especially if the teacher's efforts of inclusivity go no further than this. Finally, "essentializing" occurs when one culture is represented primarily by singular elements of that culture. An example of essentializing might be a teacher presenting a unit on Native American music by presenting all Native Americans as peoples who live on reservations, wear traditional regalia, hunt their own food, and play traditional musical instruments. Essentializing fails to recognize the diversity of lived experiences within a culture.

Perhaps the most important tool for avoiding othering, tokenizing, and essentializing is to establish direct communication with students and community members whose cultures are being represented. Instead of assuming that the Syrian student identifies with traditional Syrian music, an open conversation may reveal that she is actually quite fond of Lebanese hip-hop, for example. Yet, communication should demonstrate an interest in and seek an understanding of the student's musical identity and should not simply use the student as the "validity check" of the music being studied (e.g., such innocuous but distasteful questions as, "isn't this how your people do it?"). This sort of communication can become tokenizing or essentializing. In such a case, the teacher may treat the student as an adoptive "culture bearer," or practicing expert of a musical culture within the classroom, but without the student's willingness (or expertise) to participate in this role. Of course, if a student communicates an interest and willingness to share his or her musical knowledge, and can capably discuss it, the student should absolutely be encouraged to do so; but this relationship risks becoming problematic when the teacher assumes that the act of representing this student's culture automatically becomes a bidirectional relationship wherein the student is treated as an expert on the musical tradition simply because of his or her membership within that culture.

Re-Examining Band and Orchestra as Instrumental Paradigms

In American schools, music educators often refer to a "holy trinity" or "trifecta" of musical participation which includes band, orchestra, and chorus. With this view it becomes apparent, whether implicitly or explicitly, that the ensembles which are to be superlatively valued are the three which comprise the trifecta, while those that lie in their periphery are merely extracurricular.[6] Jazz bands, for example, are pervasive in American schools, but are still considered auxiliary to traditional wind and concert bands. Also existing peripherally to this trifecta, a newfound interest in mariachi (both extracurricular and for-credit) has promisingly found a way to break into the public school "mainstream," in many cases being offered directly alongside jazz bands and other smaller ensembles. Nevertheless, sweeping changes in multicultural musical offerings are often hard to come by, especially within indoctrinated school music programs. These barriers to exploring alternative means of musical participation arguably narrow the conception of what is to be valued as worthwhile within an instrumental music program.

Truly, so-called auxiliary ensembles are quite capable of holding their own weight in music education curricula, as has been demonstrated by the relatively recent inclusion of popular music as a curricular offering in many schools. For example, an organization known as *Little Kids Rock* has established a full "Modern Band" curriculum for teaching guitar, bass, drums, keyboard, and vocals, and provides a body of repertoire that claims to reflect the musical desires of American students. When compared to the notation- and reading-based traditions maintained within wind bands and orchestras, the curricular inclusion of popular music powerfully demonstrates the potential for more informal styles of musical learning in schools. Overall, traditional ensembles have been slow to adopt many of the important skills gained from participation in nonformal musical practices, such as aural learning, improvisation, and composition, perhaps largely because the musical goals of the band and orchestra traditions minimally include such forms of participation. In effect, instrumental educators arguably pursue musical goals that reflect the needs of the ensemble, instead of musical goals that reflect the necessary skills of developing musicians. This is certainly not to say that skills learned in nonformal and informal musical environments are better or more important than those developed in traditional ensembles; however, they do reveal that there is much that traditional ensembles could gain from a re-examination of the musical outcomes from which students are intended to benefit.

But an acknowledgement of these important skills, as well as the know-how to implement them without sacrificing the needs of the existing ensembles is hardly straightforward, as many instrumental teachers may have already reckoned. Indeed, given the teacher's finite time and resources during the school year, changing the *modus operandi* of traditional ensembles and/or implementing new "non-traditional" ensembles into the instrumental curriculum is often impractical because it risks "taking away" from the success of the school's already well-established musical trifecta (i.e., band, orchestra, and chorus). While the authors certainly acknowledge and empathize with this difficult position in which instrumental educators find themselves, perhaps this presents an opportunity for teachers to challenge the thinking within the profession. After all, it could be argued that such concerns perpetuate the assumption that the school band, orchestra, and chorus *should* be the cornerstone of any worthwhile music program. To challenge and question what it should mean to have a "successful" instrumental ensemble in an elementary, middle, or high school music program should be the regular practice of the mindful music educator. It can tell educators more about what might be missing from their music programs just as much as it can remind them of the importance of their current musical pursuits.

Certainly, the school band and orchestra has historically developed to become a foundation of the American school music system, and administrators indeed find much economy in these ensembles. After the initial large investment to attain them, instruments can potentially be used for decades, and instruments can often be shared between students. Further, a school band program can be quite chameleonic, able to easily morph to fulfill an array of ritualistic and celebratory roles that the school may seek: They are featured at annual performances during school music concerts; they can be borrowed and adapted for ceremonial events (such as welcoming a public figure to the school, performing at a convocation, or playing at commencement); they can become the marching band for homecoming, and the pep band for football games; and they can shrink down into small chamber groups for small events, or into the pit orchestra for the school musical. Even most school jazz bands select their players from within the school band. Truly, the wind band tradition is incredibly economical, especially to an administrator who seeks to balance the costs of the school's significant annual events with continually depleting budgets.

Happily, students who are drawn to traditional band and orchestra instruments are given plentiful opportunities to practice their desired instruments in school. But what of students who are not drawn to such instruments or styles? What of the first-generation Irish student who has grown up learning to play the Irish fiddle? Is her bowing style, or her desire to tap her feet while playing simply "wrong?" What of the recently emigrated Korean American student who takes *gayageum* (or *kayagum*; Korean zither) lessons at home? Would he be considered "unmusical" by school standards because he cannot perform on one of the conventional instruments represented within the school ensemble? Surely, while not all musical choices must by necessity reflect the specific identities of the student body, it is nevertheless important for students to see the music with which they most closely identify—whatever it might be—to be equally as valued as those styles which are already pervasive in instrumental curricula.

Beyond instrument selection, what does the repertoire of the traditional triumvirate implicitly say about the music that our society values? It is no secret that an overwhelming majority of the music written for orchestra was composed by men of European descent, and the same is largely true for music of the wind band canon. Thus, the message that is tacitly communicated is that the music valued in schools should be primarily of Anglo-American (and male) origin. But before such an assertion raises deep contention, these statements absolutely do not to suggest that these canonical musical exemplars of Anglo origin should be excised from music curricula. Indeed, they have built an important foundation for the so-called high art culture of European and American music. And to be sure, musical practices all around the world have adopted many principles and practices of the Western classical canon. Therefore, by no means does this book intend to act as a treatise to demote these musical traditions or discourage ensembles from performing them. Instead, the desire is to promote, from a socially conscious perspective, a more holistic and thoughtful consideration of what musical repertoires are selected, and for what purposes.

Indeed, to establish a music program in America that does not perform music from Western traditions would be arguably just as imprudent as a music program that does not perform music from any other cultures. Given these considerations, a primary thesis of this book is that a focused consideration of the students in the classroom should be of initial importance when selecting musical traditions on which to focus. And while student bodies within many communities may not reflect a predominantly Eurocentric majority, we ought not forget that many American communities *do* in fact represent an Anglo majority, and these students equally deserve to have their cultural identities musically represented as well. Yet, by thinking of school music ensembles as a fixed triumvirate of band, orchestra, and chorus, teachers essentially neglect to acknowledge the intensely diverse array of musical potentials that might exist in places no further than their students' own homes and communities.

A Matter of Redefining Excellence

One of the most pertinent questions surrounding the music education profession at-large seems to surround the notion of "excellence." As mentioned, many instrumental music directors value festival competitions as a primary measure of worth and success, largely because they favorably demonstrate tangible measures of the music program's achievement. Unfortunately, focusing primarily on rewards-based goals can sometimes be problematic for the development of an instrumental program for several reasons. First, many teachers acknowledge that in "teaching to the performance," musical skills are taught with an end goal in mind, and so key concepts tend to be taught because they are found within the chosen repertoire, instead of being chosen for the developmental needs of growing musicians.

Second, months of planning and preparation typically culminate in a relatively short performance that is evaluated by impartial adjudicators and based solely on the quality of the music. As many teachers and students lament, these often high-stakes performances demonstrate little about the holistic strengths of the ensemble or program, and merely measure the group's demonstrated efficacy in-the-moment. Further, when it comes to competition, efficacy is often indirectly affected by inequitable social privileges. For example, many high-performing instrumental programs in the United States are those which have a high proportion of students that can afford to take private lessons, attend summer music camps, attend music concerts, have parents who participate in band functions (including attending booster meetings, and transporting students to rehearsals and events), and have the means to acquire high-quality instruments.

Therefore, the following question is posed: If excellence in music education is dependent upon access to resources, might the music education profession's current notion of excellence be inherently inequitable? Furthermore, if the population of students at underfunded schools is primarily students of color, are current conceptions of excellence in music education placing barriers on who is, and who is not, given an opportunity to achieve? Finally, if instrumental music programs are mostly focused on festival performances, where does that leave other musical expressions and repertoires that do not lend themselves to such presentational formats?

The authors argue that current understandings of excellence should expand to encompass broader ideals of musicianship, and as such needs to look beyond current models of so-called musical excellence. For example, what value ought to be placed on music programs that are able to successfully connect the school to the surrounding community? What worth should be attributed to programs that aurally teach steel pan music in parallel with chamber orchestra? How much importance does the skill of composing and improvising carry? These are the questions which festival- and rewards-based assessments are largely unable to answer. If music programs fail to value the multiple ways of musically participating, their true effectiveness and worth may never be fully—or holistically—understood.

Looking Beyond the Triumvirate

While band and orchestra are pervasive in school music programs, community schools, and conservatories, there exist many other worthwhile examples of instrumental ensembles existing just beyond—or even within—the walls of the classroom. The resurgence of mariachis has previously been discussed, but many other highly successful "alternative" instrumental ensembles can similarly be boasted by music programs throughout the United States and Europe. Such groups include steel pan ensembles, West African drumming groups, Indonesian gamelan ensembles, and so on. These programs can serve as meaningful models for approaching World Music Pedagogy in a way which works in tandem with revitalized conceptions of traditional band and orchestra paradigms.

Often, the teacher need not look any further than the surrounding community to find alternative modes of musical participation among different cultural groups in the area. Depending on the cultural makeup of the community, one may find a number of ensembles performing musical styles that may be unfamiliar to the music teacher, but "close to home" for many of the students. These ensembles may be professional, but they could also be amateur and equally valid. They might include a mariachi that performs regularly throughout the city or region, a small group of Irish musicians in a local pub, or a parent who plays with the Chinese *erhu* as a hobby. Beyond facilitating meaningful (and of course enjoyable) musical exchanges, these interactions can often open doors to further relationships with "culture bearers" (see the "Doing Fieldwork" box earlier in this chapter). Culture bearers can become an unrivaled resource for approaching unfamiliar musics with students in any classroom.

Approaches to Culturally Responsive Teaching

Funds of Knowledge

The *Funds of Knowledge* approach focuses on legitimizing student experiences by drawing on their "household knowledge" and using it to build a familiar knowledge base that can be used to enhance their own learning (González, Moll, & Amanti, 2005, p. 43). For many students (particularly those of color), resources that allow for their cultures to be honored in the classroom are essential for their ultimate engagement in these settings. For music teachers—who often serve as "gatekeepers of culture" in schools—this means understanding the different ways that cultural expressions might manifest themselves within traditional ensembles. This includes providing spaces and opportunities for students who might be uninterested in performing on a traditional band or orchestra instrument, but is musically eager in his or her own way. When student knowledge—including cultural knowledge—becomes a central resource for their own learning, the result becomes truly empowering for all.

Community-Based Learning

In many aspects of education, particularly pre-service teacher training, there is a growing interest in *Community-Based Learning* (CBL), which recognizes that the often-incongruous nature of teacher-student demographics leads to tension within the classroom (Cooper, 2007). Because of this, proponents of CBL develop cultural immersion experiences for their pre-service teachers as a way to learn about the wealth of knowledge that exists within the communities they teach. Indiana University has developed several of these types of programs, including the *American Indian Reservation Project*, the *Hispanic Community Project*, the *Urban Project*, and the *Overseas Project* (Sleeter, 2001). In music education, a similar program was developed at the University of Washington called *Music Alive! In Yakima Valley*. Participation in this program was embedded within a required music education course for pre-service music teachers.[7] The activities were centered on learning music from the world's many cultures and developing a reciprocal learning process between the university students and students throughout the Yakima Valley, who were largely of marginalized Native American and Mexican American descent. The partnership provided opportunities for Yakama[8] students to reclaim their heritage through shared experiences with their music, while the university students developed their teaching skills by refining theory learned in the classroom with practice gained in the field.

Surely, such programs represent full-blown curricular designs, and understandably may not be feasible for busy music teachers to fully implement into their own communities. However, small-scale activities (discussed in greater detail in Chapter 6), are a useful approach for providing music educators with opportunities to learn about their students' communities, as well as to develop meaningful musical experiences that will be of immense worth to students of diverse backgrounds.

Ideas, Approaches, and Concepts to Cultural Diversity in Music Education

Multicultural Education in Music

Within the efforts of multicultural education, teachers are charged with the responsibility of understanding, empathizing, and developing mindful instructional goals which reflect the needs of a diverse student body. To be sure, this is no simple task, with student identities reflecting a host of intricacies ranging from race, gender, age, social class, sexual orientation, and so on. While educators may acknowledge these complexities within their students, they often fail to seek a deeper understanding of how such aspects of identity may ultimately inform student learning—or conversely, how these understandings ought to inform the teacher's approach. Whether educators are aware of them or not, surface-level perceptions and associations are often made in regard to students—including their chosen style of dress, manner of speaking, body language, and so on. These perceptions are often shaped by personal biases, portrayals in the media, and socially constructed assumptions, and can lead to harmful tensions between the teacher and student if not tempered through open-mindedness and in-depth interactions with students.[9] Uncovering the rich layers beneath any student's identity allows teachers to become more successful in their journeys of teaching culture through music by examining their own teaching practices within the unique contexts of their individual classrooms.

Multicultural education, then, is far more involved than merely seeking to represent the multiplicity of cultures within the classroom or larger society. Instead, it most directly seeks *change* and *transformation*. It attempts to not merely show the faces of minority populations and oppressed social groups, but to actively pursue equity on behalf of and hand-in-hand with them. When applied to an instrumental music curriculum, the efforts of multicultural education provide both the capacity to reveal weaknesses and inequities within the status quo of the discipline, as well as the impetus to inspire change from within. Spearheading much of the work in activism-based cultural equity in education is James Banks (2004), who offers five dimensions of multicultural education: (1) content integration, (2) the knowledge construction process, (3) prejudice reduction, (4) equity pedagogy, and (5) empowering school culture and social structure (p. 5).

The *content integration* dimension refers to how teachers use examples from different cultures to explain various concepts within their subject. Within instrumental music, this could be sardonically referred to as the "Taco Tuesday" approach, where students are merely exposed to a different style of music as a way to reinforce certain musical concepts found in instrumental school music styles. This approach, while providing students with exposure to various cultures, falls short in leaving them with an in-depth cultural understanding of why the music exists, how it came to be, and what makes it significant or meaningful within that particular culture.

The *knowledge construction* dimension takes cultural understanding to a deeper level by examining how and why certain practices and approaches are privileged over others within certain disciplines. It also aims to understand inherent biases and how they influence the construction of knowledge within a particular practice (e.g., which musical styles and traditions are performed, which types of ensembles are offered). In an instrumental ensemble, the teacher might engage meaningfully in this discipline by choosing to perform a piece by a marginalized composer and facilitating a discussion about how and why this composer's music might be subjected to the social biases which prevent his or her music from becoming truly represented within the music community. While such discussions may understandably reduce the time available for rehearsal, they can become empowering pathways for students who also find themselves underrepresented.

Third is the *prejudice reduction* dimension. This dimension emphasizes the importance of critically examining students' racial attitudes and developing more democratic values. Activities that focus on gaining an in-depth understanding of the music of different cultures through participation and extensive exploration become particularly useful here. This dimension goes beyond surface appreciation of musical elements and delves into deeper understandings of how certain cultures may have developed their musical practices and traditions, what functions they serve, and what aesthetic standards are valued within that culture. Rather than using the European Art tradition as the normative yardstick, this dimension calls for each musical tradition to be valued on its own terms.

The fourth dimension, *equity pedagogy*, relates to the pedagogical practices that teachers use to connect with and improve the academic achievement of students from diverse cultural and socioeconomic backgrounds. This dimension often entails a modification in method to engage students who have varied learning styles. Instrumental music pedagogy within the Western tradition has historically valued a more rigid "master-apprentice" model in which students are intended to eventually attain musical mastery (if they possess ample talent, of course). Furthermore, students immersed within this tradition tend to work within a "closed-form" of musical learning (Allsup, 2016)—one in which the master decides for the student how particular musical conventions are to be approached, how the score is to be appropriately interpreted, and what constitutes high-quality performance. Such an approach, although appropriate in particular contexts, fails to consider the array of different approaches to musical learning with which students may more closely identify. For instance, many cultures around the world prioritize the salience of the music's social meaning over a performer's virtuosity, and closed-forms of musical learning by-and-large fail to adequately regard these alternative musical value systems. Thus, in addition to marginalizing students who have a divergent understanding of the function of music, pedagogical approaches not rooted in equitable aims can hinder students' progress at developing their own musical meaning in musical settings.

Finally, the *empowering school culture* dimension expands the scope of multicultural education efforts from within the music classroom to the larger school community and focuses on efforts to restructure both the organization and practices of the school to achieve a culturally empowering climate that seeks educational equity. The school music program is uniquely situated to make an impact in this area because it can symbolically be thought of as the heartbeat of the entire school culture. Through performances at school functions, school ensembles can share music that honors the cultures of the student body. This might look like programming performances of a popular *banda* tune at the football game of a primarily Latino school, having traditional Native American powwow dancing as an opening performance for a pep rally, collaborating with a community *lion dance* group during Chinese New Year, or perhaps even by programming the jazz ensemble to provide backing for a lunchtime hip-hop open mic performance.

What Kind of Culturalism Is the Best Culturalism?

The educational buzzword "multiculturalism" has been used extensively in discussions surrounding world music education over the past few decades. Only recently has the term begun to be replaced by another within music scholarship, which many scholars, educators, and policymakers argue to be more suitable: *cultural diversity*. Some argue that this term more aptly contains a wider spectrum of multicultural possibilities—anywhere from a focus on a single culture to a commitment towards the integration of multiple cultures. Within his framework, Banks offers that the *content integration* dimension of multicultural education is often the most used (and sometimes only) dimension used to teach multiculturalism, and it is insufficient for moving education towards equitable ends. Indeed, the United States is already a multicultural society to begin with, and it is this cultural pluralism that is simultaneously regarded as a gift by many, as well as a hostile detriment by others. The latter represents the views of isolationism, xenophobia, and even racism, all which are admittedly very much present in today's society. Thus, a society can be multicultural but not always embracingly so. When viewed as a one-dimensional educational remedy, multiculturalism goes no further than becoming successful in teaching *about* other cultures. It proclaims a pluralistic society, but not necessarily a harmonious one.

Moreover, multiculturalism might include anywhere between two and an infinite number of cultures, and as Huib Schippers (2010) points out, it is a matter of degree. For example, it may regard "between cultures," such as Asian and Middle Eastern populations both living in America, but it can also regard "within cultures," such as Northern and Southern Americans. Each has their own highly individual cultural identities, despite both being considered "American." In music, we see the attempted fruits of multicultural education quite commonly: consider an elementary string ensemble playing one song from Japan, another from Ireland, another from Russia, and so on. The songs are performed one after the other, independent of one another. This is what multiculturalism in music education quite often looks like: A method of performance, a list of repertoire, and often little more.

And certainly, such an approach is not necessarily mis-educative. There is always a benefit to employing multicultural approaches to music education; by singing songs from other cultures, students develop an ear for melodies, harmonies, rhythms, and meters that are potentially different from their own musical backgrounds, and they arguably learn cultural empathy and competency in the process as well. But as long as these cultures stand on their own, not interacting among one another, they remain multicultural at most. A prime non-musical example of multiculturalism can be found in Disney's *EPCOT World Showcase*. Walking around the park grounds, guests can "visit" Italy, Japan, Germany, China, Mexico, Morocco, Norway, and so on. A visitor can get a glimpse of each country by sampling their cuisine, hearing their traditional music, and admiring their architecture. Yet, here lies a perfect example of good intentions resulting in questionable outcomes. Certainly, Disney has the best of intentions in mind for the entertainment of its guests; however, it disputably raises the red flag of essentializing these other cultures in the process.

Like Banks's concept of multicultural education, the concept of cultural diversity similarly exists along a continuum of practice from least-to-most integrated, constantly striving to move closer to cultural equity. From this vantage, multicultural efforts progress toward *interculturalism*. In this form of cultural diversity, cultures begin to interact and exchange with one another, resulting in potential musical fusions such as Afro-Peruvian jazz or Tex-Mex *conjunto*. Finally, beyond interculturalism lies *transculturalism*, which involves a more in-depth exchange of cultures. Through transculturalism, two or more cultures blend together such that all or both are on an equal footing, and neither are marginalized against the other. This conceivably results in a newly created culture, altogether different from either of the two by themselves.

While transculturalism may often be the intended goal of many globally conscious music programs, it certainly does not maintain that intercultural, multicultural, or even monocultural experiences are unfavorable. In many circumstances, a meaningful but limited "glimpse" of another culture is precisely what is desired. At other times, a monocultural approach might be most fitting. For example, high school students taking an Advanced Placement Music Theory class must prepare for a rigorous examination that focuses on Western music theory, making a monocultural approach perhaps most appropriate within the context. As long as these students are reminded that they will be learning about the theories of "this" particular music (in this case, Western classical), and not "all" musics, there is perhaps little harm in this monocultural approach for the sake of utility and practicality.

Thinking and Talking About Music

With the acknowledgement that other musical traditions beyond the Western canon are important, the ways in which musicians discuss musical practices must become more carefully considered in following. Once a classroom finds both familiar and unfamiliar musical traditions coexisting within its walls, no longer do general statements about music carry absolute truth. No longer can a culturally conscious music educator begin a sentence by saying "In music . . ." or "All music . . ." These statements must mindfully be replaced by more particular statements of fact: "In *our* music . . .," "In *this* music . . .," or "In *some* musics . . ." Once music is discussed from the global perspective, universalities seem to evaporate. For example, one may confidently say "in the Western tradition, it is proper etiquette to refrain from clapping until the musical selection has completely finished." But one cannot say "in music, we only clap at the end of the piece," because this is simply not true if talking about the audience's traditional role in a jazz concert, African performance (Nketia, 1975), a rock show, or an Egyptian vocal performance (Wade, 2009). Or, for that matter, even Western classical music before the 19th century[10] (Small, 1998).

It becomes immediately apparent that once a commitment is made to creating a culturally responsive instrumental program, far more is involved than just selecting more diverse repertoire. First, it is important to understand that what different cultures might regard as "music" to begin with is highly distinctive. Some cultures believe that music ought to be a packaged entity, performed by a few highly skilled musicians and consumed by the rest. They tend to view music as a chosen career; something people do for a living. In countless other cultures, music is a natural part of life; an activity in which every member of the society is expected to participate. For some in the former culture, music might be a tangible aesthetic product that is meant to be esteemed as-is, like a cultural artifact protected behind museum glass. For many in the latter culture, it is regarded as something that is constantly evolving; something that often cannot be definitively articulated because it is always changing.

Christopher Small (1998) articulated such a nuanced view of music with the term "musicking," which sought to redefine music from a noun to a verb: Something that people do; an *activity* in which they engage. In India, the word *sangita* encompasses both music and dance inextricably. In Christianity, prayer through music is considered a way to actively become closer to God (as the Christian adage goes, "he who sings prays twice"), while in the Islamic worldview, the melodic recitation of the *Qur'an* would not be considered a musical act whatsoever[11] (Wade, 2009). In Sub-Saharan Africa, the phenomenon of *ngoma* encompasses the highly-social acts of singing, dancing, drumming, and dramatizing throughout their performances.

In being mindful about the language being used to describe music, musicians must also become mindful of the aesthetic assertions and judgments made about music at-large. In the Western tradition, someone might consider an aesthetically pleasing instrumental performance to be one in which all instruments are played in-tune, instrumental balance is achieved, and resonant sonorities ring throughout the performance space. Yet, each of these aesthetic valuations might take on a different level of importance in other forms of music or carry no importance whatsoever. For example, the pitches in Indian classical music are tuned according to the *raga* that is being performed. To the untrained Western ear, the use of microtones in Indian classical music might sound "out of tune"; an altogether myopic perception. In terms of balance, the role of the highly ornate *gong ageng* in Indonesian gamelan music takes on a nearly subliminal musical role. The largest gong in the ensemble, it is intended to lie underneath the rest of the ensemble, giving support to the group and providing the metrical foundation, but ultimately intended to exist more-or-less outside of the listener's aural perception. A music critic unfamiliar with gamelan might comment on the irony of the *gong ageng* and other highly ornate gongs that are visually striking but whose sounds appear to be "lost" in the complexities of the mallet percussion in the foreground. Finally, regarding the desirability of timbre, the incredibly powerful nasal quality of many African, Turkish, and Arabic styles of singing brings into question whether open sonorities of Western traditions are truly the most evocative and desirable.

Interestingly, music educators are typically fully aware that there are no universalities when it comes to music, yet the language that teachers elect to use when discussing music often suggests otherwise. For example, any band director who has been charged with the responsibility of concurrently directing a jazz band may have experienced difficulties in teaching what a "proper" tone, style, or articulation might sound like between both musical genres. A rule-of-thumb in wind band performance typically maintains that a desirable attack is one in which the tongue does not stop the sonority of the note from resonating. Except when desired for effect, the result is usually an undesired "clipping" of the note. But in jazz articulation, this tongue-stop is often precisely the articulation that is sought. In other words, articulations in classical forms of playing (e.g., wind band, orchestra, chamber music) tend to adopt phonetic syllables such as "*tu*," "*du*," "*ku*," and other open-vowel attacks. In jazz, however, many phrases will end with a consonant, such as a "*doit*" or "*dat*" articulation. Therefore, speaking in universalities could come at the price of student confusion when the educator is not mindful about describing musical conventions as being style-, genre-, and culture-specific.

A Time and Place for World Music?

Now that a thorough discussion about world music has been laid out, when and where does it belong in an instrumental curriculum? This question will be revisited throughout the book, but it warrants immediate attention from the very beginning. Should band and orchestra teachers reserve one performance a year the be the so-called Music Around the World concert? Should they program Native American songs in November, African American music in February, Irish jigs in March, and Mexican mariachi on Cinco de Mayo? Should attention to non-familiar musics be reserved for the times of the year when we must be reminded to pay special attention to those cultures? And perhaps most challenging to answer: Is it better to attempt non-perfect renditions of unfamiliar musics and risk misrepresentation, or ignore these musics altogether out of fear of doing them injustice?

The latter question is one that will be continually examined throughout the pages of this book. But pertaining to the "time and place" for global musical engagements, experiences can and should occur in a number of settings, over various periods of time, and in several circumstances. They may be presented as a part of a unit, with the music teacher planning small visitations of a culture that lead to in-depth experiences and performance opportunities woven throughout the school year. To be clear, these experiences should not occur *solely* during national holidays (e.g., Mexican music during *Cinco de Mayo*), specific times of the year (e.g., Chinese music during Chinese New Year), and during harvest seasons (e.g., Native American music during Thanksgiving), although their appropriateness might be evident during these times in addition to others. Additionally, experiences can occur interdisciplinarily as the music teacher plans to combine activities with other subjects (e.g., history, social studies, literature, language departments) to provide a more immersive view of a given culture (see Chapter 6). Finally, they can and should occur when students ask about other cultures, or perhaps when they make ill-informed assumptions about certain musics that can be adequately amended through a brief visitation of that tradition.

Indeed, it is a blessing in disguise that there seem to exist no formal schemas which seek to assess these global music experiences. Learning cultural diversity through music is a holistic craft, not a reductionist one, and the freedom from the pressures of receiving a gold rating for masterfully performing Thai *piphat* music, for example, is a freedom that will allow World Music Pedagogy to survive and thrive in music ensembles for a long time to come.

World Music Pedagogy in Instrumental Music Education

The questions posed in the preceding pages set the stage for what is to be discussed at great lengths ahead: A culture-rich, holistically conceived, and socially responsive approach to instrumental music education. It represents an initial attempt to frame the craft of instrumental music education through the eyes of the World Music Pedagogy approach, as envisioned by Patricia Shehan Campbell (2004). World Music Pedagogy, or WMP, is an approach to teaching music and teaching culture with shared perspectives in music education and ethnomusicology. Therefore, the primary goal of this book is to provide instrumental music teachers, musicians, students in undergraduate and graduate music education courses, and administrators with a much-needed and long-overdue resource for mindfully and purposefully implementing World Music Pedagogy into the instrumental music classroom. By no means is this text intended to represent a "recipe book" of world music integration—nor should it, given the previously discussed problems associated with a one-size-fits-all curriculum. Instead, it is intended to be a guide of highly personalized and unique musical journeys.

Each of the following chapters will deal with a specific dimension of the World Music Pedagogy process. Each will begin with a brief vignette of the WMP dimension in-action—demonstrating what it looks like when instrumental students and teachers work through the simultaneous efforts of maintaining a traditional instrumental ensemble and entering into the unfamiliar-but-exciting territory of culture-rich ensemble approaches.

Chapter 2 will frame an important discussion around what it means to listen actively, especially with unfamiliar musical soundscapes. This will include suggestions for musical "visitations" and warm-ups that bring the musicians a glimpse of potentially unfamiliar musical models—all with the goal of achieving "cultural awakenings" that will inspire the remainder of the WMP process. Chapter 3 will discuss ways that instrumental programs can more fully embody these cultures through "participatory musickings," followed by strategies for preparing full performances of world music in Chapter 4. Chapter 5 will take these listening and performance concepts a step further, promoting continued musical journeys through composition, improvisation, and arranging. Chapter 6 will continue to endorse the "next steps" in World Music Pedagogy, which aims to make the music one's own as experiences potentially approach deepened transcultural expressions. This will involve the immersive integration of global musical cultures into the instrumental music program, including exposures to interdisciplinary study and experience that lead to cultural understanding and empathy. Finally, Chapter 7 will attempt to resolve the many questions and seemingly insoluble problems that will inevitably arise through a discussion of these issues.

In executing a successful culturally diverse curriculum within an instrumental ensemble, a thoughtful demonstration of respect, appreciation, and valuation for a wide variety of musical cultures is certainly a primary goal. However, in discussions that question the status quo, the tendency is to take for assumption the abasement of what has always been done. This simply should not be so. The importance of the Western art music has been briefly mentioned and must not be understated. Implementing World Music Pedagogy does not mean discounting the genius of Bach, Beethoven, and Brahms—or Husa, Sousa, and Maslanka—but it does involve realizing that theirs is merely one form of musical genius, and other forms of musical expertise are not more primitive or simpler than theirs.

Finally, readers must be constantly aware of a two-forked discussion that will both explicitly and implicitly take place throughout these pages, especially considering the complexity of cultural representations within a diverse range of classrooms. Among the students whose identities are not reflected in the current repertoire, the authors seek representation. Of course, this has been made clear throughout the chapter, but it is merely one part of the music educator's full responsibility. Indeed, it must go further: Of the millions of Anglo-American students throughout the United States and world whose cultural backgrounds *are* represented in current music curricula, the goal must be the development of cultural empathy, humility, and understanding. In this way, even among school districts in which 100% of the student population identifies as Anglo-American, the worth of pursuing a World Music Pedagogy is still clearly evident. Certainly, it would be equally irresponsible for the music teacher who teaches in a monoculturally White school to disregard this text as irrelevant and immaterial. Thus, the ultimate goal of this instrumental World Music Pedagogy is to ensure the understanding that musical excursions of the Anglo-American variety *are* valued and meaningful, but that musical traditions of other cultures are also highly complex, innovative, passionate, revered, celebrated, and worthy of serious study.

Notes

1 In many school districts throughout the United States, participation in a music ensemble fulfills students' only state-mandated music requirement. Therefore, many students do not need to enroll in classroom-based music classes as long as they participate in a music ensemble.

2 While discussions around cultural diversity in instrumental music have been somewhat scarcer, a commitment to teaching diverse musical cultures at the elementary school level and (to a somewhat lesser extent) in choral contexts has gained significantly more traction. These contexts seem to have made important steps toward more diverse musical repertoires, processes, and objectives, while instrumental music education has in many ways remained stagnated within predominantly Western musical realms.

3 Reed wrote the music for "La Fiesta Mexicana" based on the diverse musical styles he heard while studying in Mexico under an immersive Guggenheim Fellowship during 1948–1949.

4 New York City Department of Education. (2016). *Data about schools: Demographic snapshots.* Retrieved from http://schools.nyc.gov/AboutUs/schools/data/default.htm.

5 Washington State Office of Superintendent of Public Instruction. (2016). *Washington state report card.* Retrieved from http://reportcard.ospi.k12.wa.us/summary.aspx?group Level=District&schoolId=1&reportLevel=State&yrs=2015-16&year=2015-16.

6 This statement is made to shed light on the inherent value statements that are made within school music programs and does not intend to suggest that a refutation of the "trifecta" is essential for the development of globally minded instrumental curricula. Instead, this book will continually argue that the efforts of the World Music Pedagogy approach can in fact thrive alongside the continued efforts of traditional band and orchestra programs, in both practice and performance.

7 See Campbell and Bannerman's (2012) article "Anatomy of Mused 452: A course called 'Ethnomusicology in the Schools'". *Musik Pädagogik.* Berlin, FDR.

8 Documentation referring to the locality of Yakima (i.e., City of Yakima, Yakima Valley) is spelled differently from the recognized spelling of the Yakama People (www.yakamamuseum.com).

9 For further reading, refer to Stanton Wortham's (2003) article, Curriculum as a resource for the development of social identity. *Sociology of Education, 76*(3), 228–246.

10 See Small's (1998) discussion of how the Western concert hall came to be, including how conventions such as applauding only at the end of the piece were socially formed. Of further interest is his discussion on would-be typical audience behavior in non-traditional spaces such as the Rotunda in Ranelagh Pleasure Gardens.

11 In Islam, the term *musiqa* is a category encompassing various genres of music (Wade, 2009, p. 7).

References

Allsup, R. E. (2016). *Remixing the classroom: Toward an open philosophy of music education*. Bloomington, IN: Indiana University Press.

Banks, J. A. (2004). Multicultural education: Historical developments, dimensions, and practice. In J. A. Banks & C. A. M. Banks (Eds.), *Handbook of research on multicultural education* (2nd ed., pp. 3–29). San Francisco, CA: Jossey-Bass.

Campbell, P. S. (2004). *Teaching music globally: Experiencing music, expressing culture*. New York, NY: Oxford University Press.

Cooper, J. E. (2007). Strengthening the case for community-based learning in teacher education. *Journal of Teacher Education, 58*, 245–255. doi:10.1177/0022487107299979

González, N., Moll, L. C., & Amanti, C. (2005). *Funds of knowledge: Theorizing practices in households, communities, and classrooms*. Mahwah, NJ: Lawrence Erlbaum Associates.

Nketia, J. H. K. (1975). *The music of Africa*. London, UK: Gollancz.

Schippers, H. (2010). *Facing the music: Shaping music education from a global perspective*. New York, NY: Oxford University Press.

Sleeter, C. (2001). Preparing teachers for culturally diverse schools: Research and the overwhelming presence of whiteness. *Journal of Teacher Education, 52*, 94–106. doi:10.1177/0022487101052002002

Small, C. (1998). *Musicking: The meanings of performing and listening*. Hanover, CT: Wesleyan University Press.

Wade, B. C. (2009). *Thinking musically: Experiencing music, expressing culture*. New York, NY: Oxford.

2

Attentive Listening for Cultural Awakenings

Mr. Solie grips the steering wheel as he leaves his home and prepares for a long week at school. His 9th grade band is first that day, fresh off a successful festival performance from the week before. In his briefcase are the scores for the new pieces he will begin teaching and rehearsing today in preparation for the end-of-term concert, still several weeks away. A march and an overture are standard fare, *he thought*, and are probably suitable for his students at this stage in their musical development. *But he was having some misgivings about the third newly commissioned work, "Balkan Excursions."*

It's plenty exciting, *he thought*, replete with exotic scales and harmonies, thick percussion scoring, and meter changes. Including it as a concert selection would seem to satisfy the letter, if not the spirit, of the district's multicultural curriculum mandate. The performance challenges would occupy the group's attention for several rehearsals, and the kids would like it, no doubt.

But Mr. Solie's mind drifted to his recollection of the Metropolitan Folklife Festival he had attended over the weekend, where he saw a Madeconian troupe perform for a rapt audience. Dancers presented the Paidushko horo, *with men and women clothed in traditional garb. Musicians played a* gaida, *a* kaval, *a* tŭpan, *and an* accordion, *with missing instruments satisfactorily replaced by a synthesizer. The dancers' graceful, dramatic movements, and their infectious smiles reflected their deep joy and pride.* I didn't even know there was a Macedonian community here, *Mr. Solie thought. He had been mesmerized—caught up in the intensity of the sound and the spectacle. At the next stoplight, he looked again at his briefcase and wondered if "Balkan Excursions" could really approximate that experience for his students.*

Traffic was fairly light. His route to school took him through an older neighborhood where a growing community of Somali immigrants now live. On the sidewalk, a woman in a brightly colored shawl trekked alongside her young daughters on their way to the elementary school where, later in the week, Mr. Solie was planning to give a recruitment presentation. The woman sang as she walked, also caught up in a world of music in her head. What was that music? *Mr. Solie wondered. For the moment, that question seemed more important than whether or not the woman's two daughters would join the band.*

His favorite parking spot was still available. The early school bus had just arrived, and Mr. Solie was pleased to see many of his own students disembarking with instruments in-hand. They had practiced over the weekend, it seemed! *Meanwhile, a parent in another car pulled up to the front of the school to drop off his son. Luis had brought his trumpet home, too—but the trumpet music blaring from the car's stereo was that of a new mariachi group on the local Latino radio station. Mr. Solie hears Luis shout his goodbyes in Spanish to his father, then watches as he shuts the car door. The music, now suddenly muted, fades as Mr. Martinez drives away.*

Once in in the band room, Mr. Solie confronts the residual evidence of last week's flurry of school activities. Sheet music new and old, permission slips, thank-you cards, and junk mail all find their way to their proper place. Open on his desk is a book he purchased at last year's state music educators conference. Maybe I can read another couple of pages before the bell rings, *he thinks.*

> The word "listen" should be used from the very beginning and regularly through-out the rehearsal. In fact, I think having it painted in 8-foot letters on the wall behind the podium is a really good idea.[1]

Mr. Solie pauses. He takes out "Balkan Excursions," looks at it, and lays it on the desk. He turns to his computer and begins a search on the Smithsonian Folkways *website for "music from Macedonia." A few minutes later, Luis and two of his friends are among the first students to arrive to class.*

"What are we going to play first, Mr. Solie? Are we going to play that new music you gave us last week?"

"Pretty soon, Luis. In fact, don't get out your instruments just yet. Just take your seats, please. Let's do some listening first."

Listening

Listening is perhaps the most fundamental human response to music. Whereas the hearing of sounds is itself an acoustical and biological process, to *listen* is to pair this phenomenon with some degree of deliberate attention. For music of any culture and in any setting, listening would seem to precede just about any subsequent response, whether that be moving in synchrony to march or dance, raising one's voice to join in song, settling one's spirit to pray, or focusing one's imagination to follow the program of a symphonic tone poem. Indeed, the sheer multitude of such possibilities attests to the splendor of music. For instrumental music teachers, this also speaks to the necessity of directing students' mindful attention in a fashion which leads to their greater understanding of the music presented to them.

In a traditional school band or orchestra rehearsal, a teacher's admonition to "listen" usually presumes that students should exhibit particular subsequent behaviors that follow from what they heard. "Listen to the flutes" told to trumpet players may mean that they ought to play softly enough so that the melody and countermelody are played at equal volume. "Listen to the basses" may actually be an instruction to the violins to help them stay on pulse. A conductor's wincing at the saxophones while pointing to her ear serves as a cue for the players to adjust their intonation and match pitch with one another. Even a general exhortation to the entire ensemble—"LISTEN!"—can be intended as a remedy to any number of shortcomings in music performance. Usually, due to everyone's familiarity with the music, the desired response is understood by the students even if it has not been precisely specified by the teacher.

Some musical concepts may be overly complex or abstract, and do not lend themselves to simple explanations. A teacher may not wish to encumber rehearsal with innumerable directions from the podium on how to achieve proper balance or blend, or how to play in the correct style for a given piece of music. In these situations, recordings can be invaluable instructional tools to help provide students with a "gestalt" sense of musical performance goals. Students who find themselves confused or frustrated with an overwhelming set of performance challenges may be newly inspired after hearing accomplished instrumentalists play the music. Those who are especially curious may seek out other recordings within the genre, developing both a penchant for the repertoire and a deep understanding of a given set of musical norms and expectations. Such a musical education by means of aural transmission has long been embraced by both classical and especially jazz instrumentalists and pedagogues, particularly in cases where attending live performances is not feasible or even possible. Musicians in popular music styles (e.g., rock, country)—genres which originated outside of schools and which have flourished as such ever since—have also received their "education" on their instruments by means of imitating what they hear on recordings (Green, 2002). All of these examples illustrate the vitality of listening as a key component of a musical education, regardless of genre.

Recordings in Instrumental World Music Pedagogy

For instrumental music teachers wishing to share music of an unfamiliar culture with their students, recordings can serve even more critical educational purposes. To illustrate this, consider how much student knowledge can often be assumed by teachers when presenting a recording from within an already-familiar musical genre. Even if students did not know, say, a particular Tchaikovsky symphony, and even if they could not place it as being representative of the Romantic era, they would still likely understand it as "classical music" more generally. They would be able to identify the ensemble as an orchestra, and would probably correctly imagine a conductor, a concert hall, and an audience listening to the music offered in a presentational (non-participatory) setting. Or, upon hearing a new recording of popular music, the student might not know the particular artist, but probably would be able to identify the correct genre (rock, pop, reggae). He or she might have seen a music video from a similar music group, and thus is able to imagine the attire the musicians would wear, or the style of their hair. The music may inspire a particular manner of dancing (or fist-pumping or head-banging), which the student would know. The lyrics are probably in a familiar language, and they offer further clues as to the intended message of the song. In short, a great deal of the ambient culture in which the young person has been immersed throughout his or her life has already facilitated his or her understanding of what he or she is hearing.

Students with some degree of musical training would also bring their knowledge and skills to a new piece of Western music, even unwittingly. They may snap on beats two and four, or they may conduct a 3/4 pattern along with a waltz. They may recognize the tonality as major or minor, or they may comment about subtle elements of the composition or the performance—an arpeggiated bassline, a bluesy guitar solo, a bridge in the subdominant key. Conversations with other knowledgeable musicians would expand and refine their musical vocabulary, lending richness to their listening experience. Over time, the student becomes acculturated to a particular set of musical values and attitudes, especially if the music heard represents a performance standard to which the student aspires.

Initially, hearing music from far-away or "foreign" musical cultures may prove challenging or even frustrating for new listeners. The instruments they hear and the timbres those instruments produce might seem strange and unfamiliar, with pitches often falling "between the cracks" of Western tonality, and with rhythmic patterns that do not fit neatly into simple recurring units as does much of Western popular and art music. Or, the music may be inspiring and delightful to students, yet still misunderstood—encumbered by stereotypes learned from mass media, or even by ignorance imparted by friends or family members. The students' willingness to enter deeply into the musical experience may be limited by what they perceive to be the relevance and utility of this music, and by their lack of familiarity of the people and the cultures from which this music comes. They may see this as "someone else's" music, not "our" music—and since it's not even like our music, why study it? Why spend time with it? How does this help us become better people, better musicians?

Thus, our first stage of World Music Pedagogy in instrumental music ensembles is *Attentive Listening*—a deliberate and careful (although flexible) approach to providing students with an initial encounter that piques their curiosity and engages their imagination. It is, first and foremost, a direct experience with the music, preceded at most by the teacher's very brief and simple questions to help guide their listening. Notably, the presentation of the music is not delayed by first providing extensive background information; rather, the cultural context is discovered vis-à-vis the sonic experience itself and through the attendant questions that arise from the listening sessions. The recorded examples are, at first, of a limited duration (often 30 seconds or less), so as to provide these experiences in manageable, "bite-sized" portions. (Longer or full-length recordings can be explored later at the teacher's discretion, or could be offered as optional experiences for individual study.)

Questions, Tasks, Activities, and Goals

The questions for students in a band, orchestra, or other instrumental music setting are simple and straightforward, such as the following: *Where did this music come from? How many instruments do you hear? In what sort of setting would someone likely perform this music?* The teacher can also pose open-ended, personal, and even visceral questions as well: *What sort of emotional or feelingful effect do you get from these sounds? What sort of effect do you think the performers were trying to convey? Is this music for celebration or for mourning, for marching or for dancing, for prayer or for protests? Do you know anyone in your school or community who knows or plays this music? In our community, where might we go to hear this music performed?* Of course, many other questions are certainly possible, too.

Speculative or creative answers from students ought to be encouraged. The teacher can patiently provide "correct" answers as needed, or better yet, he or she can encourage discussion, prompting students to respond to their classmates towards discovering richer perspectives and more accurate information. The idea is to present the music to students as directly as possible, with the general goal being to have students engage with what they hear through their heightened awareness of what seems familiar or unfamiliar to them. Done with some degree of regularity, Attentive Listening can help students develop perspectives and attitudes that will facilitate their openness to diverse music and to the various peoples and cultures from which the music comes. This approach can also instill certain habits of mind that will help establish a context for students' further musical study.

For older adolescents especially, and/or for students who have already developed some degree of skill and fluency on their band or orchestra instrument, particularly rich discoveries can be made by making mindful comparisons between the music of other cultures they hear and the Western-centric music with which they are likely most familiar. Any given WMP listening experience will reveal at least surface-level similarities and differences in relationship to Western musical practice. Guided by the teacher's focused questions—and honed by repeated listenings to selected recordings—students can delight in understanding more deeply the nature of those "other" musical cultures, which in turn yields greater perspective on their own developing musical skills, and on the diversity of musical practice throughout human-ity. For example: *How* is a *kamancheh* (Iranian spike fiddle) bow held, and how does that compare to a violin bow hold? Listen to the sustained tones, and imagine the speed of the bowing as the tone color changes. Or, listen to the *shakuhachi* (Japanese end-blown flute) player. How does the musician manipulate his or her embouchure to create the range of timbres you hear? Is such a wide range possible on the instru-ments we play? What does this tell us about the components of virtuosity, both in that culture and in ours? Is the sense of "collaboration" heard on a performance of Iranian traditional music akin to a string quartet, or a jazz combo, or a symphony orchestra? Or something else entirely? How so? Such bold explorations are uniquely possible in a secondary-level instrumental music classroom, and they are wholly suited to the intellectual development and musical curiosities of students at this age.

At the Attentive Listening stage, playing along with the music (or humming along, or even tapping along with the pulse) is postponed—not discouraged per se, but only suspended for the moment, with the full knowledge that students' more complete involvement with the music will proceed in due course (i.e., in the Engaged Listen-ing and Enactive Listening stages; see Chapter 3). Certainly, the desire to join in making music with their own voices or instruments is entirely natural and laudable, and some students will want to quickly attempt to do so, even regardless of their own musical skill level. But grappling with the music intellectually—that is, engag-ing by listening, engaging with their hearts, their minds, and their vocabulary—is also a natural response, albeit one that often must be encouraged. To that end (and as illustrated in the opening vignette), teachers may wish to ask students to leave instruments in their cases during dedicated listening times. It may be particularly beneficial to establish such procedures as a matter of regular classroom practice, so that students come to expect that a portion of every rehearsal day will be devoted to listening. Verbal cues and/or agendas written on the chalkboard or whiteboard can help in this regard. Recall again that unlike for Western classical or popular music, most students do not bring to their initial encounters with a given "world" music selection a shared understanding of its general background or purpose. Attentive Listening processes serve to help establish this context first, before proceeding further.

It should be noted that such listening activities are not meant, and should not be approached, as merely "exposure" to this music, or as exercises in "music appreciation" for students, at least not in a casual sense of that term. Nor are these sessions intended to directly affect their musical preferences—although indeed, many students will come to love much of this music as a result of their deeper understanding of what they hear. Contrary to the common saying, music is not, in fact, a "universal language," much less a universally understood language (or even a "language" at all, strictly speaking), a fact confirmed by recent behavioral and neurological studies (e.g., Demorest, Morrison, Beken, & Jungbluth, 2008; Morrison, Demorest, Aylward, Cramer, & Maravilla, 2003). Still, music is a universal phenomenon, and music of a particular culture can be universally understood (or nearly so) given the listeners' greater familiarity with the music and its context. More precisely, to "appreciate" a given style or genre of music means to *place value* on it—that is, to recognize its origins, to know something of its form and function and expressive system, to be able to speak intelligently about the instruments and the people who play them, and to see and hear even in the most foreign of musical sounds (wherein "beauty" is acknowledged as local and enculturated) elements of a shared humanity.

As such, the overall objectives for these activities are as much attitudinal in nature as they are behavioral. Indeed, the shaping of attitudes (and their concomitant behaviors) is a critical component of any educational program (Madsen & Madsen, 2016). The most important attitudes for WMP are not necessarily targeted to a specific musical culture or selection, but rather are general qualities that indicate the learner's humility (i.e., a recognition of the extent and limits of one's own perspectives and knowledge) and his or her willingness to learn from an external source. Achieving such objectives, both among individual students and collectively as an ensemble as a "community of practice" (Wenger, 1998), is accomplished via the totality of the experiences, rather than through any one given listening exercise. Again, the regularity and the intentionality of listening as a consistent part of rehearsals are key, as is the attitude that the teacher models for the students.

Teachers can certainly still insist upon students' acquisition and demonstration of specific knowledge elements that accrue as part of these listening experiences. Specifying particular terms (such as names of musical instruments) or geographic locations (e.g., identifying a place-of-origin for a musical example presented aurally) may be appropriate behavioral objectives, and articulating them as such may be beneficial in designing a listening "lesson" and/or may be helpful when presenting an accounting of instructional planning to administrators. Note, however, that similar objectives may have been in place for music classes at much younger grade levels. If replicating such expectations at the secondary level represents a needed extension of students' knowledge and skill base, inclusive of a world-inclusive repertoire of music, teachers should be prepared to explain as such to parents, colleagues, administrators, and other stakeholders. It may be helpful to note that many references to understanding context (inclusive of particular cultural contexts) are embedded within the "Responding" and "Connecting" strands of the National Core Arts Standards (2014), even for traditional ensembles such as bands or orchestras.[2] It would stand to reason that especially as a teacher ventures into less-familiar musical styles and genres as a topic of study for his or her ensembles, listening activities and expectations for students thereof may seem very basic in form even though they may in fact be occasions of profound musical and intellectual growth. The Standards also call for more personal and sophisticated responses, appropriate for older students.[3] In any case, although comprised of discrete activities, Attentive Listening is best conceived as a long-term and immersive experience.

What follows in the remainder of this chapter is not a set of prescribed activities, but rather a set of possibilities. Here, they are presented in the context of specific musical examples. The thoughtful teacher is encouraged to adapt each activity according to the features and the context of the particular music under study, and according to the age and skill level of the students as appropriate. Generally, these Attentive Listening activities are meant to lead to Engaged and Enactive Listening (Chapter 3) and eventually to full-on performance (Chapter 4), and even more extensive forms of musical participation (see Chapters 5 and 6), although in some circumstances the teacher may find it preferable to focus on listening more exclusively. Here, as in all chapters throughout this volume, we present music of several different cultures. It is for the teacher to decide whether to "tour" a variety of selections from throughout the world, or to use a several of these strategies on a more limited number of musical examples from a single culture. Generally, our preference is the latter approach, so as to achieve greater depth of understanding.[4] Here, the strategies we suggest center largely around discussions and question-and-answer sessions, with some opportunities for outlining, sketching, locating on a map, and similar pre-performance activities. Again, appropriate to particular curricular values of the school or district, the creative teacher may wish to extend some of these ideas into group presentations, written assignments, or independent seek-and-find or show-and-tell projects, all as an adjunct or a supplement to the ensemble's regular performance activities.

Where to Begin?

Of all the world's music from which to choose, where should the globally conscious band or orchestra teacher begin? More precisely, what should guide an instrumental teacher's choice of music to present to students for listening? The dimensions of these decisions are somewhat different as compared to the process of selecting regular performance literature. By virtue of their own lifelong immersion in school music, most ensemble teachers have some sense of what constitutes "standard repertoire" for their genre, and what particular selections might be considered "masterworks" that students ought to encounter at some point in their playing careers. Challenges and opportunities for each piece are evident and can be considered relative to the strengths and weaknesses of the ensemble members. Moreover, there exists a vast support system to help guide teachers in these decisions—notably music publishers, with their print advertisements, emails, and website resources. Other aids include prescribed literature lists, recommendations from colleagues, and music reading sessions at state conferences. Again, though, what should an ensemble teacher do for World Music Pedagogy in the absence of such resources?

When possible, the teacher's own interest in music of a particular other culture is likely the first and perhaps the best place to start (or at least the most convenient), especially if the teacher him or herself affiliates with that culture and thus is, to some extent, a "culture bearer." Whether the music seems to "translate well" to school ensembles need not be a concern; indeed, finding and creating "bridges" from seemingly distant music to the realities of bands and orchestras is the very subject of this volume. Or, the teacher may have developed a special interest in another musical tradition, independent of his or her own cultural background. In either case, the teacher's own knowledge, curiosity, and demonstrable enthusiasm can sustain and inform his or her instruction throughout the long term. Few things are more rewarding than sharing one's own love of a particular music with young people, especially when they express their own interest in turn.

But as mentioned in Chapter 1, even more powerful than "looking within" is for the teacher to consider carefully the students in his or her own ensemble, and to consider if among them or their families are musical traditions which have yet to be honored, studied, and celebrated within the school's music program. Minority students within a majority culture may be recent immigrants (or Native Americans) whose cultural traditions are very close to them. Or, they may be a few generations removed from having immigrated, with memories of their culture-of-origin retained in family traditions, houses of worship, or cultural centers. Whether they assimilated recently or long ago—or whether they assimilated at all—they may be accustomed to the school as an institution unto itself, with its own traditions and with little room or interest in others. Having a teacher sincerely (and delicately, as necessary) express interest in learning more about their musical backgrounds and traditions, with an eye towards welcoming this music as a bona fide part of the music curriculum at school, can be an especially powerful experience for these families and for the entire community, particularly if this interest and this relationship is sustained over a long period of time. The teacher might also wish to make a special effort to seek out music from families whose children are not participants in the school's music program, given that minority students (especially Latino students) are underrepresented in American high school bands, choirs, and orchestras (see Elpus & Abril, 2011).

More practical considerations may influence the selection of particular world music traditions to present to a band or orchestra class. A nearby community or cultural center might be a place where a given music is heard regularly, and where its denizens can speak knowledgeably to a curious music teacher about representative recordings or about the meaning of particular musical selections. Live performances may present an opportunity for a "field trip" for a school music program, or perhaps the teacher could arrange for a performer from the center to come to the school and play or sing for sing for students. Teachers would do well to prepare students for these occasions with listening experiences garnered from several recordings, and to follow-up the visits with further listening opportunities to extend and enrich student understanding of this music and of the people to whom the music belongs. Where possible, music teachers may wish to collaborate with school colleagues in other subject matters towards creating cross-curricular learning experiences for students. If teachers elsewhere in the school are already taking advantage of community resources in this fashion for their classes, band or orchestra teachers can complement these lessons by seeking out recordings of music from the culture.

Or, such opportunities might be more temporal in nature, informed by news of community and world events. The opening of a new ethnic market in town can inspire a curiosity of the proprietor's culture. The deployment of military service men and women (perhaps students' parents or other family members) can be an occasion for discovering more about the native sounds of the far-away lands they will visit. Even the release of a new animated movie can prompt an examination of the extent to which music of other cultures is accurately suggested or portrayed. In using occasions such as these as curricular material, the school's music program becomes less insular and more reflective of the world and of the people throughout the world who make music. Indeed, the need to impart a thoroughly musical education to instrumental music students is borne not only from a sense of locality or of temporality, but also from a concern for universality—that is, from a desire for students to be able to utilize musical knowledge and skills toward learning something of the great (and little) musical expressions of the world's cultures, in addition to learning the rich traditions of Western art and popular music.

Finally, the traditional band or orchestra literature that a school ensemble is rehearsing can also present the need for "excursions" to music from other parts of the world. Perhaps a given selection features authentic melodies from another culture as source material for the composition. Examples for band might include John Barnes Chance's "Variations on a Korean Folk Song," which features the Korean folk song "Arirang,"[5] or Jan Van der Roost's "Rikudim," with originally written melodies inspired by Israeli folk songs; for orchestra, consider Johannes Brahms's "Hungarian Dances" (drawn from both semi-authentic folk strains and others written in the *style hongroise*) or Alexander Borodin's "In the Steppes of Central Asia" (a symphonic tone poem with his own "Russian" and "Eastern" themes). More troublesome cases might be any number of purportedly Native American–themed compositions (or similar movie theme arrangements), with stereotypical open-fifth harmonies in repeated eighth notes. (Where possible, it is usually best to avoid such selections in the first place.) In these and similar cases, the thoughtful teacher will want to seek out recordings of more authentic presentations of those same melodies and of other music from the represented culture—not for the purpose of merely supplementing or "enriching" the study of the ensemble literature, but rather to allow the music of that culture to stand on its own, and to afford students as much of an opportunity as possible to encounter it directly, in an unmediated fashion.

Classroom circumstances will inevitably vary for each teacher. But for all, Attentive Listening starts, alas, with listening. Please note that the descriptions for each of the selections that follow are intended as focused introductory material, not as definitive commentary. For this material and for recordings of any other music (culturally familiar or otherwise), readers are encouraged to "dig deeper" and conduct their own investigations in order to find more information which helps guide their listening. Note also that the Attentive Listening strategies featured for each of these recordings are examples of approaches that could be used when presenting music to students. Depending on the particular example chosen (and depending on the musical readiness of the students), many of the strategies here could be interchanged with one another.

Please note that unless specified otherwise, each procedure-point consists of playing the recording for students (usually just the first 30 seconds or so) together with an accompanying question or task presented by the teacher. Usually, the question precedes the presentation of the recording, so as to help focus students' listening. The teacher may wish to judiciously reverse this order on occasion in order to allow for more open-ended student responses. In any case, the teacher should take care to not burden the listening experience with excessive verbiage. Listening to the recording multiple times at each point (with ample opportunities for guided student responses throughout) is also encouraged.

Examples for Attentive Listening

"Mi Gente," Héctor Lavoe

"Mi Gente" ("My people") was one of the signature songs by Héctor Lavoe (1946–1993), a famous Salsa singer from Puerto Rico. *Salsa* (literally, "sauce"—an indication of the "spiciness" of the music, although the term is not embraced by all players of this musical style) is a fusion of several Cuban and Puerto Rican traditional dance music traditions, together with influences from Latin jazz. Lavoe's life inspired a 2006 biographical film, *El Cantate*, starring Marc Anthony as Lavoe and Jennifer Lopez as his wife, "Puchi."

This selection us performed by Lavoe on lead vocals, who is backed by the Fania All-Stars, a group comprised of musicians who worked for Fania Records (a New York–based record label that specializes in Salsa music). Listen for the bravado of the solo vocalist and the multiple layers of ostinato parts in the rhythm section (in particular, the *son montuno* piano and bass lines against the percussion, Figure 2.1).

Figure 2.1   Bassline and piano montuno to "Mi Gente" (0:18)

Episode 2.1: Salsa in the Classroom (Learning Pathway #1)

Specific Use: Instrumental ensembles (e.g., band, orchestra, jazz); Grades 4–12

Materials:

- "Mi Gente," Héctor Lavoe (Puerto Rico/Caribbean)

Procedure:

1. Ask in advance: "Where is this from, and how can you tell?"

   This is a good "standard" opening question to initiate nearly any Attentive Listening experience. For "Mi Gente," many students will likely recognize the Spanish language, and/or they may identify the rhythm section of the ensemble as playing Caribbean music of some kind.

2. Play track (beginning to about 0:30, at the beginning of the first verse).

3. Ask, "What 'Western' components are there here? And, what is distinctly Afro-Caribbean?"

    Here, we are starting with what's "familiar," before proceeding to what's "different." The reverse order could be employed as well. The two questions could be asked and answered simultaneously, or in sequence. Western components include most instruments (piano, bass, brass, etc.), the instrumentation (salsa band which is derivative of jazz bands), and the general tonalities (note the pedal dominant throughout the introduction); Afro-Caribbean components include percussion instruments such as bongos, congas, and timbales. Güiro and especially claves are common in this style, but are not heard on this recording. (The clave rhythm is implied and felt by the players, even if not heard.)

4. Play track (same segment).

5. Ask, "What is adventuresome about this music? More precisely, what grabs your attention, what 'sticks out'? What seems to 'break the rules'?" Note the non-chord tone in the piano, and the characteristically "edgier" brass.

6. Play track.

7. Ask, "What do you think the soloist (Héctor Lavoe) is shouting at the very beginning of the tune?" The teacher can ask non-Spanish speaking students to listen carefully to the tone of the exclamation, and to the cackle-like laughter. Like much of Salsa music, the singer is asserting himself and expressing his own pride and masculinity: "¡Cuidado que por ahí vienen los anormales!" [Roughly, "Watch out . . . here comes a crazy person!"] Then, for added imagery, in a mix of Spanish and English "y con a straightjacket!" ["And with a straightjacket!"] This "sets up" the main text of the song. "Oigan, mi gente, lo más grande este mundo, siempre me hacentir un orgullo profundo." ["Listen, my people, the greatest of this world, I always feel a deep pride."]

In any music where lyrical content is prominent, it is natural to attend to the words of the song to discover the meaning of the music. But "meaning" is contextualized in many different audio clues, including the instrumentation, the particular style of the music (and the context that precedes that style), and the "attitude" conveyed by the performers.

"Tulina's Carmona," Kinan Azmeh

Born in Damascus, Syria, clarinetist and composer Kinan Azmeh traverses a range of musical styles, described as "Arabic music fused with jazz, opera, folk and classical music."[6] He studied at the Arab conservatory of Music in Damascus, then later at the University of Damascus (where he double-majored in electrical engineering and music), the Juilliard School, and the City University of New York. "When it comes to my musical world, the whole idea of dialogue and being open to the other is actually what shapes my musical journey," Azmeh says. "I maneuver between Arabic music and jazz and classical . . . and I feel that I am equally connected to all these different cultures. So dialogue is a concept I live with—live *by*, in a way. Especially making my music."[7]

Kinan Azmeh performs on clarinet, joined by Kyle Sanna on guitar, John Hadfield on percussion (hand drum, shaker, triangle, box drum, et al.), and Petros Klampanis on string bass. Here, Western instruments are performed in Middle Eastern styles, in a fusion of jazz and Syrian musical influences, with a melody reflecting Arabic *maqam* modes.

Episode 2.2: Contemporary Syrian Music (Learning Pathway #2)

Specific Use: Instrumental ensembles (e.g., band, orchestra, jazz); Grades 4–12

Materials:

- "Tulina's Carmona," Kinan Azmeh (Syria)

Procedure:

The teacher will need to gauge the students' ability to entertain divergent questions while remaining focused on the listening tasks. At times, more direct, convergent questioning may be prudent.

1. Ask in advance: "What kind of music is this?" (Or: "What part of the world is this music from? Is this traditional or modern music?")
2. Play track (beginning to 0:35; first three statements of melody).
3. Play track again, still temporarily withholding the identity of performers. *(Not disclosing the performers' names forces a more direct, focused, and imaginative listening of the music itself, unbiased by cues or clues.)*
4. Encourage students to imagine possible styles and places-of-origin. Possible answers might include jazz, Arabic music, fusion; modern music with traditional flavors. Klezmer is proximous (i.e., not accurate as a place-of-origin for this music, but geographically nearby and possibly related and/or influential on this style).
5. Play track again (same segment).
6. Ask, "What cultural influences do you hear? What cues from the music suggest those cultures?" *Encourage students to use musical vocabulary. Percussion, syncopation, and instrumental texture (clarinet with rhythm section) suggest jazz; modal scalar passages suggest Arabic music; clarinet colorings (e.g., growl, bended notes) might suggest klezmer; guitar stylings may suggest Spanish influences.*
7. Ask, "What aspects of their performance are virtuosic?" Obvious answers include "fast notes" (or more precisely, accurate execution of rapid passages).
8. Play track again and repeatedly.

9. Encourage students to hear both individual and ensemble characteristics. For both percussion and clarinet especially, note the wide range of instrumental colors, and the rapid and dramatic changes in dynamics for expressive effect. Note the precision in the harmonized lines between clarinet and guitar.

10. Discuss and ask: "The clarinet soloist is the composer of the piece and the leader of this group; his name is Kinan Azmeh. How is his clarinet playing similar to and different than the kind of playing our clarinet players normally do?" Similarities include precise intonation, breath support and tonal control; differences may include pitch bending, tonal colors, stop-tongue articulation (which is more common in jazz stylings).

Resources for extended study:
Artist's website: kinanazmeh.com

"Tulina's Carmona" illustrates how virtuosic performers can play non-Western (in this case, Syrian) music on instruments often associated more-or-less exclusively with Western styles.

"Chemtengure," Lora Chiorah-Dye and Sukutai

This recording is drawn from an album entitled *Safarini in Transit: Music of African Immigrants*, where musicians from various cultures and countries throughout Africa—now living in the United States—perform songs they recall from their childhood as well as other contemporary songs. ("Safarini" means "on a journey.") The selection "Chemtengure" (also spelled "Chemutengure") is performed by Lora Chiorah-Dye and the Sukatai Marimba Ensemble, which includes (among others) three of her children, Tendai Maraire, Danai Maraire, and Dumi Maraire, Jr., all on *mbira* and/or vocals. "Chemtengure" is a traditional Shona melody (sung in the Shona language), which Chiorah-Dye recalled singing in first grade. Chiorah-Dye wrote words to the song, remembering a vendor named Vajeke who brought familiar treats like sweet potatoes to children living in boarding schools far from home.

Listen for the call-and-response form, with freely harmonized responses and multiple layers of rhythm (i.e., polyphonic textures) among the vocal leader, the vocal responses, and the *mbira* and *hosho* (shaker) (Figure 2.2).

Episode 2.3: Zimbabwean Shona for Band (Learning Pathway #3)

Specific Use: Instrumental ensembles (e.g., band, orchestra, jazz); Grades 4–12

Materials:

• "Chemtengure," Lora Chiorah-Dye and Sukutai (Zimbabwe)

Procedure:

1. Ask students and discuss: "Do you remember any particular song you sang (or one you heard sung to you) in your very early childhood? How long ago? What were the songs about? Did only certain people sing them? Did you sing them, and did others sing with you? If asked, could you play the song on an instrument now? (Or, is it so personal that you might not even want others to play it?) Were they folk songs of sorts, or were they melodies from a favorite television show, or were they originally created songs? Have they ever been notated? Were they passed orally from an earlier generation?" (Consider asking students to ask their own parents/guardians these questions, and ask if they would consider sharing their findings in class.) *Such a discussion could constitute a lesson unto itself, and/or could "contextualize" the more technical aspects of the music that they will hear in this recording.*

Figure 2.2   Layers of sound within the opening of "Chemtengure" (approx. 0:09–0:10)

2. Play track (first 30 seconds).

3. Ask, "Where is this from, and how do you know?" Students may recognize this as generally "African." With added listening experiences drawn from throughout that continent, students can be led to trace the origin of this music more specifically as Zimbabwean. (Note again that this was actually recorded in Seattle in 1996.) The *mbira* (sometimes Anglicized as "thumb piano") is native to south-central Africa, particularly the Democratic Republic of Congo, and Zimbabwe. Note also the various timbres and tessituras of the *mbiras* heard. Listen to the ring of the metal and the resonance of the wood, and the "rattle" that accompanies the performance of each note.

4. Play track again (same segment).

5.   Listen and feel: Allow the layers of sound to "wash over" them. Later, more focused listening on the polyrhythms will reveal the complexity of the music.

6.   Play track again (same segment).

7.   Ask, "How many layers of rhythms do you hear?" *For now, encourage only a verbal response. If the class proceeds to Enactive/Engaged Listening stages with this particular selection, students may attempt to notate three layers of rhythm.* What else contributes to the "wash" of sound in the music? Note the alternating thumbs in the *mbira* performance, creating a multi-voice effect. The off-pulse accents (perhaps more felt than heard) also contribute to an expansive sense of time.

8.   Play track again (same segment).

9.   Note the general call-and-response pattern. Ask and imagine: "How were the responses likely learned by the performers?" Note the "counterpoint" between high and low voices in the responses. Singers may have already known a general sense of harmonization for this style, which they then adapted specifically for this song, improvising at key points. It is unlikely that particular harmonies were ever notated.

The call-and-response pattern is probably a rather salient feature for many listeners with musical experience. Less obvious are the subtleties of the pulse (and the delicate-yet-solid sense of ensemble among the performers), made up of layers of rhythms which reveal themselves more clearly upon repeated listenings. Attempts to describe the music using vocabulary specific to Western musical traditions (e.g., counterpoint, polyrhythms, meter) can be helpful at first; soon, however, limitations of the vocabulary may become evident.

"Sea of Spring" ("Haru No Umi"), Performed by Tomoko Sunazaki

"Haru No Umi" (rendered variously as "Sea of Spring," "Sea in the Spring," "Springtime Sea," and so on) was composed in 1929 by Japanese musician Michio Miyagi (1894–1956). Blind since he was eight years old, Miyagi wrote this duet based on his visual memory of the Sea of Tomonoura (an inland sea near Hiroshima). Instruments heard are the *koto*—a plucked stringed instrument (Figure 2.3) which Miyagi played and here is performed by Tomoko Sunazaki, and the *shakuhachi*—an end-blown flute, traditionally made of bamboo, somewhat similar to a recorder but with only five finger holes (Figure 2.4), here performed by Masayuki Koga. "Haru No Umi" represents an example of the *Shin Nihon Ongaku* movement, a blending of Japanese and Western musical influences in the early 20th century.

Note the tone color variations in *shakuhachi*, heard especially in long sustained notes, and the virtuosic and expressive use of vibrato.

Figure 2.3 Japanese *koto*[8]

Figure 2.4 Japanese *shakuhachi*[9]

Episode 2.4: Japanese "Art Music"

Specific Use: Instrumental ensembles (e.g., band, orchestra, jazz); Grades 4–12

Materials:

- "Sea in the Spring," Tomoko Sunazaki (Japanese art music)

Procedure:

1. Days prior to playing the recording, ask students to compile an inventory of Western classical music pieces inspired by the sea. (Less experienced students will need more help with this.) Examples might include Debussy's "La Mer," Mendelssohn's "The Hebrides (Fingal's Cave Overture)," Vaughan Williams's "Sea Symphony" or perhaps his brief work for band, "Sea Songs." Ask students to identify common elements among those disparate compositions. Answers could include selected use of modal harmonies, slow dynamic changes and generally soft dynamic profiles overall, and undulating accompanimental motifs.

2. Briefly explain the inspiration for the composition of "Sea in the Spring."

3. Play track (beginning to about 0:30).

4. Discuss and see if students identify similar elements in "Sea in the Spring" as they did with the compositions discussed earlier.

5. Play track.

6. Ask: "Is this a composed or an improvised piece? Is it modern or traditional?" *This is a modern, composed piece; many musicians have performed and recorded "Sea in the Spring," which is perhaps Miyagi's most famous work. The point of this question is to help students recognize that other cultures have "art music" traditions as well, and that not all non-Western musical examples are folk music.*

7. Play track.

8. Listen carefully to the changes of timbre in the sustained notes of the *shakuhachi*. Ask, "How might the performer accomplish that?" Virtuoso performers manipulate the timbre through changes of airstream, embouchure, blowing angle, and fingerings (including half-holes), all made that much more difficult by the limited resistance from the instrument. *Students can get a better sense of this challenge by attempting to make similar timbral changes on a recorder (or on a* shakuhachi, *if one is available), or on the low register of a flute.*

9. Play track.

10. Listen to the vibrato, both in the *koto* and the *shakuhachi*. Ask, "How does this compare to vibrato in Western music?" Vibrato in this performance of "Sea in the Spring" is generally wider and more varied in speed than is often heard in Western art music. Like Western music, however, vibrato is withheld and employed purposefully, for expressive effect.

Resources for extended study:
Miyagi Michio Official Website: www.miyagikai.gr.jp/eng-top
Jinko, K. (1986). Some innovations in musical instruments of Japan during the 1920s. *Yearbook for Traditional Music*, *18*, 157–172. doi:10.2307/768527

In some respects, "Sea in the Spring" represents music which is "most distant" from Western practice, beginning with a floating, non-metrical sense of time. Its harmonic system seems somewhat more familiar, perhaps reflective of Miyagi's passion for blending Japanese and Western elements in his compositions. Students typically prefer musical styles that have more (rather than fewer) elements in common with Western norms. When sharing music that at first seems most difficult to understand, it would seem important for teachers to quickly call students' attention to sonic or contextual elements that might provide points of familiarity with their own musical experiences.

The use of the pentatonic scale is another salient feature of this selection. Teachers who elect to focus on this musical element would do well to explore the particular arrangement of pitches, and to discuss how this differs from other five-note scales found in other cultures. Teachers should combat broad stereotypes that pentatonic scales are "Asian" scales, or that they are somehow reflective of "simplistic" music (notwithstanding the entirely appropriate use of such scales in established pedagogical traditions such as the Orff-Schulwerk approach or the Kodály Method).

"Eternity," Ghazal

Ghazal is a trio, comprised of Kurdish-Iranian *kamancheh* ("spike fiddle") player Kayhan Kalhor (Figure 2.5; Kalhor is also a member of the Silk Road Ensemble, like Kinan Azmeh in Episode 2.2), and Indian musicians Shujaat Khan on *sitar* and Swapan Chaudhuri on *tabla*. (Sandeep Das plays *tabla* in this performance.) "Eternity" is the last of three selections on Ghazal's 2003 live album *The Rain*, which was nominated for a Grammy Award. The word "ghazal" refers to a style of pre-Islamic poetry that originated in the Arabian Peninsula and was brought to South Asia along the Silk Road; these musicians' adoption of this word as the name of their group reflects the collaborative nature of this ensemble, bridging Persian and Hindustani traditions.

In the brief excerpt, notice a gentle and nuanced sense of "dialogue" between Khan on sitar and Kalhor on *kamancheh*, and over the full selection, a grand sense of structure that culminates in a "blazing finale."

Figure 2.5   Kayhan Kalhor performing on the *kamancheh*[10]

Episode 2.5: Persian and Hindustani Instrumental Music

Specific Use: Instrumental ensembles (e.g., band, orchestra, jazz); Grades 4–12

Materials:

- "Eternity," Ghazal (Persian and Hindustani)

Procedure:

1. Play track (beginning to about 0:30).
2. Ask, "How many instruments do you hear?" Students may be surprised to learn that there are only two instruments in this excerpt (the *tabla* does not enter until later); the sitar's sympathetic strings provide a rich accompaniment to its own melodic line.
3. Play track.
4. Listen to the back-and-forth between Khan and Kalhor, each improvising over a simple motif (1–2–1–3), with each solo of varying durations (some brief, some long; some simple, more melismatic). Notice the sense of restraint, with each musician only modestly embellishing the melodic statement in each iteration. Their patience allows for a broader sense of form and drama to the composition.

5. Play track.

6. Listen to the contrasting timbres between the plucked *sitar* and the bowed *kamancheh* (sometimes played plucked or "pizzicato"); notice also the variations of the *kamancheh* tone as Kalhor accents certain passages. Ask, "When does the *kamancheh* sound more like a violin (often in upper registers), and when does it sound more voice-like?" (The bow can be set to various tensions, allowing for different timbres.)

7. Play track.

8. Ask, "How else do the musicians sustain the listeners' interest throughout the composition?" Notice more frenzied strumming later in the piece, yielding percussive and "ringing" moments as high points. The ever-present drone of the *sitar* provides a sense of stability as the musicians improvise over selected motifs.

9. Ask, "How is this different than more traditional music from India, or from Kurdistan?" Much Indian music makes use of very long rhythmic cycles; here, shorter, syncopated rhythmic patterns seem more common. Notice, however, the variations in the *tabla* patterns later in the piece.

Ghazal represents a beautiful (and popular) collaboration of musicians who are from regions of the Middle East and the Asian subcontinent known that are known today for a great deal of political and ethnic strife. The study of this piece can lead to separate explorations of various Iranian and Indian musical traditions, as well as to other instances of cross-cultural music-making.

"Tujang Biru," Gamelan Angklung, Mas Village (Bali)

The island of Bali (in Indonesia) is home to a Hindu enclave amongst the most populous Muslim-majority country in the world. The Mas village musicians heard in this recording (gathered in Bali in the 1960s by ethnomusicologist Ruby Ornstein) were mostly farmers, and were all men and boys who played this music from memory. "Gamelan" means a set of instruments, and "Angklung" refers to a particular type of portable ensemble. Music of this style is often performed specifically for religious and ritualistic purposes. "Tujang Biru" ("Blue Flower") is *kuno* (traditional) music that accompanies particular ceremonies such as temple rituals or funeral processions. Ornstein describes the ceremonies as follows:

> It is a festive and deliberately noisy scene, a desirable form of confusion called ramé. . . . Ngaben, or rites for the dead, also requires the services of the gamelan angklung. . . . The [body ready for cremation] sits atop a platform supported by a network of bamboo poles so that it can be carried by a group of men and boys. The procession to the cremation grounds can include hundreds of people, or even more if the deceased is of noble birth. Women carrying dishes of food lead the procession, and they are followed by the gamelan angklung. . . . On the same day, or on another auspicious day, the gamelan angklung leads a procession that brings the ashes to the sea.[11]

Featured instruments include two metallophones played in unison (the *gangsa*, and a *kantilan* an octave above), and a third metallophone (a *jegogan*, an octave below) plays on every other beat. *Réyong* (tuned gong-chimes) ornament the melody in a style called *kotékan*; other gongs called *kempli* and *kelenang* mark the pulse.

Episode 2.6: Gamelan Angklung

Specific Use: Instrumental ensembles (e.g., band, orchestra, jazz); Grades 4–12

Materials:

- "Tujang Biru," Gamelan *Angklung*, Mas village (Bali)

Procedure:

1. Prior to playing the recording (similar to Episode 2.4), discuss types of religious music, perhaps specifically types of music heard at funerals. In modern American practice, the family of the deceased often chooses the music to be played. The style and "mood" of the music may vary according to the family's preferences, or may be specified according to a particular religious custom. A selection that is celebratory in nature is somewhat less common; an exception might be the "second line" tradition in New Orleans "jazz funerals." Festive music to accompany cremation and burial (as in this recording) would seem quite extraordinary to many Westerners.

2. Play the entire track. (It is only a minute-and-a-half in duration.)

3. Ask, "How many layers of sound do you hear?" Discuss and describe, playing the recording repeatedly as needed. (Four layers are described previously.)

4. Play the middle portion of the track (about 0:30 to 1:00).

5. Note the asymmetrical phrases (another characteristic of the *angklung* style), and imagine the challenge posed by needing to memorize a particular, specific melodic pattern, only partially repetitive, on such a limited set of pitches.

6. Play just the opening five seconds of the track. That very brief opening pattern, played on the *gangsa*, functions as the "title" of the composition and serves as the signal for the entire ensemble regarding what music to play.

7. Ask, "Are there examples of this practice in music more familiar to us?" (Possible answers could include a drum cadence to introduce a fight song, or a particular melody played by guitar at the beginning of a rock tune, or perhaps an "incipit" of a chant in a Catholic Mass.)

Whereas an earlier listening example ("Sea in the Spring," Episode 2.4) featured an unfamiliar sense of pulse, "Tujang Biru" is somewhat more familiar in this regard, but it features a more distant sense of timbre and tonality. The four- and five-note scales in *Angklung* music do not perfectly match to Western temperament. Balinese tuning is quite specific, yet can vary among different gamelan instruments; the "beats" that ensue between slightly different tunings when two gamelans play together (in Balinese, this is called *ombak*, or wave) are a deliberate and intentional part of the texture, yielding a shimmering quality. (Such intonation discrepancies are scrupulously avoided in nearly all Western music). Again, providing a sense of context to students (using familiar reference points as necessary) can be critical.

Teacher Feature: John Brindle on Offering Diverse Musical Practices in Band

John Brindle, Teacher of Guitar, Drumming, Keyboard, and Mariachi at Prairie Middle School in Aurora, CO, previously also the Interim Band Director

Q: How did you come to teach this array of music offerings at your school?
A: My previous teaching position was in La Junta, Colorado, down in the southeast corner of the state. I was teaching K–12 music to farm and ranch kids, and I largely followed the traditional model of school music offerings, using standard general music texts for my elementary students and standard ensemble repertoire for the band and choir. A few years later, some personnel shifts in our district enabled me to stay in just one school building, full-time, provided that I could teach one more class. My principal suggested that I try offering a drumming class and a mariachi class, even though I knew nothing about mariachi at the time! So I worked through that for a couple of years, try-ing to discover what this music was all about . . . what is the culture that it came from,

what does the Mariachi tradition look like, what does this mean in the world today, and what does it mean for my school.

When I moved to my current position at Prairie Middle School, I had an opportunity to teach only drumming and mariachi. This has since evolved to include guitar and keyboard offerings as well. For all of these classes, I have tried to stay true to a model of experience-based learning . . . through doing and through listening, rather than primarily through reading.

Q: Do you pursue any culturally specific approaches in your drumming class?
A: Our hand drumming especially is largely based on West African music. We create a lot of polyrhythms, and there are lots of opportunities for students to make decisions on what rhythms to imitate or expound upon when they play. I will sometimes assign particular rhythms to particular drums. I have worked with a particular resource, *West African Drum and Dance: A Yankadi-Macrou Celebration,* by Kalani and Ryan Camara (Alfred Music Publishing). I learned about this in my graduate program at Adams State University, where I also encountered *Thinking Musically* by Bonnie Wade and *Teaching Music Globally* by Patricia Shehan Campbell [both published by Oxford University Press]. I've been able to use a lot of those ideas in my teaching practice.

Q: How do you approach music listening in your classes?
A: In the same way we say that "a picture is worth a thousand words," listening to something—especially for style, especially for feel—is enormously important. I think we do our kids a disservice when we tell them that they shouldn't listen to something until they can read it, because there's so much that comes from listening to a piece of music. There's inspiration in so many different ways . . . like, "oh my gosh, this person plays or sings in this way that I really want to emulate." There's a connection to the tradition that I don't think that you can really grasp if you don't listen.

And the reality of our kids' lives outside of our music classes is that they are already listening to music all the time . . . whether at family events where mariachi music is being played, or at a park where they sit and strum their guitars with friends, or through their headphones while they're riding a skateboard to school. So we ought to use listening in an educational way, too. In my classes I share video and audio recordings of pieces that we're playing, or pieces that are in a similar style, or pieces that might be nothing like what we're playing but are still examples of exceptional musicianship.

One of my favorite recordings to share is a Mariachi Vargas video of "El Cascabel" . . . a selection that was far beyond our abilities, but I would still show it at the beginning of the term as an exemplar of what our goal was as an ensemble. Then, I played it again for them later in the semester, and they would discuss with me how they understood it differently—what they saw, what they heard—now that they had more experience with the music. So yes . . . listening is absolutely key.

Q: In La Junta especially, was your instruction informed by the kind of music that was happening outside of the school?
A: Yes. This was music that was current in the community, and it continued to be so as I taught it. Students and other community members would sometimes ask me to have the group learn and perform particular songs that were special to them.

What I find so exciting and vital and vibrant and important about many world music traditions—particularly mariachi—is that there are so many traditional songs which span several generations, yet they are still played today by even the most popular artists. And those artists write and perform their own music, too. It's folk music, but it's popular music, too, and it has its own virtuosity such that it is also like classical music. It's very rich, and it's widely embraced—it really is music of the people.

Now, Press "Play"

Diligently sharing recordings of music culled from throughout the globe remains as perhaps the easiest means of providing instrumental music students an initial, broad perspective on the world's musical cultures. Such material is now more accessible than ever before, with numerous possibilities existing for finding recordings of music performed by true representatives of a given nation or ethnic group, "unmediated" by a composer or an arranger or a movie studio. Band and orchestra directors can pursue such listening activities deliberately and regularly as an integral component of their curriculum (even if only briefly, at first), both as an end unto itself and as a prelude to further musical exploration via performing, composing, and/or improvising. With some measure of careful planning, exploring selected musical traditions of the world can be done in congruence with the regular performance program that the school ensemble would otherwise pursue. Key to the teacher's success in these efforts will be the questions to be posed to students regarding what they hear, and the discussions that will follow a given listening episode. Conveying a sense of delight and curiosity about the music is also critical; this can be paired with a sense of kinship, whereby the young instrumentalists in one's classroom come to recognize what aspects of their own musical surroundings and their own musicianship are both *similar to* and *different than* those of the performers whose music they encounter. In so doing, music listening—like music performance—embodies a true sense of play, through which students learn more about themselves and each other and the world around them.

Notes

1 Battisti, F. (1998). In J. E. Williamson (Ed.), *Rehearsing the band* (pp. 1–10; quote on p. 5). Cloudcroft, NM: Neidig Services.
2 See in particular Anchor Standard 7, "Perceive and analyze artistic work," and Anchor Standard 11, "Relate artistic ideas and works with societal, cultural, and historical context to deepen understanding." Seemingly problematic might be the term "artistic" (like the term "aesthetic"), which can seem reflective of an inherent bias in favor of Western art music. Although *listening* would certainly be a key component of quality instruction in music of any genre, culture, or style, the thoughtful WMP teacher would recognize that for much of the world, *music* is not conceptualized as a disembodied art-object, removed from the listener, meant to be dispassionately contemplated and analyzed. The Attentive Listening activities offered as examples in this chapter are not presented as such writ large. Teachers might best recognize the Core Arts Standards as a descriptive support system to help articulate, define, and defend the learning activities of an already-robust performing ensemble program, rather than as a prescriptive set of curricular mandates.

3 For example, under Anchor Standard 7, High School, at the "Accomplished" level: "Evaluate works and performances based on research as well as personally- or collaboratively-developed criteria, including analysis and interpretation of the structure and context."

4 See Chapter 7, however, for additional considerations regarding a systematic, multi-year approach to World Music Pedagogy in instrumental music classrooms.

5 "Variations on a Korean Folk Song" was a featured selection in the first volume of the popular study guide series, *Teaching Music Through Performance in Band* (Vol. 1, ed. R. Miles, 1996, GIA Publications), but interestingly, in the first edition, little is mentioned about "Arirang" beyond its title and a brief acknowledgement of the meaning of the lyrics. This was remedied in the second edition (Vol. 1, 2010), where additional context is provided regarding the history, etymology, and regional variations of the folk song. See Chapter 4 of this volume for recommended recordings of "Arirang" (also rendered as "Arrirang," among other spellings) as performed by instrumentalists and singers from Korea.

6 Daily Star (Lebanon), website, September 4, 2004.

7 National Public Radio interview, March 7, 2009. Azmeh earned a Grammy Award in 2017 as part of the Silk Road Ensemble.

8 By Smgregory at the English language Wikipedia, CC BY-SA 3.0. Retrieved from https://commons.wikimedia.org/w/index.php?curid=2539413

9 Public Domain. Retrieved from https://commons.wikimedia.org/w/index.php?curid= 10251356

10 Tasnim News Agency [CC BY 4.0 (http://creativecommons.org/licenses/by/4.0)], via Wikimedia Commons.

11 Ornstein, R. (2010). [Liner notes]. *From Kuno to Kebyar: Balinese gamelan angklung*, [CD], SFW50411.

References

Demorest, S. M., Morrison, S. J., Beken, M. N., & Jungbluth, D. (2008). Lost in translation: An enculturation effect in music memory performance. *Music Perception, 25,* 213–223. doi:10.1525/mp.2008.25.3.213

Elpus, K., & Abril, C. R. (2011). High school music ensemble students in the United States: A demographic profile. *Journal of Research in Music Education, 59,* 128–145. doi:10.1177/0022429411405207

Green, L. (2002). *How popular musicians learn: A way ahead for music education.* New York, NY: Routledge.

Madsen, C. K., & Madsen, C. H., Jr. (2016). *Teaching/discipline: A positive approach to educational development* (5th ed.). Raleigh, NC: Contemporary Publishing Company.

Morrison, S. J., Demorest, S. M., Aylward, E. H., Cramer, S. C., & Maravilla, K. R. (2003). An fMRI investigation of cross-cultural music comprehension. *NeuroImage, 20,* 378–384. doi:10.1016/S1053-8119(03)00300-8

National Coalition for Core Arts Standards. (2014). *National Core Arts Standards: A conceptual framework for arts learning.* Retrieved from www.nationalartsstandards.org.

Wenger, E. (1998). *Communities of practice: Learning, meaning, and identity.* Cambridge, UK: Cambridge University Press.

Listening Episodes

"Tujang Biru," Gamelan Angklung, Mas Village, Smithsonian Folkways. A Balinese gamelan performance featuring the *gangsa, kantilan, jegogan* (metallophones), and *réyong, kempli,* and *kelenang* (gongs). www.folkways.si.edu/gamelan-angklung-mas-village/tujang-biru/sacred-world/music/track/smithsonian

"The Rain," Ghazal, iTunes. A Persian and Hindustani collaboration featuring a trio comprised of Kurdish-Iranian *kamancheh* player Kayhan Kalhor, and Indian *sitarist* Shujaat Khan and Indian *tabla* player Swapan Chaudhuri. https://itunes.apple.com/us/album/eternity/id203000961?i=203000973

"Mi Gente," Héctor Lavoe, iTunes/Fania. A Puerto Rican salsa classic, featuring a full salsa band and iconic singer Héctor Lavoe. https://itun.es/us/Nn0aF?i=520308589

"Tulina's Carmona," Kinan Azmeh, iTunes. Contemporary piece in mixed meter by a Syrian clarinetist and composer. https://itun.es/us/iHNdP?i=688814352

"Chemtengure," Lora Chiorah-Dye & Sukutai, Smithsonian Folkways. A traditional Shona melody about a vendor named Vajeke, performed with marimbas, mbira, and voices. www.folkways.si.edu/lora-chiorah-dye-and-sukutai/chemtengure/world/music/track/smithsonian

"Sea in the Spring," Tomoko Sunazaki, iTunes. Japanese composition written by blind musician Michio Miyagi about his visual memory of the Sea of Tomonoura (an inland sea near Hiroshima), featuring the *koto* (a plucked stringed instrument) and the *shakuhachi* (an end-blown flute). https://itunes.apple.com/us/album/sea-of-spring/id201366976?i=201367003

3

Participatory Musicking

Throughout the crammed space of the orchestra room, the final notes of Aaron Copland's "Hoe Down from Rodeo" ring climactically. "Well, it doesn't get any more American than that!" Mrs. Davis exclaims as she drops her baton to the conductor's stand and closes her score. The orchestra erupts into celebration: a mixture of applause and bows slapping music stands fills the room as the students realize that their ardent performance will likely mean a gold medal at next week's state orchestra festival.

Mrs. Davis smiles, looks down at the score, and tries to identify any final areas of weakness she might be able to tidy up with the last 10 minutes of rehearsal. But fearing that she might extinguish the enthusiasm in the room by drilling more rehearsal, she closes the score again, looks up to her class, and instead begins to clap a steady ostinato in a clave pattern. "Ch, ch, ch . . . ch-ch," she repeats as the chatter subsides in the room. Soon, the entire class catches on, joining her in the clave ostinato by clapping and slapping their bows on their stands. The class apparently understands exactly what Mrs. Davis is communicating with her clave: suddenly, a trumpet player joins in with the iconic call from Héctor Lavoe's "Mi Gente"—a piece they had been working with over the past few months. Two flutes and a handful of violins join in with the montuno part they had learned weeks before. The basses begin playing the syncopated bassline, playfully swinging their massive instruments from side-to-side in unison with spur-of-the-moment choreography and laughing along with their silliness. Soon, the entire class is involved in a grand jam session of interlocking ostinatos. Stepping off the podium and to the sound system, Mrs. Davis picks up her iPod, clicks play, and the original Lavoe recording resonates throughout the room. The students all know the piece quite well by now, and they wait for their part to enter into the fabric of the recording. Soon, the entire orchestra picks up again, playing along with their ostinato of choice while Héctor Lavoe's charismatic voice struggles to cut through. Suddenly the school bell rings, and Mrs. Davis apologizes for losing track of time. Students hurriedly pack up their instruments and leave the room. Down the hall,

Mrs. Davis can still hear her students' voices receding down the hall singing, "Qué cante mi gente!" and giggling.

By this time in the WMP process, students have immersed themselves deeply in the sounds of the featured musical culture. Thanks to repeated listenings of musical exemplars in their band and orchestra ensembles, they have now "bathed" themselves deeply into carefully curated cultural soundscapes, at times allowing the entirety of the experience to envelop their senses, yet regularly focusing their attention towards particular musical elements. They have homed in on the salsa's bassline groove, the rhythmic ostinato, the melodic contour, or the progression of the form, perhaps. After plenty of repeated listenings—perhaps dozens or more (indeed, as many as the students *need* to feel sufficiently immersed within the music)—finally comes the time in the WMP process where Attentive Listening becomes purposefully active and increasingly participatory. Students are now encouraged to physically engage with the musical sounds as they continually attempt to re-create it for themselves.

Because this process is occurring within the context of an instrumental ensemble, teachers will likely begin to think of ways to transfer what the students have been hearing to their instruments. In fact, students have perhaps already begun to do so with or without the teacher's realization. Musicians naturally enjoy exploring on their instruments, taking incessant "earworms" and transferring them to their lips and fingers. But just because we may be in the business of educating instrumentalists does not necessarily mean that learning must occur in this way alone. Students can and should be encouraged to *sing* and *move* in addition to playing on their instruments. In fact, any way that students can find themselves more directly engaged with the nuances of the music should be actively encouraged. After all, musicians should pride themselves in being musical through every facet of their personal expression— with their instruments, with their voices, and with their bodies.

Surely, all musicians can attest to the power of participation. Surely it is fun to listen to music, whether passively or deeply. Consuming music moves us, excites us, and impassions us. It makes us feel nostalgic, sometimes inspires us to be more outgoing, perhaps makes us desire to be more romantic, and at the very least, encourages us to become more connected to our fellow humans. But when we actually *make* music, it does something different to us. We are dealing with the same sounds, the same melodies, and the same rhythms, but we take on an entirely new role as active participants. Whether singing, dancing, or playing along, partaking in the music makes us feel more connected to what is occurring in the moment. Moreover, it makes us feel more connected to the people with whom we are making and sharing that music. Ethnomusicologist Thomas Turino (2008) calls participatory music a "strong force for social bonding" (p. 29), noting that in the act of making music together we develop a sense of social solidarity. This feeling of connectedness with our fellow musicians— something that appears to be basic to human nature—is something which Turino argues to be "a good and, in fact, necessary thing. We depend on social groups—our family, our friends, our tribe, our nation—to survive emotionally and economically and to belong to something larger than ourselves" (p. 3).

From an early age, children can be found making music together while waiting for the bus, on their way to field trips, and during unstructured moments throughout their days. When presented with the options to engage with music by listening to it or by making it, musicians will likely always choose to make it for themselves. Thus, the WMP process necessitates not merely passive listening in an attempt to develop a familiarization with a particular culture's music; it demands active participation in order to become a truly meaningful—and perhaps even transformative—musical experience.

This chapter describes the second and third phases of the World Music Pedagogy process, known as *Engaged Listening* and *Enactive Listening*. These two phases are assuredly interrelated, but notably different in practice. After Attentive Listening, which was covered in detail in Chapter 2, Engaged Listening becomes a new focus for the student, which Campbell (2004) defines as involving "active participation by a listener in some extent of music-making while the recorded (or live) music is sounding" (p. 91). Students are at this stage engaging in the salient concepts that are being directly communicated through the music by singing, playing, moving, stepping, dancing, or grooving. They may have already begun to emerge into this phase on their own during the Attentive Listening phase, expressing themselves freely as they become instinctively inspired through multiple listenings that become increasingly familiar over time. They may have impulsively begun to tap their toes or fingers to the beat or groove, or they may pretend to play the featured instrument in the air, or perhaps have taken it upon themselves to rise from a chair and begin dancing as the inspiration strikes. This is the proclivity of a musically minded learner, and of course should always be encouraged. When students begin to demonstrate their willingness and desire to enter into this active musical process, the teacher should follow enthusiastically along.

As this approach evolves into increasingly more complete musical excursions, students will begin to demonstrate a readiness for Enactive Listening. In this phase, the goal is for students to approach a stylistically appropriate performance both alongside and beyond the use of the recording, such that the musical expression becomes not merely one of attempted recreation, but of true embodiment by the student musicians. Not surprisingly, this is considered to involve the deepest level of listening of the WMP process. At this stage, intensive listening is necessary for students to grasp the nuances of the recording as they seek to capture every detailed musical quality of the culture bearer's or traditional musician's expression. Reference checks to the recordings are integral during this stage, but the role of these recordings have now shifted from playing an informative role to playing a supportive role.

The episodes as presented in the following pages of this chapter represent a number of listening samples that allow for the potential of these phases of the WMP process to be fully realized in instrumental settings. These samples include the three Learning Pathways that are featured throughout the WMP process (as described in detail within each chapter and summarized in full in Appendix 1), as well as other noteworthy selections that can be adapted purposefully for use with instrumental ensembles from 4th through 12th grade. Yet these examples are merely that: *examples*. It is the music teacher who best knows his or her particular students, and so the musical selections that will most powerfully take hold of specific students can only be known by the music teacher him or herself. As such, teachers should feel empowered to select pieces that may entice their young musicians to "hook into" the soundscapes of particular musical practices and not want to relinquish that grasp.

Like Mrs. Davis in the opening vignette, teachers will certainly know and feel when this has been achieved.

Techniques of Engaged Listening

By the time students are prepared to enter into the Engaged Listening phase of the process, they have listened to the music repeatedly—perhaps dozens of times, or perhaps many more if the piece is particularly complex or unfamiliar. Students are able to answer specific questions about the sounds, instruments, timbres, melodies, rhythms, and possibly the form. While directed questioning during the Attentive Listening phase has oriented their ears toward specific musical elements, they have also attained a broader sense of the music through immersive listening.

As mentioned at the opening of this chapter, the natural tendency might be for teachers to enter into this phase by immediately instructing students to pick up their instruments. After all, throughout the entire Attentive Listening phase, instruments have gone mostly untouched, and both teachers and students are eager to begin transferring what has been brimming in their ears to the pieces of metal and wood with which they musically identify. Of course, this desire should not be discouraged either, but teachers should also be aware that not all engaged activities will involve the use of instruments by necessity—at least, not necessarily the students' personal instruments.

With whatever musical example that has been selected, consider the most salient musical elements which necessitate active attention towards their performance. Of course, questions raised during the Attentive Listening phase have likely already focused students' listening towards such elements, but now they are specifically being asked to re-create them for themselves. For example, students' attention may need to be focused toward the bell pattern of a Malian drumming piece, because it represents the "timeline" or "backbone" of the entire musical progression. In such instances, being able to clap the underlying pattern will become fundamental to ensuing activities.

Other selections may feature different prominent musical components, such as a particularly lyrical melodic line or memorable harmonic accompaniment. For example, the Brazilian *forró*, "Forró Beberibe" features a fast-moving melody whose "singability" increases with each repeated listening. The same can be said about Kinan Amzeh's Syrian-infused contemporary tune, "Tulina's Carmona." Whether focused on a full melody or on a short motif, such as the repeated "qué cante mi gente" line in Héctor Lavoe's "Mi Gente," students may find themselves most immediately aware of one musical component over others. Identifying these salient components will be important to planning successful initial activities of Engaged Listening.

Finding the Groove and Performing Rhythms

Many musicians tend to most naturally seek to feel the underlying beat or groove whenever they hear a new piece of music. This will often be a logical (and important) first step in the Engaged Listening phase, though students have likely already begun exploring the beat from early Attentive Listening experiences—perhaps even trying to find it while simultaneously answering other questions that have been posed. Often, finding the steady beat will be quite straightforward, as it may be with selections such as "Forró Beberibe" (Episode 3.4). For other selections, it may be more appropriate for students to focus on a repeated rhythmic ostinato or bell pattern to find the groove. Students can locate and perform with the clave (or the steady beat pulse played by the cowbell) in "Mi Gente" (Episode 3.2), the *hosho* (shaker) pattern in "Chemtengure" (Episode 3.6), the bell pattern in "Place Congo," (Episode 3.1) and the opening snare drum ostinato in "Bolero" (Episode 3.3). Yet, students will revel in the challenge of determining the underlying pulse of a piece such as "Tulina's Carmona" (Episode 3.5), which features asymmetrical beat structures. In fact, many examples of Balkan folk music feature such asymmetrical beat patterns as well, including groupings of five, seven, nine, eleven, and so on (see "Jovano, Jovanke," featured in Chapter 5). Because an understanding of the underlying beat is so important to grasping most musical models, many Engaged Listening experiences will begin with the music's groove or underlying musical pattern.

But as any instrumental music teacher can attest, solely asking students to find the beat or pulse of the music can quickly become uninspiring for students and teachers alike. One way for teachers to maintain engagement while still reinforcing the beat and pulse is to have students shift their focus specifically toward the *timbre* represented by these patterns or grooves, allowing students to explore the room and vicinity to find material objects that closely replicate this timbre. For example, while listening to the bell pattern in "Place Congo," students can search the room for ways to approximate the desired timbre of the *agogo bell.* (*"A drumstick on the snare drum stand sounds too high, a triangle beater on a music stand is too thin and sharp, but hitting this empty coffee can with a drumstick sounds just right!"*). While exploring the room for the appropriate sound, students are all the while listening repeatedly to the underlying groove, internalizing it, and referencing their substitute sounds to the recording with a critical ear.

Performing Melodies and Harmonies

When shifting focus from rhythmic elements to melodic and harmonic elements—which need not be one-directional in practice even though they may be presented in such an order in this book—teachers are likely to view these as the moments in which students may finally reintroduce their instruments. But once again, this is not necessarily the only approach. Musicians may learn a great deal about particular musical elements by humming along with the instrumental melody, or full-on singing the lyrics of a melodic phrase or section. To be sure, this is positively not to say that pre-instrumental activities *must* precede those involving instruments; indeed, both types of activities can occur simultaneously, or may even follow instrument-based activities.

Undeniably, the importance of singing throughout this process—arguably in any musical process—cannot be understated. By momentarily removing the instrument from the equation, musicians are able to focus on the specific nuances of the sound which they seek to re-create. For example, in order for a trumpet player to perform a *marcato* attack, the musician needs to understand what to do with his or her tongue and airstream in order to appropriately execute that sound. The attack, length, decay, accent, and intensity of a musical expression are some characteristics that can be reinforced in this practice because they do not need to be first "translated" through a technical understanding of the instrument. Indeed, one of the most popular techniques among band directors is to have students sing their parts in order to more accurately identify the appropriate stylistic and technical execution for each note and phrase. This allows the musician to get the desired expression "just right" for the needed context, it and allows him or her to develop a stronger sense of "groove" because the music is coming directly and purely from the human source. Especially with developing musicians who may not yet be fully aware of how to execute certain musical nuances on their instruments (especially unfamiliar ones), an ability to sing aloud is an essential tool for helping musicians embody what they seek to communicate in the first place.

ENGAGED LISTENING OF MELODY, WITHOUT INSTRUMENTS

The following activities can be utilized for students to explore the melodic contour (or full melody) and underlying harmonic structure of a selection:

1. Sing the melody or ostinato on a neutral syllable (i.e., "loo," "doo," "la").
2. If a vocal piece: Sing the melody with the given lyrics.
3. Sing the bassline on a neutral syllable (i.e., "bum," "bah").
4. Have students split and simultaneously sing any combination of 3, 4, or 5.

ENGAGED LISTENING OF MELODY, WITH INSTRUMENTS

Of course, instrumentalists require Engaged Listening activities to be translated to their instruments in order for the WMP process to be truly meaningful and worthwhile. To reiterate, this progression need not be outlined in the chronological progression as presented here. One strategy need not lead into another, but rather each strategy should carry with it its own pedagogical advantages as students are asked to focus on specific musical elements. In short, activities should be designed based on what the students are attempting to execute at a given point in time, not based upon a prescriptive step-by-step progression that ends with students *lastly* being asked to transfer learning to their instruments. That said, planning Engaged Listening activities without instruments first can often help students more easily place the melody, harmony, or rhythm on their instruments, but this may not always be the case.

The following activities can be planned to help students place particular melodic and harmonic concepts on their musical instruments:

1. Play the melodic ostinato on a fixed pitch.
2. Play the melodic ostinato as-is.
3. Layer multiple melodic ostinati together, with different instrument groups performing separate ostinati.
4. Play the full melody on the instrument.
5. Play the harmonic voice(s) along with the melody on the instrument.
6. Play the bassline on the instrument.

7. Perform the functional harmony (i.e., chord) on each downbeat (this may require some notation, and/or a discussion about which instruments should perform which pitches within the chord).

8. Play any combination of 1–6 on a different instrument (e.g., xylophone, piano, guitar).

9. Have students split and perform any combinations of 1–6.

Especially for students who may be unfamiliar with the practice of aural transmission, transferring music from their ears to their instruments will surely be a challenging step. Many students will be far more comfortable with notation-based learning, because it is likely the transmission method that has been used throughout most of their musical learning up to this point. Nonetheless, it is encouraged that students do their best to learn by ear during the WMP process, and practice placing melodies and harmonies on their instruments through trial-and-error and deep listening. While many students will likely struggle with this process of transmission at first, the goal is certainly not for students to grow so frustrated that they reject the process altogether. The task should be consistently challenging for students, but also continually rewarding. To cultivate maximally rewarding experiences, students should be encouraged to use peer teaching strategies, where students who either are more comfortable with aural-based learning or have particularly strong ears are able to assist their peers to locate the melodies on their instruments. Occasional use of notation might also be acceptable to get students started (especially with particularly difficult or fast-moving melodies), and teachers might also consider using solfège- or numbers-based learning strategies to help students clarify the movement of the melody. Above all, the teacher must demonstrate patience during this process, and encourage students to incrementally develop their aural skills at their own rate.

Moving

Puzzlingly, participating in an instrumental music ensemble tends to be a stationary activity—at least in most Western contexts. With the exception of marching band, students participating in an instrumental music program are typically seated in a predetermined arrangement and remain mostly still throughout rehearsals and performances. From a young age, music and movement are seemingly inextricable as students participate in structured and unstructured musical games and dances. But somewhere along a person's musical development—perhaps as musical learning becomes more directive and focused—the natural human proclivity for movement seems to get lost. This need not be so.

Indeed, many musical cultures around the world are heavily dependent upon movement, which is often inseparable from the music itself. Whether executed through some combination of music, dance, drumming, and pageantry in the sub-Saharan African tradition of *ngoma*, through purposeful dance with Balkan, Irish, and Greek music, or marching in a processional with Haitian *rara* music or New Orleans second line, movement in some shape or form is a common companion to music throughout the world.

As expected, young instrumentalists who are simultaneously working through their social identities may sometimes be hesitant to do something beyond what is typical or comfortable. But once movement becomes understood to be a regular part of any music-making process, students will begin to discover how movement can bolster their musical experience and understanding. The following suggestions may be used to incorporate movement into this stage of Engaged Listening:

1. Step, march, or dance to the steady beat or groove.

2. Use dynamic movement to explore the contour of the melody, or the articulation of the rhythm (e.g., short movements for staccato, long flowing movements for legato, uneven movements for asymmetrical rhythms), in a Dalcroze-like fashion.

3. Have some students perform any instrumental activity from the earlier sections, while others move, step, march, and dance.

4. Allow students to conduct the entire ensemble or small groups to gesturally embody the beat or pulse of the music.[1]

Engaging in Part Work

The ability for students to participate in one Engaged Listening activity while others participate in another is an important skill for musicians who are progressing towards fluency with a given musical culture. Because of the inherent challenges of simultaneity, part work exercises may be best saved for later activities, but this need not be the only trajectory for part work exercises to be successful. For example, it may take time for students to perform part work involving the simultaneous performance of the full melody and ostinatos, but they might be able to more immediately perform rhythmic part work, with half the class performing the steady beat and the other half clapping the ostinato or bell pattern. Part work can involve any combination of these activities (including those involving movement), which allow students to participate in the multidimensionality of the musical tradition. Additionally, part work exercises can involve both (1) dividing parts between sections, and (2) asking students to perform both activities on their own at the same time. An example of the latter may be as straightforward as stepping the beat while clapping an ostinato (e.g., stepping the beat and clapping the clave during "Mi Gente"), or as complicated as performing two interlocking bell patterns at the same time (e.g., performing both *agogo bell* patterns in "Place Congo"). Thus, in some of the activities listed later, "Part 1" and "Part 2" could refer to a 50/50 class split, or a single student performing both musical tasks simultaneously. Some specific activities may include the following:

1. Part 1 performs the steady beat (i.e. steps, pats, plays); Part 2 performs the rhythm.

2. Part 1 performs the steady beat; Part 2 performs the ostinato.

3. Part 1 performs an ostinato or rhythm; Part 2 performs the melody (i.e., sings or plays).

4. Part 1 performs the melody; Part 2 performs the bassline or harmonic accompaniment.

5.   Part 1 performs the melody; Part 2 performs the rhythm or ostinato; Part 3 performs the harmonic accompaniment and/or bassline.

6.   As number 5, but a fourth part engages in a movement activity (i.e., dance, step, march).

Truly, the possibilities are nearly endless. The key is for the teacher to be creative in a way that allows for this process to feel continually fresh and consistently challenging every time. Some students may be capable of executing many of these activities by themselves almost immediately, while others will struggle to simply play the beat or ostinato with the melody playing at the same time. The most important consideration in planning part work activities, therefore, is to allow for students with various ability levels to be successful in their own way.

From Engaged to Enactive Listening

Once students have focused their immersive listenings towards active musical experiences that featured playing, singing, humming, clapping, stepping, and dancing, they will have embodied the music in such a way that they are now capable of performing it largely on their own. Now comes the time for Enactive Listening, in which the students' focus is directed more specifically towards nuances as they seek to create the music for themselves and on their own. Listening becomes more intensified here, and recordings shift from being at the very center of the students' musical activities, to becoming references against which students measure their own performances. During the Enactive Listening phase, "students benefit from opportunities to listen to timbral qualities of instruments and voices, their attacks and delays, the dynamic flow of a piece, its melodic and rhythmic components, and the interplay of multiple parts" (Campbell, 2004, p. 126). Enactive Listening exercises may begin with short snippets of a selection, but will continually seek full-and-complete musical "images" that may be performed as a cohesive idea. These efforts may result in full-and-exact, beginning-to-end performances of the selection (eventually without the recording, when possible), or perhaps, for more challenging and complex selections, may involve a performance of the manageable elements from the recording in a way that achieves a satisfying musical unit. For example, with the brief episode featuring Ghanaian drumming with an American jazz orchestra (Episode 3.1), it may lie beyond any timely and realistic possibility for students to aurally learn and perform the jazz band's intricate harmonies as an Enactive Listening exercise. However, the bell pattern from the start of the recording can be successfully combined with the drum set's swing pattern and the primary melodic line (starting at 0:37), which would create a musically satisfying performance without the intricate harmonic introduction performed by the flutes and reed instruments (0:19–0:37).

In practice, some activities within the Engaged Listening phase may very well lead themselves naturally into the Enactive Listening phase, and teachers should feel empowered to follow these impulses as students demonstrate a willingness and readiness to proceed. The episodes in this chapter represent several ways in which both engaged and Enactive Listening activities can be seamlessly planned for students.

Many Enactive Listening experiences will eventually result in removing the recording from the mix, so that the student musicians become the primary source of the live musical creation. However, this need not be the goal of every Enactive Listening experience. In some instances, there may be little melodic or harmonic context remaining when students are only performing a singular musical component such as an ostinato, bassline, or bell pattern. When the component-of-focus is the melodic line, for example, it may be wholly appropriate to isolate this component without the recording in an Enactive Listening activity. However, if focusing on a clave pattern or a short ostinato, performing this alone without the recording will feel largely meaningless without the other musical elements which support it. By combining other Engaged Listening activities over time—perhaps one that focuses on the rhythm or groove, another which isolates the bassline, and another which practices the main melody—multiple activities layered together approach a fuller representation of the complete musical work. As students are able to perform each of these activities simultaneously, they are evolving from focused attention toward singular musical components to understanding how multiple components fit together on a "macro" level. By this time, gradually removing the recording will preserve the context of the music because the essential elements of the music will all remain intact.

As a reminder, the basic progression of the selections in this book tend to largely follow a *familiar-to-unfamiliar* trajectory. In every chapter, experiences often begin with the sounds and traditions which students already recognize, and then progress into more unfamiliar territory over time. Of course, teachers should be reminded that, first, familiarity is contextual and subjective depending on the listener, and, second, that musical cultures *themselves* should not be viewed as "familiar" or "unfamiliar" broadly—because such thinking can create dualistic otherings of "our music" versus "their music"—but instead should examined as being practice and context specific. This means that teachers should implore students to investigate what specifically sounds familiar or unfamiliar within a musical practice by asking themselves questions such as, *what specific element or elements seem familiar or unfamiliar? Is it the melodies or harmonies (or scales)? The complexity of the rhythm or the steadiness of the groove? The timbre of the instrument or vocal quality?* In this way, students become better served expressing unfamiliarity in terms of musical concepts rather than cultures. For example, it is better for a student to say, "the sound of the microtones in this Hindustani music is very unfamiliar to me" rather than "Hindustani music [broadly] sounds so strange to me." The latter risks othering the culture, whereas the former expresses the musical concept of which the learner seeks to develop greater understanding.

The first featured episode involves an innovative collaboration between American jazz musician Wynton Marsalis and Ghanaian drum master Yacub Addy. The result is an inventive album that celebrates the power of interculturalism from a historical perspective.[2] The resulting blend here is West African drumming with American jazz, the latter which largely attributes its stylistic origins to the former. Therefore, in some ways this collaboration represents less of the synthesis of two different cultures in the pursuit of creating something entirely new, but rather what might be considered a "back to the basics" ethos with American jazz becoming reunited with one of its musical ancestors. Students should understand that the result of this collaboration is ultimately not intended to represent "Ghanaian music," just as it is not meant to represent "straight-ahead jazz." Instead, through intercultural efforts, the result is something in which each musical culture has been influenced and altered by the other.

Episode 3.1: Ghanaian Drumming Meets American Jazz

Specific Use: Instrumental Ensembles (e.g., band, orchestra, jazz); Grades 4–12

Materials:

- "Place Congo," from *Congo Square* with The Jazz at Lincoln Center Orchestra with Wynton Marsalis; students' instruments
- Optional: claves or rhythm sticks

(Engaged Listening)

Procedure:

(*Note: Teachers may engage in as many or as few of these steps as desired, and may layer them over multiple class sessions and weeks. They are not intended to be all performed in a single lesson.*)

1. "Tap or clap the rhythm of the *agogo bell* that you hear at the start of the recording (it is the lower-pitched bell). It repeats over and over again, so join in whenever you can feel the ostinato."
2. Play track, approximately 0:00–0:37.
3. Repeat until students can confidently tap the rhythm.
4. "This is known as the 'bell pattern.' In many styles of sub-Saharan African music, a bell pattern provides the underlying pulse of the music. Because it also the pattern upon which musicians layer other parts, it is sometimes also known as a rhythmic 'timeline.'"
5. "Try to step the steady beat as you continue to tap or clap the bell pattern. In what type of meter does the steady beat sound to be grouped?" (It becomes easier to identify once the drum set enters around 0:11).

   (Answer: 3/4).

   "The steady beat is how we usually feel the underlying pulse in Western (and many other) musical styles."
6. Play track.
7. Repeat until students can confidently perform the part work. By both stepping the steady beat and clapping the bell pattern, students are essentially embodying the music through two different traditions.
8. "Now focus your attention on the higher-pitched *agogo bell*, which sounds like it is playing its pattern in a different meter but is remaining steady on its own. Clap or tap along with this new bell pattern."
9. Play track.

10. Repeat until students can hear and perform the second bell pattern.

11. "Now let's have half the class perform the first bell pattern while the second half performs the second pattern."

12. Play track.

13. Repeat as necessary *(this may take many tries, and indeed perhaps many class sessions).*

14. *Optional/More Advanced:* "Now, a few percussionists may listen to the drum set part performing the triple pattern on the high hat and playing a rim shot on beat 3. When ready, you may layer this part on top of the two other parts."

15. Play track.

16. Repeat as necessary.

(Enactive Listening)

Procedure:

1. "In two sections, perform the two *agogo* bell patterns without the recording."

2. "Now layer the drum set part on top of these parts."

3. Play track to reference the performance. Have students assess how successfully they were able to re-create the rhythms in the recording.

4. "Now let's hum or sing the main melody on a neutral syllable along with the recording." (0:36–1:04, or beyond).

5. Play track.

6. "Let's do that again, but at some point, I will fade out the recording. Please continue singing even when the music has been turned off." Repeat, eventually fading the recording out while students are singing. At first, fade short sections in-and-out, progressively fading out longer sections, or until students are able to hum/sing the entire section without the music.

7. "Now try to find this melody on your instruments. Even if the melody transfers between different parts, please continue to play the melody in its entirety." *This step will likely take some time as students slowly are able to place the melody on their instruments. As discussed, students should be encouraged to engage in peer teaching in sections to help each other out. They should also be encouraged to simplify melodies as needed, later aspiring to a fully nuanced performance over time.*

8. "Focus your attention to the bassline during this section. Sing the bassline on a neutral syllable."

9. Play track, repeat as necessary.

10. "Please try to find the bassline on your instruments." (This should include all instruments, not just low-pitched instruments.)

11. "Now let's have half the class perform the bassline on their instruments, while the other half plays the melody."

12. Play track, fading in and out as in step 6, until students can perform the section in full without the music. Repeat as necessary.

13. "Finally, let's add in the bell pattern and percussion parts." Split the ensemble into equal parts and play track. Fade in and out as before, and repeat over many class sessions.

Note: Because this selection is a full big band arrangement, it is of course not necessary to grasp the harmonies and intricacies of the arrangement wholly by ear. While developing an ability to perform the nuances of the recording is desired, it will be unexpected for students to be able to grasp onto every element. However, an ability to perform the nuances of the melody as well as the stylistic approach is of most importance with this selection.

The next episode centers around the highly popularized and seemingly ubiquitous tradition of salsa music. Whereas the participatory goals in Episode 3.1 focused largely on specific musical elements (i.e., the bell pattern and interlocking melody), this episode seeks a more holistic performance of the piece in full, including all musical elements. Such an approach is possible in this case because the selection is comprised of already available (or easily attainable) instruments (i.e., brass instruments, conga, claves), and its performance calls primarily for simple repeated ostinatos that can be easily learned and layered.

Episode 3.2: Salsa in the Classroom
(Learning Pathway #1)

Specific Use: Instrumental ensembles (e.g., band, orchestra, jazz); Grades 4–12

Materials:

- "Mi Gente" by Héctor Lavoe; students' instruments
- Optional: claves, cowbell, conga (or substitutes)

(Engaged Listening)

Procedure, "Qué cante mi gente" response:

1. "Listen for the repeated response to Héctor Lavoe's solo (*coro*), which repeats every four beats. Hum this response every time you hear it."

2. Play track, approximately 1:14–2:08.

3. "The words are 'qué cante mi gente.'" [display the words on a whiteboard]. Let's sing this response every time you hear it."

4. Play track.

5. "The melody you hear starts on the pitch *fa³* [concert A-flat], with an upbeat on *low sol* [concert B-flat]. Find the first two pitches, and then try to figure out the rest of the response on your instrument." *(Note: The notation can be seen in Figure 3.1. However, it is a powerful exercise for students to attempt to work out the melody by ear, even if Puerto Rican salsa is now a largely notation-based tradition in practice.)*

6. Allow students to find this melodic phrase on their instruments, independently or in small groups.

7. "Now I will play the recording, and you should play this response on your instrument every time you hear it."

8. Play track and repeat as necessary.

9. *If students are ready for an additional challenge:* "As you can hear, the singers are performing this response in harmony. If you can, try to listen to one of the harmonic lines, which are sung in mostly parallel harmony with the melody." *Teachers might need to provide the starting pitches for each of the inner voices from top to bottom: re [concert F], ti [concert D], and la [concert C].*

10. Play track and repeat as necessary.

11. "Now, let's try to sing one of the inner voices with the words." *The teacher may need to simultaneously play the desired inner voice on a piano to reinforce the pitches. With parallel harmonies such as this, it can be difficult to hear the movement of each line, and a piano can be a useful tool for bringing out these voices.*

12. Play track and repeat as necessary.

13. Repeat steps 6–8 so that students can place each part on their instruments (independently or in groups).

14. *After each of the inner voices have been isolated, have the students put all four voices together. The teacher may choose to assign each part to an instrumental section, or students may be given the opportunity to choose their desired part on their own.*

15. Play track and repeat as necessary.

Figure 3.1 "Que cante mi gente" response in harmony

(Enactive Listening)

Procedure:

1. "While the [choose instrument] section continues to perform the "que cante mi gente" response, everyone else should perform the *montuno* part." [Each of these layered components (i.e., montuno, bassline, clave) should be approached through its own Engaged Listening activities like the exercise outlined previously.]

2. Play track, starting at 1:14 (until about 2:08, or as necessary).

3. "Let's do that again, and this time let's perform the bassline all together."

4. Play track.

5. "Now let's add in the percussion, one by one." *Layer in each of the percussion parts: congas, clave, and cowbell.*

6. Play track.

7. "Now let's put it all together to perform the *coro* section in its entirety: the response, the *montuno*, the bassline, and the percussion. At some point, I will fade the recording out. Please continue playing even after the music has been turned off."

8. Play track and repeat, eventually fading out the recording while students are performing.

To demonstrate the appropriateness of the World Music Pedagogy process not just in the teaching and learning of global musical traditions, but of musical practices from any tradition or origin, the following episode will feature the Classical composition, "Boléro," by Maurice Ravel. Surely, Western classical works with complex harmonies, melodies, and forms may not be wholly appropriate for the aurally focused approach of WMP; however, by choosing a piece with memorable melodies and easily followed forms, the WMP process can present a unique and educational aural challenge for students.

Of course, published notation for "Boléro" can be easily found for a variety of instrumental settings. However, in line with the spirit of the WMP approach, it is reiterated here that students learn as much of the music by ear as possible. While such a tactic may not necessarily maintain the transmission process as practiced within the largely notation-based Western classical tradition, it aptly demonstrates the possibilities of diverse approaches to musical transmission.

Episode 3.3: Ravel's "Boléro"

Specific Use: Instrumental Ensembles (e.g., band, orchestra); Grades 4–12

Materials:

- "Boléro, ballet for orchestra," by Boston Symphony Orchestra and Seiji Ozawa; students' instruments

(Engaged Listening)

Procedure:

1. "Listen for the repeated snare drum rhythm, and tap or clap it lightly when you think you have it." (Hint: it is a six-beat pattern.)
2. Play track (0:00–0:55).
3. "Now let's play that ostinato pattern as an ensemble on your instruments" (beginning with the flute, 0:55–1:43, and beyond if desired).
4. Play track.
5. "Now put your instruments down, and hum along with the main melody played by the flute" (beginning at 0:12–0:55).
6. Play track, and repeat as needed.
7. "The melody begins on a concert C. Let's try to place this melody on our instruments."
8. *Allow students ample time to find the melody on their instruments either individually or in small groups. You may consider using groups of same instruments or different instruments, but consider using instruments with the same transposed pitch to minimize discrepancies when discussing the melody. (See "Practical Considerations for Participatory Musicking" later in this chapter).*
9. "Now let's perform the melody in unison as an ensemble."
10. Play track and repeat as necessary.

(Enactive Listening)

Procedure:

1. "You will notice that there only two musical elements occurring at the same time in this piece (at least for the first 9 minutes): the six-beat rhythmic ostinato and the unison melody. With a pen and paper, write down the order of instruments as they enter into the mixture of the composition. Be sure to include what instruments are performing the melody, and which are performing the ostinato for each iteration." *Encourage students to choose their method of demonstrating this, whether writing a list or creating a graphic representation of the composition over time.*
2. Play track in its entirety.
3. Using students' responses, write the progression of the musical texture on a whiteboard or SmartBoard. "Now, let's attempt to perform the piece with the proper instrumentation, using only the guide we have created for ourselves (no notation)."
4. Play track, with students performing their closest approximation along with recording.

5. "This time, let's listen closely to the nuances and the characteristics of each iteration of the melody. Let's start with the first iteration, with the flute melody and snare drum ostinato".

6. Play track, perhaps focusing only on the A section of the melody (0:12–0:33), or (if students are ready), the entire melody (0:12–0:55). Immediately after, conduct the students in a performance of the same section (by ear), focusing their performance the articulations, attacks, slurs, vibrato, and other nuances of the performance.

7. Repeat track. As peer judges, have non-performing students compare the recording to the live performance in terms of these nuances. *Note: Be sure to make explicit that close approximations are desired, but that some elements will require years of professional practice. The goal is of course not to show students how inferior their playing is compared to professional musicians, but rather to engage in a listening exercise of the utmost concentration.*

8. Repeat steps 6–7 as needed for students to develop a stronger nuancing of the performance.

9. Repeat this process for the B section of the form, including the other instruments who perform the melody later in the piece.

(*Note: This exercise, while important for developing stronger listening skills, is intellectually exhausting. It should likely take place over a longer period time, with perhaps only one or two iterations of the form being subjected to this sort of concentrated analysis.*)

The next episode is based largely on a supplemental activity proposed by John P. Murphy in his book *Music in Brazil* (2006), published by Oxford University Press. The piece is listed as "Forró em Monteiro" in Murphy's publication, but it is the same *forró* melody as recorded here. While this selection moves students slightly further away from an immediately familiar musical culture, it contains various levels of accessible entry points for students: They may begin by successfully performing an approximation of the Northeastern Brazilian *baião* rhythm, and may gradually work towards performing it in full once they have gained more confidence.

Episode 3.4: Folk Music from Northeastern Brazil

Specific Use: Instrumental Ensembles (e.g., band, orchestra); Grades 9–12

Materials:

- "Forró Beberibe," by Reginaldo Alves Ferreira 'Camarão, et al., triangles, drums (adapted), students' instruments

(Engaged Listening)

Procedure, forró rhythm:

1. "Lightly clap the dotted-eighth-sixteenth pattern along with the recording" (shown in Figure 3.2a, top line).
2. Play track (0:00–0:32).
3. "Now lightly clap the repeated upbeats along with the recording" (shown in Figure 3.2a, bottom line).
4. Play track.
5. When students are able to perform each part separately, combine the two together. Perform the patterns on whatever drums are available. "This is a simplified version of the *baião* pattern, which is central to the rhythmic backbone of the Brazilian *forró* style and dance."
6. "Now let's listen to the triangle part. This pattern is created by dampening the triangle on certain strikes and allowing it to ring on others. Let's try to play this pattern, as follows" (below tempo):

   D D O D | D D O D | D D O D | D D O D |

   D = dampened; O = open

   (See notation in Figure 3.2b)

7. As students become more confident performing this pattern, gradually increase the tempo and incorporate the drum rhythm back into the mixture.
8. If students demonstrate a readiness, display the full *baião* rhythm (Figure 3.2b). Allow unconfident students to continue performing this rhythm, while students who self-identify as being ready may attempt other parts of the pattern, such as the *zabumba* (bass drum) or *pandeiro* parts.

Procedure, melody:

1. "Now that you've heard the melody a number of times, try to hum along with it. If it helps, trace the contour of the melody as it progresses."
2. Play track, repeat as necessary (0:00–0:48, continuing on if desired).

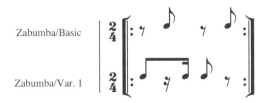

Zabumba/Basic

Zabumba/Var. 1

Figure 3.2a Simplified *baião* rhythm

Adapted from Murphy, 2006

Figure 3.2b   Full *baião* rhythm

Adapted from Murphy, 2006

Figure 3.2c   "Forró Beberibe" melody and harmony, for accordion

Adapted from Murphy, 2006

3. Display the melody for all to see, or distribute individual copies of the notation (Figure 3.2c). "Now let's play this melody on our instruments in unison, under tempo."

    Note that while the WMP process indeed values aural-based transmission practices, and this melody would likely be taught by ear in Brazil, this is one particular instance in which learning a fast-moving melody might be too time-intensive to be practically executed in the classroom. If students are able to learn the melody through aural means, including transcription, they should by all means be encouraged to do so. However, this episode assumes a limited time for learning this piece.

4. As students become more confident performing the melody, increase the tempo until many students are able to play along with the recording. For those who have ongoing difficulties performing the main melody at-tempo, encourage them to perform the left-hand accompaniment of the accordion part.

5. Along with the recording, perform both the right-hand and left-hand parts with the ensemble.

(Enactive Listening)

Procedure:

1. Break into small groups of five, providing each group with a copy of the recording.[4] Have students lead small combos of the *forró*, with one player per part (right-hand melody, left-hand melody, *zabumba* part, triangle, *pandeiro*). Students should continually compare their performance to the recording, noting how the timbres of their instruments may be similar or different from the accordion. Because few wind and string instruments can closely approximate the sound of the accordion, encourage students to note the timbral discrepancy, but to focus their attention on the articulations and phrasing of the melody.

2. Bring the groups back together, and have each group perform for the class. After each performance, engage in a discussion comparing the recording to the student performance.

    Note that students should be reminded that the goal of this phase of the WMP process is to approximate the music as closely as possible to the original recording, and that adding one's own creative contribution will certainly be valued and desired, but further down the line.

3. Conduct a web search of "*forró* dance" to view a demonstration of two-person *forró* dancing. Alternative or following step 2, while one group is performing their forró, lead the rest of the class in a *forró* dance.

The contemporary Syrian-inspired piece "Tulina's Carmona" employs an asym-metrical rhythmic structure to contribute a sense of rhythmic uncertainty. Given that many contemporary band and orchestra composers popularly use asymmetrical

Figure 3.3 Music educator Juliana Cantarelli Vita leads a *Maracatu de Baque Virado* from Pernambuco, Brazil, at the Smithsonian Folkways World Music Pedagogy Certification Course at West Virginia University

rhythms to great effectiveness in their repertoire, performing these figures may not present an altogether new challenge for students. However, learning to play fluently through changing 7/8, 9/8, 13/8, and 2/4 beat structures solely by ear will become an inspiring challenge for students (see Chapter 5 for notation).

Episode 3.5: Contemporary Syrian Music (Learning Pathway #2)

Specific Use: Instrumental Ensembles (e.g., band, orchestra); Grades 6–12

Materials:

- "Tulina's Carmona," by Kinan Azmeh; students' instruments

(Engaged Listening)

Procedure, rhythmic structure:

1. "Can you tap the beat along with the recording?"
2. Play track (0:00–0:59; melody begins at 0:11).

3. "Are all of the beats even, or do some appear to be longer than others?"

4. Play track. (Answer: The third beat is longer than the others; i.e., *short-short-long*)

5. Place this pattern on the board and have students chant "one-two, one-two, one-two-three" with the music to feel the pattern. "What time signature might we call this?" (Answer: 7/8)

6. Play track and repeat as necessary.

7. "Does the 7/8 pattern hold throughout the entire melody, or does it seem to change? If you hear it change, can you raise your hand whenever you hear it do so?"

8. Play track and observe students' responses

9. Write the changes in time signature on the board for students to see which measures are 7/8, which are 9/8 or 13/8, and which are 2/4. "Now let's clap and say the rhythmic pattern of the melody" along with the recording:

    ‖: 1–2, 1–2, 1–2–3 | 1–2, 1–2, 1–2, 1–2–3 | 1 + 2 + |
    | 1–2, 1–2, 1–2–3 | 1–2, 1–2, 1–2, 1–2–3 | 1 + 2 + |
    | 1–2, 1–2, 1–2–3 | 1–2, 1–2, 1–2–3 | 1–2, 1–2, 1–2–3 |
    | 1–2, 1–2, 1–2, 1–2, 1–2, 1–2–3 :‖

10. Play track; repeat as necessary.

Procedure, melody:

11. "Does it sound like the opening of the melody ascends by steps or skips? While you're thinking about it, can you sing along with the melody on a neutral syllable?"

12. Play track. (Answer: they ascend by step).

13. "The melody is written in concert a-minor. On your instruments, see if you can find at least the first six pitches of the melody (which repeats in the fourth and fifth measure) on your instruments." *Allow students adequate time to find these notes, reminding them that they are in fact ascending by skip. When students are able to play it, ask them to help a neighbor if he or she is struggling.*

14. Play track; allow students to play quietly along with recording to check their pitches.

15. Repeat steps 3–4 for each part of the melody until they are able to play the melody in its entirety.

(Enactive Listening)

Procedure:

1. "What sorts of expressive characteristics is Kinan Azmeh giving to the melody when he plays it on the clarinet?"

2. Play track. (Answer: He sometimes "falls" quickly off of the top note of the melody; he "growls" at the end of the second repetition of the melody.)

3. "Let's try to sing the melody along with the recording, trying to perform all of the falls and growls that Kinan Azmeh performs."

4. Play track and repeat as necessary.

5. "Now let's try to add these expressive techniques and ornamentations to our performance on our instruments."

6. Play track and repeat as necessary. Continually compare students' performances to the recording.

The final episode for this chapter presents the Engaged and Enactive Listening exercises for the Zimbabwean Shona tune, "Chemtengure." This selection clearly illustrates call-and-response techniques used in the composition of *mbira* music. Structurally, it utilizes the repetition and variation of small melodic units with an underlying pulse from the *hosho* (shaker). As the students listen they should be guided to pick out the various melodic parts that comprise the polyrhythmic structure of the piece.

Episode 3.6: Zimbabwean Shona for Band (Learning Pathway #3)

Specific Use: Instrumental Ensembles (e.g., band, orchestra, jazz); Grades 4–12

Materials:

- "Chemtengure," Lora Chiorah-Dye and Sukutai; students' instruments

(Engaged Listening)

Procedure:

1. "As you listen to the piece, focus on one instrument or voice for as long as you can (it is helpful to understand that the melodic fragments are varied). Try to focus on its most basic structure."

2. Play track (first 30 seconds), repeat 2–3 times as needed for students to adequately hear the part they have chosen.

3. "Let's listen again, and this time, try to sing the part that you have been focusing on. Remember, it may be different from what your neighbor has been listening to."

4. Play track.

5. "Can someone share the part they were listening to by singing it?" Allow students to demonstrate their part. "Can you raise your hand if you were focusing on the same part?" Afterwards, try to have the students identify which instrument or voices are performing each of the parts of focus.

6. "Let's listen again, and this time, try to figure out the part you have chosen on your instrument. Be sure to play softly so that we can still hear the recording."

7. Play track, repeat as needed for students to become comfortable performing their parts. *The teacher might need to facilitate this by briefly rehearsing each of the elements that the students are performing one by one.*

8. "Now, try to perform a different part on your instrument—one that you weren't focusing on before."

9. Play track and repeat.

(*Note: Encourage students to focus on the three major melodic parts of the song: the* mbira *accompaniment, the call (from Lora Chiorah-Dye), and the response (from the choir). This activity could be considered complete when the students are able to identify and perform each part of the song's texture. The Enactive Listening exercise that follows will focus specifically on translating the* mbira *part to the band.*)

(Enactive Listening)

Procedure:

1. "Now we are going to focus on performing just the *mbira* part alone. Like the piano, it is played with two hands—typically the thumbs. In fact, that's why the *mbira* is also known as the "thumb piano." During the opening, there is an interlocking melody played by the two thumbs. Try to sing along with this part once you have it."

2. Play track, 0:00–0:04.

3. "Now let's do the same for the lower part that comes in afterwards. Try to sing along with this part once you have it."

4. Play track, 0:04–0:08.

5. "Now let's try to figure these two parts out on your instruments." Give the students ample time to complete this task, either by working in groups or individually. If students appear to struggle, partial notation may be provided, but the authors reiterate the importance of learning through aural transmission during this process.

6. "Now, with our instruments, let's split these two parts in half. Half of the ensemble will play the main melodic part (the first part), and the other half will play the countermelody (the second part)."

7. Play recording. *The teacher can decide how to facilitate this, from pre-assigning parts, to having students come up with the instrumentation themselves.*

8. "Now let's play along to the recording to see how well our parts fit." Have the students play along with the recording to check their execution of the style.

9. Play track, repeat as needed.

10. "Now that we are comfortable with the *mbira* part, let's try to perform it on our own. We are also going to record it so that we can compare it to the recording and check our stylistic accuracy."

    (*Note: Recording and comparing to the original is another technique for engaging students in a critical examination of their performance. This can be used in conjunction with, or instead of, fading the recording in and out.*)

11. "Now let's compare our recording to the example. Do we sound like an *mbira*? Why or why not? What are some ways that we can improve our performance to sound more like the ensemble in the recording? Is it ever really possible to obtain the 'true' sound of the *mbira*? Why or why not?" Have the students listen to their performance and compare it to the example. Have them discuss ways to improve and rehearse in their own groups.

12. Repeat this process until students are satisfied with their performance.

(*Note: The focus of this lesson should be to acquire an understanding of how to reproduce the sound of the* mbira. *Since the* mbira *is a plucked instrument, it has a percussive attack that gives way to a mellow buzzing sound. The students should consider how they might use their instruments to create this sound. Additionally, the piece lends itself to an exploration of compositional techniques used in Zimbabwean* mbira *music, such as repetition and variation. By focusing on the repetition and variation of these musical concepts, the students can focus on how their parts fit rhythmically with others, and can work towards creating a cohesive polyrhythmic texture.*)

Figure 3.4 Notation of *mbira* part to "Chemtengure"

Practical Considerations of Participatory Musicking

Choosing Quality Repertoire

As discussed in the previous chapter, because the WMP process is so strongly grounded in aural transmission, selections ought to be chosen for their strong listenability. The best selections are those which have a strong aural "hook" which pulls the listener into particular elements of the music. Arguably, this is increasingly more important as the music becomes less familiar. Instrumental music teachers might consider choosing repertoire which features melodic, rhythmic, and textural simplicity over complexity, repetitive figures that focus the listener's ear, and timbral clarity. Of course, this does not mean that each selection must contain each of these elements, but rather that the musical concept of focus should be strongly discernable for the listener over a number of repeated listenings. For example, the bell pattern in "Place Congo" may be challenging to decipher in its entirety, but by focusing attention towards the lower *agogo bell* first, the listener is able to make greater sense of the musical pattern from the start. While carefully constructed questions raised in the Attentive Listening phase allow students to hone in on specific musical features and concepts, the phases of Engaged and Enactive Listening present new challenges for students because they are expected to *do it*: To actively participate in the music through some performative, kinesthetic, or tactile response. Because of this, considerations for selecting quality Attentive Listening selections ought to be further considered for the practicality of eventual participation. After all, the goal of most WMP experiences will be for the students to journey through all five phases of the WMP process, or at least the first three, to foster a musically fulfilling experience.

Ensemble Size and Makeup

Teachers of instrumental ensembles are no strangers to large class sizes. Enrollment in school bands, orchestras, and especially marching bands can sometimes reach into the triple digits, making it not only difficult to develop a meaningful relationship with many students, but also challenging to develop practical, aurally based musical tasks that students can successfully execute. Because ensemble classes in schools are typically designed to be more rehearsal-based than lecture- or discussion-based, the teacher may understandably become stymied by the task of leading a large group of students in an Engaged Listening experience in which they focus on a singular musical pattern and then respond with a meaningful participatory response. Likewise, there are challenges to bringing a large ensemble together in the Enactive Listening process that requires the focused attention of many students to a recording in order to learn their parts among the multiple parts that are simultaneously played by the various sections. While issues of ensemble size will be discussed in greater detail in Chapter 4, practitioners of the WMP approach have proclaimed its successful implementation in small and large groups alike. With attention and interest in these enticing musical cultures acquired from the start, the WMP process ought to be equally possible with students in the hundreds or more.

Traditional or Adapted Instruments?

Now that the WMP process is progressing from primarily passive responses (Attentive Listening) to focused and active participation (Engaged Listening and Enactive

Listening), the natural question of instrumentation arises. Especially in Enactive Listening experiences, where the goal is to approximate the sound of the recorded instrument as convincingly as possible, it becomes immediately evident that using Western instruments is often inadequate to reaching this goal; in such instances, it is understandable that some instrumentation choices will result in closer matches than others. For example, a violin may prove to be a close sonic match to the Chinese *erhu*, while substituting a trumpet for an animal horn played in a *Xhosa* ensemble will require a slightly greater departure from the "authentic" sound, as would the use of reed instruments (i.e., clarinets, oboes, saxophones) to approximate the sound of a Scottish bagpipe. Here as before, the successful implementation of the WMP process will appropriately embrace approximation, so long as these approximations are made with integrity towards the musical tradition in question.

Embracing approximation is also essential because, in most cases, obtaining access to traditional instruments will be nearly impossible for many musical cultures of study—and this especially true for teachers seeking to include numerous musical cultures within a school year. The teacher might otherwise feel like he or she is stuck "between a rock and a hard place," so to speak, with inevitable timbral inauthenticity on the one hand and unattainable resources on the other. Citing a fear of doing the musical tradition injustice, teachers might elect to allow a lack of resources to win over a so-called inauthentic presentation of the musical culture (Campbell, 2004; Schippers, 2010). They find it safer to avoid the culture altogether and prevent showing shortcomings, rather than facilitating an experience that they recognize to be inauthentic at best.

However, "playing it safe" is not what the WMP process is truly about. Instead, the approach contends that samplings and immersions of both familiar and unfamiliar musical cultures contribute to a more wholesome understanding of what music is, how it functions, and who gets to create it across cultures. In other words, proponents of World Music Pedagogy believe that experiences ought to be organized in a manner that offers the most holistic and accurate of musical journeys, but concede that the attainment of *truly* authentic experiences is both impossible and impractical (nor is it necessary). After all, a beautifully envisioned performance of a source-piece that pays close attention to the nuances of its melodies, the supportive use of its harmonies, and the enticing nature of its rhythms—but which uses adaptive instrumentation—would ultimately be celebrated as a fulfilling and genuine rendering of the music. Myopically obsessing over timbral inconsistencies, then, detracts from what is likely experienced as a wholly satisfying musical experience for students, teachers, and audiences alike.

In this way, demonstrating integrity toward the musical culture in question allows the teacher to recontextualize the musical practice in a way that maximizes both the intended musical experience as well as the students' ability to interact with it. Indeed, culture bearers are largely "on board" with recontextualizing the music in an appropriate manner to allow students to meaningfully engage with the experience (Campbell, 2004). For example, when Senegalese drummer Thione Diop works with groups on traditional drumming patterns found throughout Senegal and West Africa, he happily does so with what is available—which, in a school context, is often an assortment of various types of drums, from traditional *djembes*, to Brazilian *baterias* and Middle Eastern *doumbeks*. These instruments are unable to yield the same desired timbres of "tone," "slap," and "bass" that are central to playing the *djembe*, but the experience can still become meaningful because (1) the group is actively participating within the ethos of a collective drum circle as socially intended, (2) they are learning to perform authentic Senegalese rhythms, even if on inauthentic instruments, and (3) comparisons to the "real thing" are consistently made through live demonstrations by the culture bearer on traditional *djembe*, *sabar*, and *tama* drums. Thus, participants are engaging in the musical tradition in a meaningful fashion but are constantly reminded of how the music would sound in its home context.

Transposing Instruments, Difficult Keys, and Fast Tempos

Teachers of instrumental ensembles—particularly in bands—are also faced with a challenge that is simply not an issue within non-instrumental musical contexts. First, the need for musical material to be transposed into different sets of pitches for different instruments can present a challenge for teachers and students alike. Especially when working with younger students who may not yet understand the concept of transposing instruments, placing melodies on instruments can prove to be difficult when notation is used, or when an explicit discussion of absolute pitches is necessary. Moreover, it may be difficult for younger students to perform along with a recording if the original track is performed in a challenging or unfamiliar key, or at too fast a tempo.

Teachers can prepare for these challenges in a number of ways. For example:

1. At first, when working in small groups, the teacher may choose to create groups of instruments functioning with the same transposition to facilitate ease of discussion (i.e., trumpets, tenor saxophones, and clarinets [B-flat instruments]; flutes and trombones [C instruments]; alto saxophones [E-flat instruments]; French horns [F instruments]). However, creating groups in this manner quickly reveals that instrument groups may not necessarily create the most pleasing of timbral mixtures. For this reason, students and teachers should be encouraged to practice some of the additional techniques described later.

2. Encourage the use of solfège- or numbers-based pitch identification (or another system, such as Indian *sargam*) over absolute note names. Of course, if students are not used to communicating in this manner, or translating solfège to their instruments, this process may take time. Yet, as many instrumental teachers would agree, the benefits to fluently communicating in this manner is useful well beyond the scope of a world music context.

3. Especially for less experienced students, choose selections that are in transposition-friendly keys—that is, keys that are relatively accessible for any instrument group within the ensemble. For example, keys of C, D, and G major might be most familiar to instrumentalists in orchestra (and other non-transposing ensembles), while the keys of B-flat, E-flat, and F major are most immediately familiar to musicians who play in transposing wind bands. Careful attention toward selected keys will allow students to focus less on note-specific translations of the melody to their instruments, and more on the holistic capturing of the melodic line on their instruments.

4. Of course, quality recordings are not always made in student-friendly keys. While the preference is of course for students to perform the music in its original key (for some cultures, specific keys may have a particular significance), teachers may choose to adapt the recording to be placed in a more familiar key

for a more successful learning experience. This can be done by uploading the recording to a software system such as Audacity, which can change the key of the music without significantly changing other elements of the recording.

5. Similarly, teachers may choose to utilize software such as Audacity to slow down the tempos of selections that are too fast for young students to attain by ear. While it is almost always preferred to maintain the original recording as-is, slowing down the tempo of a song might be a necessary modification to help students succeed—especially when such small modifications both (1) facilitate the most productive learning process for students, and (2) *do not hinder the overall character or identity of the music.*

From Participatory Musicking to Immersive Performance

The two phases of the World Music Pedagogy presented in this chapter—Engaged and Enactive Listening—are among the most immersive of the WMP approach. These phases seek for band and orchestra students to become active participants in the musical culture with which they are interacting, and to assume the performative roles of those who make the music within that culture's society. These are exciting stages in the process to be sure, where students have the opportunity to fervently "get their hands dirty" with the musical culture brimming in their ears. Still, consistent throughout these phases is the importance of context. Students must be constantly aware of why this music exists, what it is used for, who gets to make it within that culture, when it is performed, and in what settings. As the WMP sequence is presented, these matters might appear to be saved for the final stage of the methodology, Integrating World Music (Chapter 6). However, as has been discussed throughout this book, the phases of the WMP process ought not be viewed as a strictly linear one, but as an interwoven one. Conversations of context should appear throughout the process, entwined within and between listenings, such that students become imbued with the music's meaning and significance from the very start.

As it happens, as instrumental music students foray more deeply into the WMP process, they naturally begin to demonstrate a yearning to understand the contextual meaning of their playing. They seek to understand how their playing can become more realistic and nuanced, and work tirelessly to achieve what they perceive to be an authentic reproduction of the music. At times, their ears might even grow to become more critical than those of a more forgiving educator.

When students begin to demonstrate an aptitude for placing what perhaps were once-unfamiliar musical practices on their instruments, and can communicate with fellow musicians (young or old) in and through that musical culture, they are fully experiencing the goals of participatory musicking. Now the process progresses to the next step in the sequence—the goal of bringing these musical experiences to the level of full performance. Such is the purpose of the following chapter.

Notes

1 Be sure in such instances to communicate clearly that the act of conducting may not be utilized by many musical cultures, and is largely an activity of large, Western ensembles. However, this does not mean that conducting activities cannot be utilized to help students feel and embody the musical pulse of any musical tradition.

2   The album "Congo Square" is intended to represent the historical Congo Square in New Orleans, in which enslaved Africans were permitted to socialize on Sundays. Gatherings at Congo Square would involve an open marketplace with singing, dancing, and drumming.

3   Of course, you may use whichever system with which your students are familiar (if any). While solfège knowledge is not a requirement to be successful in this activity, it does help maximize efficiency when students attempt to place the pitches on their transposing instruments. More on this is discussed in the section "Practical Considerations for Participatory Musicking" later in this chapter.

4   This can be accomplished by renting computers from the school library and loading each with a flash drive that contains a copy of the track.

References

Campbell, P. S. (2004). *Teaching music globally: Experiencing music, expressing culture*. New York, NY: Oxford University Press

Murphy, J. P. (2006). *Music in Brazil: Experiencing music, expressing culture*. New York, NY: Oxford University Press.

Schippers, H. (2010). *Facing the music: Shaping music education from a global perspective*. New York, NY: Oxford University Press.

Turino, T. (2008). *Music as social life: The politics of participation*. Chicago, IL: The University of Chicago Press.

Listening Episodes

"Place Congo," Jazz at Lincoln Center Orchestra with Wynton Marsalis, featuring Yacuub Addy and Odadaa!, Jazz at Lincoln Center/iTunes. An intercultural collaboration of an American jazz and Ghanaian drumming, composed as part of a suite to celebrate the history of Congo Square and the roots of American music. https://itun.es/us/EK8Bw?i=376424841

"Boléro," Boston Symphony Orchestra & Seiji Ozawa, iTunes. Orchestral ballet from the Romantic era featuring a repeated melody over a recurring rhythmic ostinato. https://itun.es/us/vlzLr?i=295015258

"Mi Gente," Héctor Lavoe, iTunes/Fania. A Puerto Rican salsa classic, featuring a full salsa band and iconic singer Héctor Lavoe. https://itun.es/us/Nn0aF?i=520308589

"Forró Beberibe," Reginaldo Alves Ferreira 'Camarão, Joana Angélica, Leo, Quartinha, Zeca Preto, Menininho, Paulo Guimarães, and Arlindo dos Oito Baixos, iTunes. A traditional *forró* melody from Northeastern Brazil, featuring accordion, *zabumba* (bass drum), triangle, and *pandeiro* (tambourine). https://itun.es/us/xO4Ubb?i=1102810475

"Tulina's Carmona," Kinan Azmeh, iTunes. Contemporary piece in mixed meter by a Syrian clarinetist and composer. https://itun.es/us/iHNdP?i=688814352

"Chemtengure," Lora Chiorah-Dye & Sukutai, Smithsonian Folkways. A traditional Shona melody about a vendor named Vajeke, performed with marimbas, *mbira*, and voices. www.folkways.si.edu/lora-chiorah-dye-and-sukutai/chemtengure/world/music/track/smithsonian

4

Performing World Music

On a humid Friday afternoon, Mr. Kauffroath sat alone at his desk in a dusty office. The poor circulation caused the air to sit heavier than the weight on his shoulders. He dropped his pencil that was scribbling notes on a score and firmly pinched his furrowed brow between his thumb and forefinger. Doubts about his students' upcoming concert began to swirl in his mind. This was his third year teaching at the school and he wanted to really connect with his students. The previous band director was adored and his students spared no moment in letting Mr. Kauffroath know this. Every success thus far had been hard-won. He was following the advice his mentors offered to not change anything for the first three years, but he was growing increasingly impatient following in his predecessor's shadow. He wanted to make this band his. *Dropping his pencil on his desk and standing up wearily, he said to himself, "At least I have tickets to see Rebirth Brass Band this evening." Gathering his belongings, he headed for his car—the last one left in the lot.*

He drove home that evening in desperate need of inspiration to alleviate his growing doubts. There was little more that he loved more than New Orleans second line music. He longed for the controlled chaos that occurs when a crowd, compelled by the boom of the bass drum, the snap of the snare, the lightning fast licks from the horns that crack the air, extemporaneously emerge and join in on a parade performance. As he blasted Rebirth Brass Band's latest album on the drive home, he said to himself, "I wonder if my students would like this."

Later that night, as he walked to the entrance of the concert hall, he shuffled past a local brass band busking on the corner. He listened for a minute, dropped a dollar in a trombone case lying open on the ground, and headed through the double doors with his ticket in hand. Inside, season ticket holders were cued in the wine line waiting for some last-minute refreshments before settling into their seats for the night. The warning bell buzzed to indicate five minutes until show time, signaling a mad dash to the hall. The night of the concert began like any other he had seen in the hall before, but as the audience shuffled in, he immediately noticed how small the five members of the Rebirth

Brass Band looked on the massive stage. As the band began their first tune, "Do What You Wanna," the infectious rhythms coursed through his veins, causing his body to bounce in his seat. "Man," he thought, "I need to dance!" He looked around the room and could see that others seemed to feel the same way. Only a minute into the song he noticed a color-coordinated group of individuals bravely stand up and make their way to the stage. "That is the band from before," he thought. When the group arrived at the edge of the stage they were stopped by a hefty security guard. Seeing this, the saxophone player for Rebirth looked directly at the band and shouted, "Get up here!" With a beckoning wave of the hand the security guard swiveled as if on a hinge, and the group rushed the stage. This move signaled to the crowd to free themselves from their seats and join the dance party that had just broken out. As Mr. Kauffroath joined the rest of the concertgoers, the familiarity of the crowd consumed him. At that moment, a spark lifted his spirits. "If this can happen here, why can't I do this at my concert? Why can't I do this with my kids?"

As the junior band shuffled into Mr. Kauffroath's class that Monday they were greeted with unfamiliar music blaring unusually loud. "What is Mr. Kauffroath doing with his trumpet out?" one student yelled over the din of brass music filling the room. "I've never seen him play before. This is kind of cool!" At the front of the classroom, the projector listed several instructions: Take out your instruments. Leave your chairs, stands and music. Pick a part in the song and quietly hum (or tap) along. The students quickly followed the instructions and a drone of voices searching for notes eventually blended into emerging melodies.

A few days later, Mr. Kauffroath played the same recording at the start of class. "Play along if you're ready!" he shouted. As students figured out parts and coordinated their fumbling fingers, Mr. Kauffroath circled the room reinforcing melodies to his students with his trumpet. Within minutes, the students' playing overtook the recording and they were performing a tune they had never heard in a style they were completely unfamiliar with. With a large gesture, Mr. Kauffroath cued the end, and students— confused, exhilarated, and engaged—cut off in one giant unison hit.

"What was that?!" one student eagerly asked.

"That's second line!"

For the jazz portion of the concert the following month, Mr. Kauffroath decided to end with a second line, complete with an impromptu parade around the auditorium. Students grabbed audience members, thrusted a tambourine or pair of claves in their arms, and paraded around the room and out the back doors into the lobby. The cheers filled the atrium at final downbeat, telling Mr. Kauffroath that it was well-received. The audience loved it! He had never seen them so engaged at any of his concerts. This moment he knew that the risk had paid off and that he had made his mark on both his students and the community. He finally felt that this was his school band, performing more of the world's musical practices than was historically standard, and performing with focus, musical expression, and spirit. Because they could!

World Music Pedagogy and Performance

At this point in the WMP process it should be apparent to instrumental music teachers that learning by ear is critical, as is acknowledging music across the world as a largely oral (and aural) tradition, as is embracing listening as a means of getting to the heart of music in all its nuances. The focus of earlier chapters has been the importance of repeated listening through Attentive, Engaged, and Enactive means. With the development by students of skills and understandings through continuous listening, study, and particular types of participatory experiences, the potential for public performance of musical cultures from across the world is readied for realization. After experiencing the gradual release from playing along with recordings in Enactive Listening exercises in Chapter 4, this chapter provides teachers with suggestions on taking the next steps to transform these exercises into full performances in secondary instrumental settings. Patricia Shehan Campbell (2004) implores music teachers to ponder the question, "What is music, if not wrapped around the performance of it?" (p. 125). This is a powerful query that cuts at both the experiential and existential underpinnings of our practice. Since there can be no music without performance at some level, this question seems central to our efforts as musicians, educators, and consumers.

Musical Performance as Social Practice

In World Music Pedagogy, the goal for successful performance is founded on an in-depth understanding of the musical intricacies within a specific culture that ultimately leads to an *accurate approximation*. As mentioned previously, an additional goal of this volume is to also help secondary instrumental teachers to explore music as a culturally universal phenomenon and experience how performance of diverse musical styles can help to develop an appreciation of culture. Approaching musical study from this perspective allows for a deeper understanding of how cultures ascribe values and assign specific functions to musical practices to imbue them with profound meaning. For example, in Indonesian gamelan music the *gong ageng* (large gong) is said to house the spirit of the gamelan. Moreover, there is strict protocol regarding how one can physically move around the ensemble because it is strictly forbidden to step over any of the instruments. Acquiring an understanding of music in this way illuminates what cultures prioritize, why they maintain these beliefs, and how this eventually is enacted through performance.

This approach can also reveal how engagement in music allows members of cultures to learn values and behaviors that allow them to successfully become a member of their respective societies. John Blacking (1973) argued that musical properties such as pitch and rhythm relationships often reflect the social structures from which they emerge. In his study of the Venda (ethnic group from South Africa), he examines how the use of different musical scales reflected a process of social change in which different groups were incorporated into Venda society (p. 73). He also described how communal dancing helped young individuals to develop their capacity for cooperation. In the Philippines, music tends to reflect social structures, whereby instrument construction and tuning systems reflect the temperament of individual performers as opposed to strict guidelines for intonation (Santos, 2012). This allows for the concept of harmony to be shifted from the sonic relationships between notes to social relationships between people. From these perspectives, musical performance can be viewed as a *social practice*: A site where individuals are able to create cultural meaning through participation in a common activity.

Music is not only organized sound but also a profound distillation of cultural attitudes. By incorporating other aspects of culture in musical performances developed through the WMP process, students, teachers, and audiences are left with a deeper understanding of music not as a culturally neutral "universal language," but rather a nuanced expression of the innermost insights of how cultures make sense of the world around them. As schools become increasingly diverse, the expansion of musical performances that center around this perspective could help provide spaces for students to share these unique insights with their classmates. Furthermore, students developing their skills to perform the music of a particular culture are not only re-creating specific sounds but temporarily acquiring membership within that group through the development of *music-in-identity*. This construct refers to how individuals use music in efforts towards *self-making* (MacDonald, Hargreaves, & Miell, 2002). In other words, it describes how music is used to develop obtain, enhance, or embody new identities. Acquiring an insider perspective in a musical manner such as this can provide students with valuable insights that can lead to more sympathetic interactions with diverse peers.

The Process of Developing WMP Performances

Musical performance in the WMP process is an outgrowth of Enactive Listening, with activities focused mainly on re-creating the nuance of a musical tradition through a gradual release from performing along with a recording to playing without a recording. After multiple listenings, opportunities to play along, and comparative "check-ins," students enter the performance stage ready to create fully developed performances of their own. When expanding Enactive Listening activities for actual performance, there are several items to be considered. For example, how will decisions to establish a song form be approached? And, how will decisions regarding instrumentation be made? A clearly established plan will help to create meaningful performance experiences for both the performers and audiences.

While there are several ways in which such performances can be created, the activities in this section will focus on splitting these questions into two different categories for developing concerts: Musical nuance and concert production. For the purposes of the WMP process, musical nuance refers to all of the intricacies of song form, choreography, sound production, and what Charles Keil (1995) refers to as *participatory discrepancies*: The feelings, grooves, ornamentations, and accompanying dance steps of a musical traditions that breathe life into sound and transform it to music.[1] This seems to already be central to the efforts of music teachers in that most rehearsals focus on capturing the nuance of the pieces being performed. These important details of performance that often exist beyond structural elements are what allow individuals to differentiate between musical styles of diverse cultures—to tell the difference, for instance, between a Beethoven sonata and *sandaya* (Burmese-style of piano).

It is worth mentioning here that each performance will inevitably have its own requirements, so these suggested considerations should be approached with flexibility rather than viewed as a stringent protocol when developing ideas for concerts, informances, or presentations. Furthermore, some of the following items might be excluded or new ones might emerge that will help the transition of the music from the classroom to the concert hall or community center. While specific issues of arranging and composing will be covered in Chapter 5, this section introduces music teachers to initial considerations in organizing Enactive Listening into full-fledged performances for the fall, or winter, or spring program.

Addressing the Details of Performance: Musical Nuance

Establishing Song Form

Earlier Enactive Listening Performance Activities helped to immerse students in learning a musical tradition through the performance of carefully curated moments of a recording. These previous activities were chosen to illustrate salient features of a musical tradition and help to convey the essence of that practice to eager ears, voices, and bodies. However, in order to truly embody these musical experiences the students must be allowed to present fully staged productions on their own. A primary consideration for expanding these activities into full performances is the establishment of a song form. Every musical tradition in the world has specific forms that vary based on culturally specific performance outcomes. For example, jazz music often utilizes repeated forms based on a sequence of chord progressions (e.g., 12-Bar Blues, ABA, AABA, etc.), which facilitates improvisation. In this tradition, basing songs on these specific musical elements allows performers to musically explore expansive creativity within a (mostly) bound and (not always) predictable harmonic framework.

Other musical traditions such as *son jarocho* from Veracruz, Mexico follow simple *verso* (verse) and *estribillo* (chorus) structures that, rather than adhering to a strict form, remain musically open to allow performers to improvise on instruments, with poetry, or through dance. This open-ended structure allows space for improvisational ideas to develop and musical interactions to occur between singers, dancers, and musicians. In other cultures, such as the *Ewe* in Ghana, dancers and musicians engaged in the performance of *gahu* (an *Ewe* musical genre) rely on rhythmic cues from the master drummer playing the *atchimevu* (large drum played with a hand and stick) to indicate shifts in the song form or choreography. While there are no set parameters to clearly define the form of a musical tradition, a general understanding of how form functions musically will help teachers in making their own performance decisions.

The three Learning Pathways featured in this chapter (Performance Activities 4.1, 4.2, 4.4) build on previous Attentive, Engaged, and Enactive Listening activities and provide illustrations of how music teachers can take the complex and lengthy arrangements found on the recordings and reduce them to key musical moments. These "visitations" might feature the song form, some of the stylistic nuances, and possibly extended repetition (and variation) in order to give the listening audience a proper duration of experience in which to enjoy the music. Imagine: A piece learned entirely by ear that can be shaped into an enjoyable performance piece! It should be noted that both of these examples combine arranged sections and space for improvisation while keeping in line with cultural conventions of the performance practice. By incorporating both of these structural elements into the form, students are able to perform pre-existing melodies with attention given to participatory discrepancies and also create their own musical expressions through soloistic exploration.

Issues of Instrumentation

In an ideal situation, music programs engaged in the WMP process will have access to authentic instruments with which to perform. However, access (or lack thereof) is not an insurmountable obstacle. Keeping the idea of *accurate approximation* very much in mind, music teachers will often need to rely on their students' instruments to perform the specific sounds within a musical culture. Because of this, in developing performances of diverse musical cultures, many music teachers will find themselves unsure of how to cleanly transfer certain musical practices that often exist in small ensembles with culturally specific instruments, to large ensemble settings with traditional Western instruments. A keen ear, musical creativity, and profound familiarity developed through multiple listenings will be crucial in guiding teachers to make sound musical decisions. Learning Pathway #2 provides an example of one way to accomplish this goal (Performance Activity 4.1). In this instance, the piece "Tulina's Carmona," which was originally composed for clarinet, nylon string guitar, electric bass, and percussion has been expanded to provide parts for the instruments in a typical string orchestra. While these instruments have been selected to augment the ensemble, the majority of musical parts can be performed by the pre-existing ensemble (e.g., band, orchestra, jazz ensemble).

Performance Activity 4.1: Contemporary Syrian Music (Learning Pathway #2)

Song: "Tulina's Carmona"

Performance Context: A simplified version of the song form was arranged to facilitate the performance by a high school orchestra performing music at a medium difficulty level.

Form:

| Drum Intro (A) ||: A (x 2) | B (x 2)| C | C' :||: Solo (B') :|| A (x 2) ||

This structure was arranged in this way because it distills the form to a basic loop that cycles through all sections and then repeats. A solo section was added after the second time through the repeated section so that students can explore the intricacies of this style through improvisation (see Chapter 5). The piece then ends on a repeated A section, which functions to reiterate the introductory theme.

Instrumentation: The instrumentation of "Tulina's Carmona" is easily adaptable to string orchestra because it was composed for a small ensemble with melodic instruments (clarinet, nylon string guitar, bass guitar) and percussion. These parts can easily be transferred to the different sections of the orchestra but the ensemble will need to be augmented with a clarinetist (or several) and percussionists to capture the feel of the original.

1. *melody*: clarinet, violin 1.
2. *countermelody*: violin 2.

---

3. *harmonic accompaniment*: viola 1, viola 2, nylon string guitar (this could be substituted with a vibraphone or marimba).

4. *rhythmic accompaniment and bassline*: cello, contrabass.

5. *percussion*: cajón, *derbakki* (goblet shaped drum) or snare drum with the snares off, triangle, suspended cymbal, clapping.

Choreography: While the Syrian *dabke* (line dance) could easily be adapted for this piece, there is no accompanying choreography for this particular performance.

Performance Tips: Like most music from this region, "Tulina's Carmona" relies heavily on an asymmetric meter to provide a lively feel. Because of this, it is suggested that the students listen to the percussion section to navigate the ensemble through the various sections of the arrangement. This will help the students to internalize the pulse of the meter and provide them with a better sense of feel in this music. Some students could also be selected to clap the main pulse of the meter so that it is clearly marked for those performing the melodic material.

Resources:
Video: *Music Beyond Borders: Voices from the Seven* www.seattlesymphony. org/beyond-borders/live-stream
This performance provides examples of and considerations for how music from cultures in the Middle East can be adapted for large ensembles.

Another strategy for rectifying concerns of ensemble size is to create smaller ensembles within the larger group that are responsible for arranging, rehearsing, and performing a different musical tradition for the concert. For example, in a concert that features music from Mexico, one piece could utilize a small group that focuses on performing marimba music from *Chiapas* (see Performance Activity 4.3). Since marimba ensembles from this region are typically comprised of three musicians, the parts could be doubled to involve six musicians on two marimbas. To facilitate performance of a marimba piece by a concert band, the ensemble itself could also be expanded to include student performers on other percussion instruments such as the *güiro* (notched gourd), shakers, snare drum, bass drum, or cymbals. Meanwhile, the winds (and brass) sections could provide harmonic accompaniment or double the melody. There are many ways that diverse musical traditions can be modified to accommodate the size and diverse instrumentation of a concert band, and it simply takes mindful planning to accomplish these goals. So long as the students have listened repeatedly to the origin piece or source recording—for example, the Mexican marimba ensemble—drawing this music into the context of a concert band is effectively transferring the rhythms and melodies from one set of instruments to another—all the while maintaining the musical style intact.

Incorporating Choreography

As mentioned in Chapter 3, many of the world's musical cultures also incorporate dance into traditional music performances such as *flamenco* music from Spain, *gamelan* music from Indonesia, and country-western music from the United States. In fact, dance is so connected to music that in some cultures, such as the Wagogo of Central Tanzania or the Yoruba of Nigeria, there is no distinction between the two, but rather, an all-encompassing term that refers to both: *Ngoma*. While this may seem like a distant concept for those trained in Western music, it is important to remember that many of the song forms that are performed by classical musicians today were associated with dance forms of the past. The musical suite in the Western art music tradition, for instance, is based on several dances including the *Gigue, Allemande, Sarabande,* and *Bourée*. Adding choreography to performances developed through the WMP process allows for individuals to engage an additional mode of cultural expression in their efforts to completely embody a musical practice.

The importance of movement to music is still—and must remain—relevant because they are not mutually exclusive expressions, but rather, they are intertwined aspects of culturally specific aesthetic features. One example, a 2009 TED event performance by the Teresa Carreño Youth Orchestra (under the direction of Gustavo Dudamel) illustrates this concept during a concert featuring Mexican composer Arturo Márquez's *Danzón No. 2* (see Performance Activity 4.2). Near the end of the piece, all members of the symphonic orchestra, after being invited by a mischievous grin from the maestro himself, suddenly leapt to their feet and began to dance along to a rhythmic ostinato that marked the 2–3 clave pattern. This maneuver not only catapulted the performance with striking, visual energy, but also re-connected the music to the dance form that served as the inspiration for the composition. For music teachers, this can serve as an example of how an understanding of the importance of dance to musical performance is necessary not only for the WMP process, but also for existing musical experiences in which they may already be engaged.

Performance Activity 4.2: Salsa in the Classroom (Learning Pathway #1)

Song: "Mi Gente"

Performance Context: The following example illustrates an adaptation into full performance of the piece "Mi Gente" by Héctor Lavoe. This song is arranged for a concert band that is performing music at a medium-advanced difficulty level.

Form:

| **Introduction** ||: **Verse** :||: **Bridge** :||: **Chorus** :||: **Solo** :||: **Chorus** :||

This arrangement features repeated Verse and Chorus sections that allows for dance and improvisation to be incorporated into the performance. This provides an opportunity to engage the audience in a participatory experience through movement.

Instrumentation: The basic musical parts were identified and assigned to various sections:

1. *Percussion* : *güiro, conga, bongo, campana* (cowbell), *montuno* (performed on marimba, vibraphone, or piano).
2. *moñas:* These melodic fragments played in the horns on the recording will be assigned to the high brass, trombones, and woodwinds.
3. *tumbao*: This bassline will be performed by the low brass, low woodwinds, and, if available, contrabass.
4. *vocal melody:* Rather than singing the words, the vocal melody will be performed by a solo trumpet player.
5. *coro*: During the chorus section of the form individuals from each section will sing the words "que canta mi gente."

Choreography: Since movement is an integral part of music from Puerto Rico, the musicians will perform basic dance steps along with the piece. The following example is the fundamental step pattern that is found in most dance styles from Puerto Rico, particularly salsa.

1. *Think:* 1–2–3–4
2. *Step:* Right—Together, Left—Together

Performance Tips: Since this particular arrangement was created with a concert band in mind, the music teacher will lead the students throughout the performance. One suggested accommodation is that instead of conducting with a baton, a clave will be used to mark the fundamental rhythm of the piece and keep the students together.

Resources:
Video: *Danzón No. 2* by Arturo Márquez, performed by the Teresa Carreño Youth Orchestra, under the direction of Gustavo Dudamel
www.ted.com/talks/astonishing_performance_by_a_venezuelan_youth_orchestra_1
This video illustrates how movement can be incorporated into large ensemble settings.

The first step in the decision to incorporate choreography is to determine whether the musical tradition being performed has an associated dance to begin with. This can be determined through album liner notes, careful research on the Internet, and conversations with a culture bearer. Next, the music teacher will have to determine how the steps will be learned. In some performances, this process might be easier than in others. For example, in the performance of "Mi Gente" (Performance Activity 4.2), the students are required to perform a basic dance that is little more than a four-step pattern that alternates between feet. Although the steps are simple, they are the foundational movement from with all other salsa steps are derived. The dance step associated with the performance of "La Rascapetate" (Performance Activity 4.3) is a bit more involved than the previous example. In order to teach effectively, this piece will have to be learned carefully through repeated viewings of dance videos or the recruitment of a culture bearer to assist with the steps.

Performance Activity 4.3: The Mexican Marimba

Song: "La Rascapetate"

Venue and Performance Context: The following example illustrates how the piece "La Rascapetate" by Marimba Chiapas can be arranged for concert band.

Form: The form of this piece is repetitive enough for students to adhere to the original arrangement on the recording.

$$\|: A :\|\|: B :\| C \mid D \mid C \|: E : \|$$

Instrumentation: Depending on the size of the ensemble, this piece can be expanded in several ways. The following assignment of parts is one of many possible arrangements:

1. *marimba 1* : *picolo* (melody), *centro armonica* (chords), *bajo* (bass).
2. *marimba 2*: *picolo* (melody), *centro armonica* (chords), *bajo* (bass).
3. *percussion*: snare drum, bass drum, crash cymbals, *güiro*.
4. *high woodwinds/brass 1*: melody.
5. *high woodwinds/brass 2*: countermelody and harmony.
6. *low woodwinds/brass:* bassline.

Choreography: The percussive dance step *baile rascapetate* (scrape the straw mat) could be learned and incorporated into this performance. Utilizing colorful folkloric dress also adds a dramatic visual component to the dance because the skirt is fanned in rhythm with the song.

Performance Tips: After the students learn all parts through the WMP process, the piece should be performed at a lively tempo but not so fast that the dancers will have difficulty marking the triplet figures in their feet. In terms of tempo and transitions, the marimba players should lead the piece and cue all important musical transitions. This will allow the students to focus on the interlocking rhythms and the overall feel of the piece. The music teacher could join in on a percussion instrument to help ensure that the tempo remains steady.

Resources:
Video: *Carlos Mejía Discusses Marimba Traditions*
https://folkways.si.edu/marimba-traditions/latin-world/music/video/smithsonian
This video provides played examples and discussions of regional marimba performance variations.

Directing the Ensemble

The ways in which musical ensembles are led also tend to be culturally influenced. In collectivist societies such as the *Ewe* in Ghana, musical performances require many people playing small fragments of highly interacting rhythmic structures in order to create a musical whole. The drums themselves are even thought to represent hierarchical familial relationships. This points towards attitudes that emphasize the importance of all group members in creating a complete unit but also the need for a leader to direct. In this musical practice it is the master drummer on the *atchimevu* (drum) who also represents the wisdom of the grandfather. In music from individualistic societies, such as American jazz, the emphasis tends to be placed on the expression of a single individual leading the energy of the group: The soloist. While this may be the case, there is still a high level of interaction and musical negotiation among the group to ensure that the performance has an organic ebb and flow.

In instrumental music programs, which emerged out of curricular reforms that favored large groups of people performing specific functions, ensembles are typically large and rely on a conductor to keep the musicians together. Since many musical cultures being used in WMP performances often come from smaller ensembles that are participatory in nature, the role and function of the leader will vary greatly depending on the setting of the classroom and the musical tradition being introduced.

In highly participatory musical styles, such as *son jarocho*, musicians often perform in the absence of any one leader. This specific tradition relies on key musical moments for each song to be known by all participants to navigate the transition between sections. In this way, it might seem that every individual is responsible for leading the performance through his or her in-depth knowledge of musical conventions. Other musical cultures, such as Brazilian Samba, have clearly defined leaders. In these ensembles, the leader often directs all aspects of performance through rhythmic cues played on a *repique* (small high-pitched drum played with a stick). When developing performances of their own, it is necessary for music teachers to have a general understanding of how the ensemble is led. This aspect of musicking is just as important as musical nuance, oral/aural transmission, and movement in providing the students with an understanding of music as culture.

In Learning Pathway #3, which features the song "Chemutengure" (Performance Activity 4.4), students of band or orchestra (or any other assemblage of instruments), who have all learned the essential "core" of the musical selection, are now encouraged to perform without a director. After all, traditional Shona music does not typically have a conductor and performers rely on listening to each other to remain together.

Students can be enabled to do so, too. Since "Chemutengure" relies mostly on repeated rhythmic motifs, the need for visual cues is minimized—and as such, memorization should be expected. Moreover, this deep listening will help to instill students with a profound sense of musical feel as well as facilitate the incorporation of movement into the performance.

Performance Activity 4.4: Zimbabwean Shona Music for Band (Learning Pathway #3)

Performance Context: This piece has been arranged for an intermediate concert band performing in a concert based on the Virtual Field Experience

Form:

||: Introduction :||: Verse :||: Chorus :||: Outro :||

Instrumentation: Shona *mbira* ensembles are typically small and comprised of two or three performers on *mbira*, one on *hosho* and singers. The vocal melodies and interlocking rhythmic patterns of the *mbira* can be isolated and arranged for a large ensemble. The following is a suggested instrumentation:

1. *melody:* high woodwinds and brass 1.
2. *mbira 1:* high woodwinds and brass 2, low brass and woodwinds 1, mallet percussion 1.
3. *mbira 2:* high winds and brass 3, low brass and woodwinds 2, mallet percussion.
4. *hosho:* snare drum, shakers, bass drum, hi-hat.

Choreography: Traditional Shona music has accompanying dance steps that can be incorporated into the performances. These steps can be learned from a local culture bearer or from one of the many videos available online.

Performance Tips: Zimbabwe has a rich police band tradition that is known for adapting traditional Shona music for wind band. The Zimbabwe Republic Police Band has several videos online that could be utilized as models to capture the style for arrangements of this music. Since this music is based on small ensembles, the students should be encouraged to perform without a conductor. To stay together, the students should move along with the music in a basic choreographed step routine.

From the Classroom to the Concert Stage (or Community Center)

Through their carefully sequenced WMP listening adventures, instrumental music students will have completely immersed themselves within the musical selections over 30, 40, or 60 listenings! Their teacher has carefully selected short sections from larger works, and has ensured that the music can be played by every student on his or her particular instrument. Thus, the music is able to be performed in ways that are described in Performance Activities 4.1 to 4.4, becoming featured selections in school concerts. As with all other aspects of performance explored in this stage, the instrumental music teacher will have some decisions to make as to when, where, and how to present these performances. The following recommendations should, again, not be viewed as sequential, stringent, and linear but as suggestions that can be tailored by the thoughtful instrumental music teacher to the specific performance needs of individual ensembles. They have in common the intent to "press the envelope" a bit and to suggest that school band and orchestra concerts, whether in elementary, middle, or high school settings, can be shaped in a variety of innovative ways that celebrate musical and cultural diversity without losing sight of the core of these ensemble practices.

Selecting a Performance Space

For all musical presentations, it is important to understand how the performance context influences the concert experience. Most musical traditions have developed to accommodate a variety of social factors which determine the setting and the manner in which certain songs are performed. For example, the *Yoreme* from northwestern Mexico apply specific performance conditions such as the construction of an *enramada* (shelter) made from dizziness-inducing cottonwood branches. These sacred leaves are thought to assist the musical performer in visualizing and creating a music composition while simultaneously contributing to the inducing of trance in the audience. Because of this, it is important to understand that global musical expressions that are adapted for school-based performances often reflect environments that are fully participatory, interactive, or serve functional purposes within the culture. When these musical traditions are arranged for and performed in formal concert settings in school, it is important that they maintain elements of their participatory nature and function within the new setting.

Typical concerts at the secondary instrumental occur in auditoriums and gymnasiums with clearly delineated roles for both performers and audience members. While this may be appropriate for most concerts in the Western art music tradition, other performances (particularly those that come from participatory musical traditions) might be better suited in a space where both audiences and performers can freely interact. Indeed, when school ensembles provide musical accompaniment for sporting events, local parades, and pep assemblies, they are performing in a space that allows for audience participation in the musical activities and, thus, a participatory setting. Approaching WMP performances with alternative spaces in mind should help ease the tension of engaging in musical activities outside of typical concert venues.

The first selection, featured in Learning Pathway #1, "Mi Gente" (Performance Activity 4.1), could be adapted so that part of the performance is given over to the audience for participation through dance. Taking into consideration that most traditional concert spaces allow little room for audience movement might influence decisions regarding the space where the performance is held. In this way, school foyers, hallways, courtyards, playgrounds, and nearby parks become open territories for performance use. Another example can be found through the New Orleans–styled second line music featured in the opening vignette. While it is possible to hold a performance featuring second line music in a concert hall, performing in an outdoor setting on campus could provide several opportunities for audience participation and movement, including an impromptu parade or dancing. Lastly, the use of small ensembles such as a marimba trio or jazz combo (see The Mexican Marimba, Performance Activity 4.3) could also affect the chosen performance location. Since small ensembles typically offer greater mobility, a performance featuring these types of groups could occur in a number of locations on campus or in the community.

Selecting a Performance Approach

In order to provide both students and audiences with an enriching experience, there are several ways that the presentation of concerts can be approached. The following section offers a list of suggestions that might serve as a starting point for other possibilities.

THE VIRTUAL FIELD EXPERIENCE

The diversity of the world's musical cultures leaves music teachers with a seemingly infinite number of options to develop their own performances. In some cases, this can result in a kind of "choice paralysis" which ultimately leads to WMP experiences being left aside for more familiar musical pursuits. Because of this, a systematic approach to developing these performances is helpful. Victor Fung (2002) provides an advantageous framework that can be used to help organize such performances. His *Virtual Field Experience* model is based on five parameters: Context, sight, sound, physical action, and mental action. The goal of this approach is to provide an accurate approximation of the original performance context through multi-sensory concerts. For example, a music performance focusing on Burmese *hsaing waing* could incorporate several cultural artifacts such as currency (*kyat*), clothing (*longyi*), and instruments (*saung gauk, hne*) to expose performers and audiences to sights, customs, and contexts. Next, a video of *nat pwe* (Burmese ritual music) performances could be projected so that audiences can observe the context associated with the performance of the music, as well as sights associated with it—including any audience interaction. From here, student performers could engage audiences in movement activities so that they can experience the music they are listening to and viewing through physical action. Lastly, presentations could be given by students to the audience to help them create cultural connections through conversations about musical transmission or other pertinent topics. To reiterate, the goal of these Virtual Field Experiences is to allow for both students and audiences to become more deeply immersed in a culture through guided musical exploration. Table 4.1 provides a sample program for a Virtual Field Experience that is based on the music of Africa.

THEMED CONCERTS

Themed concerts for elementary, middle, and high school bands and orchestras can provide a deep and immersive musical experience for teachers, students, and audience members. These concerts may include in-depth experiences with a musical culture, country, or region (e.g., "Music from Eastern Europe," "Music in the Near East," "Pacific Islander Music"); a focus on cross-cultural musical elements (e.g., "Rhythms from Around the World"); or connections to timely social topics (e.g.,

Table 4.1 The music of Africa through the Virtual Field Experience (VFE)
Recommended Ensemble: Intermediate High School Band, Grades 9–12

Musical Piece	Country	Tradition	Type of Performance	Dimension of VFE	Issues Highlighted
Presentation of music of Zimbabwe: Images of instruments, clothing, sites, people. Context information given about the references to the colonial history of "Chemutengure" (see Chapter 6).	Zimbabwe	N/A	Student presentation supplemented with video and audio technology	Context, sight, mental action	History of song, colonial history, cultural artifacts.
"Chemutengure"	Zimbabwe	Shona mbira song	Concert band	sound	The text of the song references the "coming of the West" (see Chapter 6).
Presentation of music of Ghana: Images of instruments, clothing, sites, people. Context information could be given about the history of West African influences in the music of the West (particularly jazz in New Orleans, Salsa in Puerto Rico, Cuban *son*).	Ghana	N/A	Student presentation supplemented with video and audio technology	Context, sight, mental action	History of West Africa, movement of people through the slave trade, musical similarities in instrument and organizational structures.
"Atsiagbekor"	Ghana	Ewe drum music	Percussion ensemble and dance group in traditional clothing	Sound, sight	N/A
"Gahu"	Ghana	Ewe drum music	Percussion Ensemble and dance group in traditional clothing	Sound, sight	N/A

"Musical Migrations: From Baghdad to Berlin," "African American Music of Resistance" in the Black Lives Matter Movement, "Country Roads: Bluegrass, Old Time and Country-Western Music"). Musically, such possibilities could be organized in several ways but should generally include some type of blended performance where both traditional music of the culture and music arranged specifically for the concert are presented.

A concert program that is focused on the music of Mexico could feature WMP developed arrangements of regional *banda* music. For one piece, a performance of

Table 4.2 The many musical faces of Mexico

Recommended Ensemble: Advanced High School Band

Piece Performed	Region in Mexico	Tradition	Type of Performance	Issues Highlighted
Presentation: Banda Music of Mexico. The students could present information about history and current practice of the *banda* in Mexico. Videos and other media of this practice can be shared.	Various	N/A	Concert band	History of *banda* in Mexico, cross-cultural influence, the function of music in cultural celebrations.
"Jarabe Mixteco"	Oaxaca	*Banda*	Concert band	Performing with the correct stylistic nuance in *banda* music.
"La Bamba"	Veracruz, Sinaloa	*Son jarocho*, performed in the *banda* style of Sinaloa	Concert band and vocalist	Musical diversity of Mexico.
Presentation: Marimba Music in Mexico. This presentation could discuss the history of the development of the marimba in Mexico.	Oaxaca, Chiapas	Marimba	Percussion	History of marimba in Mexico, cross-cultural connections (Spanish, African, Indigenous).
"La Tortuga"	Oaxaca, Chiapas	Marimba	Percussion ensemble with wind accompaniment	Adapting musical traditions to a different ensemble; musical variety within a similar geographical region.

the popular song "La Bamba" could be arranged in the Sinaloense *banda* style from the central Pacific coast of Mexico. To contrast with this, space could also be given to an exploration of Oaxacan *banda* performed at the *Guelaguetza*² festival such as "Jarabe Mixteco." Between presentations, students could present background information about the history and development of this music. A percussion ensemble arrangement of a Mexican marimba song like "La Tortuga" could also be developed through the WMP process and performed. By selecting a diverse representation of music from Mexico, this sample program illustrates the richness of the musical culture beyond the typical mainstream classroom representations of *mariachi* or band and orchestra arrangements of the pervasive song "La Raspa." While these two examples should be respected as important musical contributions, they are too often the terminus for mainstream attempts at musical diversity. Programming various lesser-known musical styles from a culture or country challenges the essentialist view (often reinforced by stereotypical examples) that musical practices within a culture are homogenous (e.g., West African music, Hindustani Indian music, Mexican music) and demonstrates that they are dynamic, in flux, varied, and organic traditions.

Collaborating With Culture Bearers for WMP Performances

Through globalization and the accompanying mass movement of individuals around the globe, many cities throughout the United States have found that the population size of their immigrant communities has increased dramatically. As these immigrants move into their new homes, they bring with them their cultural expressions—including music—as a way to remain connected to their homeland. To facilitate the maintenance of cultural traditions, these groups often establish community centers, connect with churches, or partner with non-profit organizations that provide opportunities to these diasporic communities for performing their musical heritage. This in turn has led to unprecedented and widespread access to culture bearers of musical traditions. Music teachers can collaborate with these individuals by inviting them into their classrooms for cultural exchanges that center on learning a particular musical tradition.

Working with culture bearers to develop performances can be deeply enriching for teachers, students, and audiences because it provides them with first-hand experience with members of the musical cultures that they are exploring (see Performer Feature: Indonesian Culture at Canyon Crest Academy). Rather than relying solely on approximation acquired through listening, collaborating with a culture bearer allows students and teachers to acquire specific cultural insight, performance techniques, and even choreography from an individual who has been musically immersed in the culture throughout his or her life.

When working with culture bearers it should be noted that music transmission practices vary from culture to culture and do not necessarily align with pedagogical methods found in most formal classroom settings. This should not be seen as a drawback, but rather as an opportunity to learn music through a culturally specific pedagogical approach. Learning music in this way allows for deeper understanding of how transmission is conceptualized within a particular musical culture in terms of formality, power distance, and attitudes toward adapting to different learning environments. Some would argue that removing musical cultures from their original context already negates any semblance of performance authenticity, and that this thought could logically be extended to pedagogical processes as well. Regardless of one's theoretical position, in practice, music teachers will inevitably need to seek compromises. In these instances, the focus should be placed on remaining flexible enough to incorporate *strategic inauthenticities* that allow for a blending of traditional and host-setting pedagogies (Schippers, 2010, pp. 50–53). Stringent adherence to either pedagogical approach does not allow for an organic integration of the two perspectives, and it limits the potential for students to have transformative experiences. The role of the music teacher, in this case, should be as a facilitator to help bridge the cultural gap and ease any tension caused by unfamiliarity with different teaching practices.

Connecting With Musical Cultures Through Community-Based Learning

While it is important for students to have opportunities to access music from all regions around the world, exploring the musical expressions that exist locally can also provide ripe opportunities to engage in fruitful collaborations. As mentioned in Chapter 1, there has been a developing interest in *community-based learning*, where spaces outside of institutions are used as sites for educational enrichment. Through these experiences, teachers and students can develop lasting relationships with *community members-cum-culture bearers* (community members who also perform music of a particular culture) who can serve to bridge the perceived gap between these settings. While gaining access to these individuals might require careful planning (and a little bit of venturing outside of one's comfort zone) the rewards far outweigh any initial discomforts. The following list provides suggested spaces that can be approached to find musical culture bearers within the community:

1. *Cultural Community Centers or Churches:* These sites often host community events and welcome outsiders to learn about their culture. In addition to these events, there are most likely volunteer opportunities as well.

2. *Local Universities or Colleges:* Schools are often home to student cultural clubs or traditional music ensembles that engage in outreach as a part of their activities. Most times these students have a section on their school's website or can be found through social media. Additionally, there are most likely professors that are working in the areas that music teachers are exploring through music in their classrooms. Connecting with these resources could prove extremely useful.

3. *Local Arts Organizations:* Local arts organizations often have connections to multicultural communities particularly if there are high numbers of refugees or immigrants in the area. A little Internet sleuthing could turn up several rewarding opportunities.

4. *Refugee Relocation Assistance Facilities:* There are several organizations around the world that help with resettling refugees. The United Nations Refugee Agency (UNHCR) has several resources on their website (www.unhcr.org), which could guide curious teachers to relocation centers near their schools. Moreover, these centers often offer programs that help refugees to integrate into their adopted communities

5. *Restaurants:* Restaurants are also a site where music teachers can explore the musical landscape of the diaspora in their communities. These are spaces where musical events are often advertised and simple conversations over a meal could open opportunities to connect with musicians.

6. *Students:* Students, teachers, and paraprofessionals in the schools where music teachers work can also serve as culture bearers. These individuals are a wealth of knowledge and are most times extremely willing to share their culture with their peers and co-workers.

Community Concerts

As the name implies, community concerts are designed to be performed in the areas that schools serve. These concerts could be presented in various ways ranging from large-scale concert band and orchestra performances in community venues, to small collaborative presentations, of chamber groups, in spaces such as cultural centers, businesses, libraries, churches, or restaurants. Because of this, community concerts are heavily influenced by context and always with an eye and ear towards collaboration with individuals who represent the musical traditions being explored. For example, a jazz band that is exploring Puerto Rican salsa might have as guest clinician and co-performer a local Puerto Rican musician. From here, a formalized program might emerge in a nonformal and communal space such as a local community center, town hall, or park. Such experiences can help students interact with community members who might open their eyes to new understandings of how music functions in various settings.

Collaborative Concerts

Collaborative concerts focus on student ensembles performing with or alongside culture bearers of a musical tradition. These performances can take a variety of forms ranging from fully staged presentations of a musical culture on traditional instruments to a shared concert that features pieces performed by both the culture bearers and school ensembles. Students can develop and present research projects on the music being performed, or the culture bearer can be the sole source of information being conveyed to the audience. Of course, each situation will vary so it is important to create clear outcomes of what the collaboration is intended to accomplish. For example, will it only be focused on performing the style of music accurately or will an understanding of culture be the central focus? Will the partnership be sustained to develop truly bi-musical students, or will the collaboration be a one-time exploration? Setting such goals early will increase the likeliness of a successful collaboration, which in turn will provide students with a positive experience with the selected musical culture.

Performer Feature: Indonesian Culture at Canyon Crest Academy

The music program at Canyon Crest Academy has been collaborating for several years with renowned Javanese gamelan master Pak Djoko Walujo to develop a full gamelan program at the high school. Through this partnership, the students are provided an immersive experience where they play on authentic instruments and learn from a master musician who engages them with Javanese music through traditional transmission practices. The annual culminating performances of this partnership also feature professional Indonesian dancers in authentic dress. While a situation like this would be ideal in most contexts, it is acknowledged that most music programs will not have access to such privileged resources. Still, this particular setting can serve as an example of what is possible when educational goals, efforts of stakeholders, and community support align.

To reiterate, developing performances through the process outlined in World Music Pedagogy does not negate the value of traditional school music performances. Rather, this approach provides an additional perspective on musical performance—one which is concerned with providing students with opportunities to embody varied musical cultures which ultimately seek to develop greater cultural sensitivity. This is often (but not always) realized through culminating productions that result from deep cultural explorations within and beyond the classroom. The performances that result from these activities are valuable for developing deeper cultural understandings in students because they not only focus on an accurate performance of context-specific sounds, but also incorporate other aspects of musical practice (e.g., function, context, movement) that imbue these cultural expressions with profound meaning. While the two perspectives of equitable inclusion and aesthetic excellence often seem to exist on disparate planes, they are not mutually exclusive in practice.

The World Music Pedagogy Process Through the Performance of Published Works

With the suggestions provided within this chapter, the intention is not to supplant participation in traditional ensembles as being central component of music education. Instead, they seek to offer activities that can help music teachers expand their musical scope to include a variety of diverse musical perspectives in their concert programs. Understandably, this can be an overwhelming endeavor to music teachers who are already stretched thin by the increasing demands of such a taxing profession. The ways in which music programs founded on the traditional triumvirate (band, orchestra, choir) have enriched the lives of students for over a century simply cannot be overstated. Both anecdotally and empirically, the benefits associated with participation in these school instrumental ensembles speak for themselves and, rightly, justify the inclusion of music in mainstream curricula.

For many music teachers, this may be the first time that they have asked questions of how (or even why) to incorporate the learning of diverse musical cultures into their music programs. For some this may lead to discomfort, confusion, or even lead them to question the viability of the WMP process altogether. Others might even feel that the authors are seeking to replace successful music programs with activities that are little more than exercises in musical mediocrity. In order to overcome these perceptions, the authors offer ways that music teachers can gently ease into implementing WMP into their music programs through the use of published works. Rather than arranging a completely new piece based on Enactive Listening activities, music teachers can use WMP activities (Attentive, Engaged, Enactive Listening) to supplement rehearsals of published pieces that are already programmed for concerts. There are several quality examples based on music from around the world that can be used for this purpose. The following *Published Works Commentaries* illustrate how performance of the following pieces can be enhanced through the WMP process.

Concert Band

"Variations on a Korean Folk Song" by John Barnes Chance (Boosey & Hawkes)

Performers: The United States Army Field Band and Soldier's Chorus

Description: Variations on a Korean Folk Song is based on the traditional Korean song, "Arirang." According to program notes from the Wind Repertory Project,[3] John Barnes Chance heard this melody while he was stationed in Korea. This piece is comprised of the melody set to five distinct variations.

Description of context/function: The song "Gyeonngi Arirang," or simply "Arirang," is just one of the many regional versions that exists. Each province in Korea is thought to have their own version, the performance of which reflects the local context.

Recommended Resources:

Reading:
Kwon, D. (2012). *Music in Korea: Experiencing music, expressing culture (Global Music Series)*. New York: Oxford University Press

---

Recordings:

"Ah-Rirang" from *Korea: Vocal and Instrumental Music*, Various Artists, available on iTunes: https://itun.es/us/QsxYm?i=214530419

"Kangwon Province Arirang" from *Four Thousand Years of Korean Folk Music*, Various Artists, available on iTunes: https://itun.es/us/9J7Qi?i=145472063

"Arirang," from *Arirang: Korean Song and Dance Ensemble*, Kuktan Arirang, available on iTunes: https://itun.es/us/kjriq?i=270602877

Performance Advisories: Since "Arirang" is based on a vocal melody, it should be sung first to provide the students with an understanding of the shape of the melody and ways that it can be manipulated for dramatic effect. Students could also learn different regional variations of "Arirang" and perform them in a concert setting to illustrate the diversity of this piece.

"La Fiesta Mexicana" by H. Owen Reed (Alfred Music)

Performers: Harlan D. Parker and the Peabody Conservatory Wind Ensemble

Description: This piece was composed by H. Owen Reed after a year of studying Mexican music through a Guggenheim Fellowship in 1948–1949. It is comprised of three movements: Prelude and Aztec Dance, Mass, and Carnival. Reed incorporated folk melodies and that he learned during his travels in an attempt to capture the diversity of music in Mexico.

Description of context/function: From the Afro-Mexican *son jarocho* in the eastern state of Veracruz, to the pre-Columbian musical colors from the *Huaves* people in the Costa Chica near Oaxaca, Mexican music is extremely diverse and spans a broad spectrum of functions and contexts. This piece mostly explores the melodies of Mexican wind bands that are popular throughout the country from Sinaloa to Oaxaca. These groups mostly perform at social functions such as the annual *Guelaguetza* festival in Oaxaca and other community events.

Recommended Resources:

Reading:

Sturman, J. (2016). *The course of Mexican music*. New York, NY. Abingdon, Oxon: Routledge, Taylor & Francis Group.

Recordings:
La Guelaguetza: La Musica Autentica del Espectaculo Folklorico Mas Importante de America (album); Various Artists, available on iTunes: https://itun. es/us/RcAWib
Lluvia de Palos (album), by Tlaltekuinilistli, available on iTunes: https://itun. es/us/XMKV3

Performance Advisories: Several moments in this piece offer opportunities to incorporate lessons learned from enactive listening activities. For example, students could be exposed to the various sonic colors of Oaxacan band music through repeated listening and play-along activities that allow them to match the sound and the feel of Mexican *bandas*.

"Islas y Montañas, Mvt. III: Seis Manuel" by Shelly Hanson (Boosey & Hawkes)

Performers: William Berz and the Rutgers Wind Ensemble

Description: This piece is based on the Puerto Rican dance called the *seis*. This dance, intended for six individuals, originated in the *jíbaro* community, a group of individuals that live in the mountainous areas of Puerto Rico.

Description of context/function: This piece was transcribed from *jíbaro* music to a concert band setting. *Jíbaro* music is often performed in a small ensemble that features the *cuatro* (a plucked stringed instrument tuned in courses), the *güiro* (a scraped percussion instrument), *clave* (wooden dowels that are struck together to maintain the pulse of the music), and voice. Traditionally, this music is taught by rote and does not rely on music notation.

Recommended Resources:

Reading:
Moore, R. (2010). *Music in the Hispanic Caribbean: Experiencing music, expressing culture* (Global Music Series). New York: Oxford University Press.

Recordings:
"Jíbaro Hasta el Hueso," from Jíbaro Hasta el Hueso: Mountain Music of Puerto Rico, by Ecos de Borinquen, available on iTunes: https://itunes.apple.com/ us/album/j%C3%ADbaro-hasta-el-hueso-j%C3%ADbaro-to-the-bone/ id262213466?i=262213664

"Soñando Con Regresar," from El Alma de Puerto Rico, by Ecos de Borinquen, available on iTunes: https://itunes.apple.com/us/album/so%C3%B1ando-con-regresar/id1146911280?i=1146911471

Performance Advisories: Attention should be given to both the rhythmic elements and articulation of the melodic solos of this piece. Jíbaro music is intensely rhythmic and emphasizes improvised exploration from the solo singer. To play with stylistic accuracy, these elements should be isolated and rehearsed.

"Arabesque" by Samuel Hazo (Hal Leonard Corporation)

Performers: Jack Stamp and the Indiana University of Pennsylvania Wind Ensemble

Description: This piece was composed by Hazo to honor his Lebanese and Assyrian heritage. As implied by the name "Arabesque," Hazo borrowed elements and concepts of Arabic music rather than directly quoting pre-existing material.

Description of context/function: Composed in three parts, this piece utilizes aspects of Arabic music for melodic material and structure for the first two sections. The first section, *taqasim*, is an improvisatory section that is often found in Arabic music. The second section, *dabka*, is a traditional line dance often performed at Arabic celebrations. Hazo also incorporates Middle Eastern hand drums such as the *darbouka* and *doumbeck* into the percussion section and microtones in the opening flute cadenza to provide culturally accurate musical elements.

Recommended Resources:

Reading:
Rasmussen, A. K. (2009). The Arab world. In *Worlds of music: An introduction to the music of the world's peoples* (5th ed., pp. 473–532). Belmont, CA: Schirmer Cengage Learning.

Recordings:
"Taqsim on the Nay," from *Melodies and Rhythms of Arabic Music*, Various Artists, available on iTunes: https://itun.es/us/TOFWp?i=264371195
"Haji Teoulli," from *Dabke: National Dance of Lebanon*, Naif Agby, available on iTunes: https://itun.es/us/BXiN6?i=983338476

Performance Advisories: Although microtones are only found in the flute cadenza at the beginning of the piece, all students should acquire a familiarity of the nuance of microtones in Arabic music through the playing of various modes. This will help them to understand how modes are used as a compositional element in such musical cultures. To capture the rhythmic feel of the *dabka* section, the students might also learn basic dance steps associated with this music.

Orchestra

"Molly on the Shore" by Percy Grangier/Arr. Edwin F. Kalmus

Performers: N/A

Description: This piece is based on two Irish reels: "Molly on the Shore" and "Temple Hill." These contrasting pieces flow into each other without pause, as would happen at a traditional Irish jam session.

Description of context/function: Irish traditional music, or *trad*, is typically played in nonformal settings where musicians emphasize rote learning in their musical transmission practices. Through these traditional sessions, musicians are able to memorize hundreds of songs.

Recommended Resources:

Reading:
Hast, D., & Scott, S. (2004). *Music in Ireland: Experiencing music, expressing culture* (Global Music Series). New York: Oxford University Press.
O'Neill, F., Krassen M., & Coleman, M. (1976). *O'Neill's music of Ireland* (New and revised by Michael Krassen, ed.). New York: Oak Publications.

Recordings:
"The Swallow's Tail/Drowsy Maggie," from *Ireland*, Various Artists, available on iTunes: https://itun.es/us/aijYZ?i=868782739
"The Queen of O'Donnell," from *Traditional Music of Ireland, Vol. I: The Older Tradition of Connemara and Clare*, Various Artists, available on iTunes: https://itun.es/us/rLBOq?i=279034335

Performance Advisories: When performing this piece, special care should be given to re-creating the nuances of Irish melodic styles, including articulation, ornamentation, rhythmic placement, and the shaping of melodic lines. To achieve this, students should be exposed to regular listening activities focused on traditional Irish music. Musical examples could also be taken from *O'Neill's Music of Ireland* and performed as warm-ups with attention given to stylistic nuance.

The Potential of Performing the World's Musical Cultures

The suggestions presented in this chapter provide the reader with a set of considerations and a flexible-but-systematic method to approach the endeavor of performing world music in instrumental music classrooms. As with any pedagogy, implementation of these principles is dependent upon specific classroom contexts. Music is a uniquely human activity that shapes the way cultures view the world while simultaneously opening possibilities for a variety of ways to exist and make sense of diverse realities. By allowing and encouraging students to perform music from various cultures, teachers are providing them with an opportunity to learn about and briefly inhabit some of the infinite modes of human existence. This can help each student to view the world from a different perspective and open their hearts to the broad spectrum of human expression.

Teacher Feature: Amy Villanova on Performing World Music

Amy Villanova, Head of the Music Department at the Grammy Signature Schools Enterprise Award Winning Canyon Crest Academy, San Diego, CA

Q: What were some of the reasons that you decided to incorporate world music into your programs?
A: Our students are increasingly becoming global citizens, and it is important that their education represents more than just our little pocket of the world. The arts are an accessible entry point to understanding about other cultures as well. Also, contemporary music draws inspiration from all sorts of world media, so providing our students a more diverse musical vocabulary is important.

Q: How do you come to learn about the music traditions that you have incorporated into your programs?
A: Some of it was luck, and some of it was related to our university experiences. All of it was dependent on finding experts in these areas who were interested and willing to share their time and talents with our students. It is important that we connect students with authentic learning experiences directly from musician master teachers as much as possible.

Q: How did you decide which types of music should be added?
A: Again, this comes down to access primarily. We had access to Pak Djoko Walujo through our relationship with the Center for World Music. In a series of events that Anne [Whatoff, the choir director at CCA] facilitated, we housed San Diego State University's gamelan instruments when they were temporarily homeless. From this were able to grow a program at CCA that justified purchasing our own instruments. Our relationship with the Center for World Music has also allowed us to bring in many Indonesian artists as they pass through San Diego to give performances and demonstrations. Our Samba batucada evolved a little differently. Since we already had a bit of a world influence in

our program through Anne's connections, we were able to develop a Brazillian group to perform for athletics and develop a sense school spirit on campus. The samba line seemed like a good blend of authentic music-making, portability, and a festive feel. We had considered a steel pan ensemble, but it was cost prohibitive to start up, and the samba group was economically a much easier choice. We also had access to guest performers and teachers from a local community Brazillian group called the Super Sonic Samba School. Our percussion instructor, Mike Atesalp, also has a variety of expertise in jazz, Latin hand percussion, and marching band that he was able to contribute as well.

Q: How do you find a balance between the expectations to perform traditional "school music" and the desire to perform world music?
A: Inclusivity is very important, even when performing in the traditional band, orchestra, and choir ensembles. These world music groups meet after school as more of a club than a class, and draw from the entire student body, including students who are not involved in any of the other campus music classes. In our traditional performance courses, we make a very conscious effort to program literature from a wide representation of composers and styles. It is not practical to think that a student hoping to major in violin performance will only play music of the Western canon. So, as much as possible, we try to give all our musicians the experience of playing quality literature from a variety of periods, composers, styles, and geographic locations. Our state and national standards require this, but we give it more than "lip service" at Canyon Crest. Our primary concern with the traditional classes is offering quality literature and instruction, and there is so much available with a little searching that it is easy to manage.

Q: What types of resources were helpful to you when you began incorporating world music into your program?
A: People were our most important resources—people to offer advice on coaching, instrument purchase, contacts to bring in performers to inspire the students and get them curious enough to start out. If we felt the students had enough of a connection and buy-in, finding the correct staff and equipment was easier. I suppose Anne and I could have done more ourselves, based on our own training, but we had access to the funding to provide our students with direct instruction from experts in those areas.

Q: Did you encounter any challenges when incorporating world music into your music program? If so, why? If not, how did your administrators and parents support you?
A: We teach in a school where the administrative direction has always been . . . GO FOR IT! If it is good for the kids and sustainable at the level our community expects, go for it. On occasion, our administration has also supported grants that funded teachers and instruments. Our biggest challenge is finding time for our students who want to do it all. The students who want in-depth explorations into other musical cultures are also the robotics kids, the speech and debate kids, the kids who are already performing with jazz band, outside bands, theater shows, etc. The hardest thing for us to manage is our students' time. We do a bunch of advocacy work to educate our parents on the importance of these programs, and they see it as such an asset too. They find the uniqueness of our program to be one of the selling points when our parent volunteers drum up donation drives.

Q: When preparing performances, how much thought do you give to authenticity of the performance? How do you accomplish this in your concerts?
A: Some performances/pieces celebrate the traditional, while others are an intentional hybrid of world influence and pop culture, so it is always a blend. Our gamelan is our most traditional, but Pak Djoko has written compositions for Canyon Crest that use the

gamelan tradition in a more modern way. He includes traditional dancers with classical gamelan selections, but also has bent tradition a bit to make performances work for our students. Our samba group will perform with a rock band/singers and do covers of current songs, only with a samba feel. I think we look at it the same way we look at performing Bach. We aren't performing on baroque instruments, and while we give as much attention as possible to correct style and performance practice, it is naturally going to be different. The way modern music pulls from a variety of influences, our groups do their best to re-create authentic style and add their own experiences to the performance.

Q: How much attention do you give to the context of the country/culture where the music originated in your concerts?
A: Not as much as we should. We talk about the pieces in preparation, provide insight, backstories as much as possible, but we don't spend as much time researching and immersing ourselves in the languages, cultures, and historical context as we could. Our class time is much more predominantly spent preparing the music. Samba students will participate in a local Brazil Day festival with music, food and dancing, but the daily classes are more focused on the music technique. Gamelan follows classroom tradition and is taught by rote, so the students are having a completely immersive experience, but I bet if we asked some of them to quickly point out Java on a map it might take them a bit.

Q: What benefits do you feel come from performing diverse musical styles in your music programs?
A: Inclusivity is the big one . . . seeing kids involved in these groups that otherwise haven't found their voice in our music program. Also, I think it gives our musicians more confidence to try new things, to listen to other music for inspiration and to bring those ideas into their own performances and compositions. It is also important for the casual student musicians, including (and probably especially) the ones who don't participate in these groups. It shows that there is value to all sorts of world cultures and arts and that we are looking beyond the traditional. We hope to encourage them to do the same in whatever area that their passion lies. A student who is looking to become a professional musician is going to have to do more than just learn their orchestral excerpts. They need to be as versatile as possible. Even if they never perform as a professional *caixa* player, having that experience in school will give them the confidence to try new things and push themselves out of the traditional musician roles.

Q: How have your students responded to performing world music?
A: It goes in waves. At first there is high interest and involvement . . . then the work comes and they get nervous about performances, downplay their interest and even minimize their previous successes. Then they have a performance and they are right back up there on the performance endorphin high. They are savvy enough to hear the difference in their emerging skills and the techniques that they are trying to emulate. Expectations versus reality can be a tough thing to get through sometimes, but we have a diehard crew of students dedicated to this craft. In our traditional ensemble classes, the more authentically sourced literature is generally the favorite of the group. It is so validating to see students come in with their own compositions or arrangements that pull from the things they have learned outside of the Western tradition. It just gives them a greater musical arsenal when they are set free to create on their own.

Q: What are some of your most memorable moments teaching diverse musical cultures?
A: The day we started our gamelan program was also Halloween, so the first time students sat behind the instruments and learned about the gamelan, about 80% of

them were in costume. It was just another day at Canyon Crest Academy. We had a multi-week unit on West African drumming and dance. Although I teach music I must say the "dance" part was definitely the students' favorite! After the unit was over, a few of the students contacted the ensemble that came and worked with us and joined their afterschool workshops as well. They had such a strong desire to keep their involvement going. In another example, we are now in a partnership to create a whole orchestral concert with *Los Hermanos Arango* from Cuba. During a clinic that they conducted for our jazz band we ended up having a conversation about the different classes we offered at the school. After mentioning that we had an orchestra, one of the members immediately stated that they wanted to create a concert with a symphony orchestra. This resulted in them contacting mutual connections to arrange their music for our orchestra to perform with them! After our performance at Canyon Crest they will then take those arrangements on tour when they travel the United States and beyond. This all starting from a casual conversation!

Q: Do you have any advice for teachers who are thinking about Integrating World Music into their curriculum?
A: Do it! Do it on whatever scale you can. It is wonderful if you can bring in authentic sources. Kids know when you are faking expertise, so if at all possible bring people in who are experts in their field, or perhaps take the attitude of "let's learn this together." If you have a classroom community where risk-taking is safe and kind of the norm, things like introducing traditional Ghanaian dance goes a little more smoothly. Our kids jumped right in because they are used to doing so, but if you are worried about the "you want me to WHAT?" attitude, then perhaps more work on that part of your classroom environment will help make introducing potentially foreign activities go a little smoother. It is also important to model risk-taking behavior for them. If you are able to hire experts, get in there and learn alongside the kids. It is good for them to see you in a student role as well.

Notes

1 Keil defines participatory discrepancies as "the notable relationships and almost entirely unnotable microinflections of groove and sound quality [that] are always there in all musicking" (1995, p. 97).
2 An annual festival in Oaxaca that features music, dance, and food from the seven main regions of the state.
3 www.windrep.org

References

Blacking, J. (1973). *How musical is man?* (1st paperback ed., Jessie and John Danz lectures). Seattle, WA: University of Washington Press.

Campbell, P. (2004). *Teaching music globally: Experiencing music, expressing culture* (Global Music Series). New York, NY: Oxford University Press.

Fung, C. V. (2002). *Experiencing world musics in schools: From fundamental positions to strategic guidelines*. In B. Reimer (Ed.), *World musics and music education: Facing the issues*. Reston, VA: MENC.

Keil, C., & Prögler, J. (1995). [The theory of participatory discrepancies: A progress report; Searching for swing: Participatory discrepancies in the jazz rhythm section;

Rhythm as duration of sounds in "Tumba Francesa"]: Rejoinders. *Ethnomusicology*, *39*, 97–104. doi:10.2307/852201

MacDonald, R., Hargreaves, D. J., & Miell, D. (2002). *Musical identities*. Oxford, UK and New York, NY: Oxford University Press.

Santos, R. (2012). *Laon-laon: Perspectives in transmission and pedagogy of musical traditions in post-colonial Southeast Asia*. España, Manila, PH: University of Santo Tomas Publishing House.

Schippers, H. (2010). *Facing the music: Shaping music education from a global perspective*. Oxford, UK and New York, NY: Oxford University Press.

Published Works Commentaries

"Variations on a Korean Folk Song," by John Barnes Chance (Boosey & Hawkes). www.boosey.com/shop/prod/Chance-John-Barnes-Variations-On-A-Korean-Folk-song/600983 Recording available on iTunes: https://itun.es/us/orVcu?i=336262258

"La Fiesta Mexicana," by H. Owen Reed (Alfred Music). www.alfred.com/Products/La-Fiesta-Mexicana—00-BDM03027.aspx Recordings available on iTunes: https://itun.es/us/-0bCk

"Islas y Montañas, Mvt. III: Seis Manuel," by Shelly Hanson (Boosey & Hawkes). www.boosey.com/cr/sheet-music/Shelley-Hanson-Seis-Manuel/24886 Recording available on iTunes: https://itun.es/us/ZHJ6A?i=451557508

"Arabesque," by Samuel Hazo (Hal Leonard Corporation). www.halleonard.com/product/viewproduct.action?itemid=4002784&subsiteid=6 Recording available on iTunes: https://itun.es/us/nBLWdb?i=1136809934

"Molly on the Shore," by Percy Grangier/Arr. Edwin F. Kalmus. www.carlfischer.com/shop/reels-and-reverie.html Recording available on publisher's website.

Listening Episodes

"Mi Gente," Héctor Lavoe, iTunes/Fania. A Puerto Rican salsa classic, featuring a full salsa band and iconic singer Héctor Lavoe. https://itun.es/us/Nn0aF?i=520308589

"Tulina's Carmona," Kinan Azmeh, iTunes. Contemporary piece in mixed meter by a Syrian clarinetist and composer. https://itun.es/us/iHNdP?i=688814352

"Chemutengure," Lora Chiorah-Dye & Sukutai, Smithsonian Folkways. A traditional Shona melody performed with *mbira*, *hosho* (shaker), and voices. www.folkways.si.edu/lora-chiorah-dye-and-sukutai/chemtengure/world/music/track/smithsonian

"La Tortuga," Faustino González Rivera, Smithsonian Folkways. A traditional marimba piece performed in the southern Mexico states of Oaxaca and Chiapas. www.folkways.si.edu/faustino-gonzalez-rivera/la-tortuga-the-turtle-son-from-the-isthmus/latin-world/music/track/smithsonian

"Jarabe Mixteco," Various Artists, iTunes. A traditional *banda* piece performed at the Guelaguetza festival in Oaxaca. https://itun.es/us/RcAWib?i=1220649148

"La Rascapetate," by Marimba Chiapas. A traditional marimba piece from Chiapas, Mexico. https://folkways.si.edu/marimba-chiapas/rascapetate/american-folk/music/track/smithsonian

5

Creating World Music

Over the past few weeks, Debbie's high school band director has been playing "Chemtengure" repeatedly at the start of every rehearsal. Today, Debbie is left with an "earworm" that rings in her head throughout the afternoon. The mbira ostinato from the opening has stayed with her all day, and, with it running through her head, she quietly begins to hum a new melody over it during study hall. The next day, she sits in the band room, putting together her saxophone while humming her simple newly composed tune. Twisting on the mouthpiece and carefully aligning her reed, she brings the saxophone to her mouth and begins to place the melody over the sound of individual warm-ups throughout the room. A few minutes later, she turns around, and finding her friend Brandell, says, "hey, can you play that mbira ostinato we learned for 'Chemtengure' last week?" Brandell picks up his acrylic mallets—the closest he can get to the percussive sound he remembers hearing from the mbira— and begins to play the full ostinato. As he falls into a steady rhythm, Debbie lays her new melody on top of it. Hearing it in the flesh for the first time, excitement fills her body as she plays her melody repeatedly, occasionally adjusting a few notes here and there. Above the cacophony in the room, Brandell and Debbie begin to establish a solid groove. As their organized sound breaks through the discord in the room, a few friends begin to gather around. Soon, one or two classmates begin trying to play Debbie's simple new melody along with her. Showing her approval with a smile, she begins to improvise small embellishments to her tune, expanding upon her ideas in the moment.

To many Western musicians, the notion of creating original music—whether by composing or improvising—is thought to be a musical capacity reserved for the gifted and elite few. In many societies, the role of the composer, arranger, or improviser is treated as a sort of specialization which typically comes after the musician has attained a certain level of proficiency in the craft of performance. As the Western tradition goes, musicians first learn conventions of theory, counterpoint, and harmony within their musical tradition. For years, they learn the rules of appropriate voice leading, avoiding parallel fifths and octaves, and knowing which pitches fit within certain chords. As it seems, only after completing these musical "rites of passage" do musicians feel capable of creating original music on their own.

Especially in the orchestra tradition, concerts often celebrate the music of the "masters"—Bach, Mozart, Beethoven, Brahms, Mahler, and Stravinsky, to name but a few. This celebration of compositional heroes seems to perpetuate the notion that there are a handful of those who have proven themselves as worthy creators of music. They are regarded as exceptional musicians with superior musical minds. Sometimes they are even paralleled with the spiritual, the transcendent, and the magical. Musical ideas are believed to originate from a heavenly source, pouring effortlessly through the pen of the hallowed composer. To many, those who create either meditatively (composers and arrangers) or spontaneously (improvisers) are seen as existing on an altogether different musical plane. Yet, as satisfying as the image of the exalted composer might be in immortalizing music as a magical and inexplicable phenomenon, such a romanticized view of the creative process does little for encouraging others to believe that they too are capable of wielding such musical gifts.

Christopher Small (1998) takes issue with this elitist view of musical creation, problematizing the role of the performer as a one-way conduit through which the musical composition passes in order to reach its final destination—the listener. There is, of course, nothing wrong with celebrating the greatness of an artist or composer. But celebration that reaches the point of canonization arguably makes it difficult for young musical learners to ultimately see themselves as being skilled in the same endeavor. Such limited notions of musical creation ultimately serve little benefit to the musical education of children and youth. Inspirational as they may be, venerating composers alone ultimately does little to motivate children to chase similar musical pursuits.

Instead, instrumental music students should come to see the ways in which composers and improvisers are just like any other kind of musician, with ideas that start small and develop into simple works, and others which expand into larger and greater works over time. Further, students should engage in the act of musical creation not only after they can demonstrate competence on a litany of other musical skills, but from the very beginning. Immersing themselves early and plentifully into composition, improvisation, song-writing, and arranging will lead to the understanding that such activities are not an exclusive endeavor reserved for the talented few. Like Debbie, musicians of all ages and on all instruments are constantly hearing music in their heads—whether strands of existing songs, or frivolous melodies of their own making. From the development of long-form works of high artistic expertise, to playful melodies entering the ear at-will, the human penchant for creating music should be regarded as a skill as indispensable as any other form of musicking.

Global Traditions of Composition and Improvisation in Instrumental Music Education

While there are many cultures in which composers and improvisers are regarded in a hierarchical manner, there are also many cultures that embrace the belief that anyone is capable of creating original music of exceptional quality. It is within these traditions that the role of creation through composing or improvising becomes central to the art form, and, as it happens, the ones in which the line between creator and performer is often blurred. These musical traditions tend to focus less on venerating a canon of "masterworks," but instead celebrate a dynamic body of music that changes, evolves, or even becomes fully replaced over time.

We suggest that the culture of instrumental music classrooms, including band and orchestra *in addition* to jazz band (which already embodies a culture of improvisation, if not original composition), are optimal settings for creative composition and improvisation. While these ensembles are replete with planned activities of group learning and rehearsals of selected works for public performances, they are also ideal settings for brief bouts of creative work by students who, inspired by the music they learn (aurally or by notation), begin to develop new and exciting expressions. The selections featured within this book are suggested launches into journeys of creative expression for instrumental music students.

Improvisation

Within musical cultures throughout South and Southeast Asia, and across the Near East and North Africa, improvisations tend to unravel in extended performances lasting several hours, often with barely a note of music being preplanned or organized (Campbell, 2004). In many other traditions, improvisation takes on a number of different roles, some which value collective group improvisation, and others utilizing individual improvisation. Some musical cultures are inherently more improvised than others, with some utilizing improvisation almost exclusively (such as Hindustani *khayal*), others engaging in small improvised sections within larger composed pieces (such as American jazz), and others utilizing no improvisation whatsoever (such as music from the Navajo people). Further, different examples within the same culture may fluctuate in approach towards and emphasis on improvisation. For example, in Japanese *nagauta* (Kabuki dance music), there is no room for improvisation and minimal room for creative interpretation. However, Japanese *matsuri-bayashi* (Shinto festival music) and *Tsugaru-jamisen* (northern folk *jamisen* tradition) utilize improvisation heavily (Hughes, 2004). Finally, one work within the same tradition might be completely through-composed, while another from the same composer will be heavily improvised. Thus, improvisation should not be regarded as *culture-specific*, but rather as *genre-specific*.

Surprisingly to some, the art of improvisation has played a meaningful role in the Western classical tradition as well. Compositional masters such as J.S. Bach, Mozart, and Beethoven were highly skilled improvisers in addition to being venerated composers. Romantic composers such as pianists Frédéric Chopin and Franz Liszt were also talented improvisers whose best-known compositions began as keyboard improvisations. Even the great 20th-century composer George Gershwin is said to have improvised much of the solo piano part at his world premiere of "Rhapsody in Blue." As the Western tradition moved through the 20th century, an interest in deconstructing the role of the composer became prevalent through chance music and *avant garde* styles that featured extended (or complete) improvisations. In short, there are few musical cultures in which improvisation exists as an absolute (i.e., the culture either utilizes improvisation or it does not), just as there are few cultures in which improvisation is handled in exactly the same manner within every musical creation.

Composition

When it comes to composition, an image that enters many people's minds is the musical score, the notated depiction of what is to be played and by whom. Within the score lives not only the composer's melodies, harmonies, and rhythms, but articulations, stylistic considerations, and expressive recommendations as well. To many, the musical score becomes the physical manifestation of intangible sounds, itself becoming venerated as an object of importance. Some imagine a composer sitting in turmoil over the blank pages, agonizingly working musical ideas into phrases, themes, and movements. (Subsequently, portraits of long-haired 18th- and 19th-century male composers may also come to mind.) Yet, as discussed extensively already, there are many musical cultures in which compositions are never written down or notated. They exist only in the minds of the performers, who carry out the composer's wishes by verbal instruction (by rote), adhering to the musical performance as fixed and unchanged in every iteration. For example, new compositions crafted by musicians across sub-Saharan Africa are sometimes developed weeks, days, or hours before a performance, and are meant to be performed intact. The composer delivers the lyrics, melody, and harmony to the other performers by ear, making adjustments to the composition as needed (yet notation is never passed between them). In other traditions, composition goes only so far as to establish a "road map," or an agreed-upon form that the music will organically take during performance.

The Iterative Process of Performing and Creating Within Global Musical Traditions

The art of composition and improvisation is very much alive in many musical traditions around the globe, supporting the idea that learning to create music *in addition to* reproducing it is a necessary goal of the musical education of instrumental students in school bands, orchestras, and other instrumental classes and ensembles. Indeed, in the United States, the National Standards for Music Education identify composition and improvisation as necessary skills for musical proficiency, although most students participating in instrumental ensembles are rarely afforded such opportunities (with the exception of jazz band). Whenever possible, the skills of improvisation and composition may be developed alongside the processes of performing, which helps remove the previously discussed stigma that the right to create original music must first be earned through years of imitation. Instead of being viewed as a sequential progression (i.e., first students learn to perform, then they may compose and improvise), performing and creating music should instead be viewed as an iterative process. In fact, many skills presented in this chapter might do well to be presented alongside (or occasionally even before, when warranted by the customs of the musical culture) others from the preceding chapter. After all, full-on performances of certain musical traditions may not be realistic without students first immersing themselves into the improvisatory or compositional practices of that style.

However, this is not to suggest that students should freely engage with improvisation willy-nilly at the beginning of musical study. Coming loud-and-clear from the voices of those who teach, participate, study, and write about global musical cultures, the message has been largely the same: Improvisation is to occur *after* competent understandings of the techniques and procedures required to perform the music. Speaking to the matter, Hughes (2004) states that "premature improvisation is not only impractical, it is also disrespectful of the tradition and its bearers" (p. 267).

Understandably, these points may sound contradictory at first. This is largely because like most matters pertaining to global musical expressions, blanket statements rarely hold true for every culture. While the approach that each practice takes towards musical creation is unique, these suggestions advocate that students should both "get their hands dirty" with the musical practices of the culture while also showing great respect to that culture by first grounding their actions in a deeper understanding of the practice.

To clarify some of these points, instead of engaging with freewheeling improvisation from the start, students ought to have meaningful interactions with a musical practice through Attentive, Engaged, and Enactive Listening experiences. While improvisation within certain musical cultures (such as Hindustani *khyal*) might occur from the start of the transmission process, recall that native learners of such styles will have already been subjected to these sounds and practices from birth. In fact, in some cultures, musical apprentices are not directly taught to perform or create their own music until the teacher has curated in the student's ears the highest quality of musical exemplars. Importantly, our students growing up with "Westernized" ears will often be unfamiliar with the sounds of many culture's musics, making compositional and improvisatory exercises within those practices meaningless without first immersing the students into that musical practice. For example, if a teacher were to present Hindustani *khyal* to a classroom of instrumental students immediately through improvisation, the exercise would be akin to asking students to make sense of a foreign language after only hearing it for the first time.

For these reasons, the Attentive, Engaged, and Enactive Listening phases do their best to replicate the immersive experiences of a culture's transmission process in an accelerated fashion. While full enculturation of the musical culture will rarely be possible given the time and curricular constraints of the ensemble, students participating deeply in the WMP process can approach—even if only on the surface—a more immersive understanding of the musical culture over time. At this point—perhaps after dozens of Attentive, Engaged, and Enactive Listening experiences spanning several weeks—making sense of improvisatory and compositional practices may become more fluid and natural for the students.

A Few Misconceptions About Composing and Improvising

There tends to be a belief that composition, improvisation, and performance are altogether separate activities, and that they are usually performed by separate types of musicians. This is simply not the case, and instrumental music students should begin to understand how, within many cultures, the identity of the composer is inextricable from the identity of a performer. Indeed, the act of performing and composing often co-exist, with the act of one leading into the other (Campbell, 2004). Such acts may occur by chance or by design, and forays into one or the other may originate from the teacher or be inspired by the student.

There is also a misconception that compositions must result in a static piece of music and improvisations must be completely spontaneous and unplanned. In fact, there are many compositions, such as across much of sub-Saharan Africa (see Teacher Feature interview in this chapter, pp. 132–34), where musicians continually compose new iterations on top of the same piece, replacing what previously existed with something brand new. As it happens, the musical piece is continually changing, and never forms itself into a fixed "product." Similarly, improvisers often recycle musical phrases and motifs that they find favorable, sometimes repeating them verbatim in various contexts, and sometimes using them as launching pads into new ideas.

Finally, the difference between composition and improvisation is often thought to be distinguished by the timing of the process. It is believed that composition must precede performance, and improvisation must only occur during performance. Yet in practice, the act of composing can occur in-the-moment while performing, as much as improvised ideas can originate from preplanned musical seeds. Essentially, ethnomusicologists find that the practices of improvisation, composition, and performing are not by necessity different processes, and in many contexts, musicians weave in and through various stages of musical creation during the act of performance (Wade, 2009).

Approaching Musical Creation in Western Instrumental Ensembles

The craft of musical creation is not necessarily a straightforward endeavor for everyone. Indeed, some instrumental music students will appear to be "naturals" at improvising, some will have compositional ideas effortlessly flow from their pens, and likely many others will become frozen in the moment, stymied by the task before them. Yet, the goal of creating original music need not necessarily be one of high-quality, product-based musical outcomes. Students can experience rewarding musical journeys by exploring new sounds on an unfamiliar instrument, within an unfamiliar musical mode, or through unfamiliar rhythmic grooves. As instrumental students develop and grow more musically, their proclivity for spontaneous creation grows along with it, forging the path for more skillful and automated musical excursions.

John Kratus (1995) outlines a seven-step developmental process for improvisation, which may serve as a useful model against which to view students' spontaneous musical development. In order, the seven steps are as follows:

1. *Exploration*: The student is free to loosely experiment with different sounds.
2. *Process-Oriented Improvisation*: The student begins to create more organized musical patterns.
3. *Product-Oriented Improvisation*: The student becomes more cognizant of more structural processes (i.e., style, tonality, rhythm).
4. *Fluid Improvisation*: The student is capable of making musical phrases more organically and automatically.
5. *Structural Improvisation*: The student begins to incorporate purposeful strategies (musical and non-musical) to develop more musical ideas.
6. *Stylistic Improvisation*: The student learns to develop improvisational fluency and nuance within a particular musical style (or styles).
7. *Personal Improvisation*: The student is able to transcend the stylistic norms of a given idiom, developing a new style altogether.

Of these levels of improvisational mastery, few musicians actually achieve all seven. Depending on the age group being taught, a reasonable expectation might be to reach the first three or four during a student's time in school. Indeed, this model is quite beneficial for helping teachers of younger students (i.e., 4–8th grade) see the value and justification of teaching improvisation in their classrooms. For an elementary band or orchestra, entering into the first level (exploration) will become a necessary step for further improvisational growth to be learned in the middle and high school years. That said, elementary teachers can also competently bring their students well into the third level of improvisational development, depending on the amount of time allocated to such activities.

By high school, students might be capable of reaching the fourth and fifth levels. Of course, the possibilities for bringing students directly into the sixth (and possibly seventh) levels are limited, given the already inadequate time instrumental teachers have with their students in public and private school settings. However, teachers can become important guides for students who seek to develop their skills further beyond the classroom. It must be remembered, however, that the attainment of the sixth and seventh levels are, for most, the products of lifelong engagement with the craft. Therefore, a school program that aims to develop at least the first few steps of improvisational expertise within their students can be considered an effective one.

An Analogy Through the School Jazz Program

Despite the rich history of composition and improvisation in many Western musical traditions, the primary setting in which instrumental music students are encouraged to develop their own creative musical ideas in schools is within the context of the jazz band. In jazz bands, improvisation typically becomes the primary endeavor for musical creation, with original composition still being a rare activity within most programs. Granted, composition for jazz can be a challenging endeavor for anyone, and when it comes to writing for a full jazz ensemble (also known as the "big band"), there is a belief that composers need to have a strong knowledge of voicings and other compositional conventions in order to begin writing. Yet, students need not be excluded from engaging in the art of composition altogether because of the apparent complexity of the big band tradition. From the perspective of jazz, the following example may serve as an appropriate analogy through which the creative efforts of various global musical cultures may be applied.

Many effective jazz compositions take the form of simple "head arrangements," which simply display a melody and an accompanying chord progression to be performed together. If creating a new chord progression poses too large a challenge for students, they can instead compose what is known as a *contrafact*, or a new melody written over an existing chord progression. For example, jazz musicians often write new melodies over "rhythm changes," known as the chord progression, to the Gershwin standard "I've Got Rhythm." Another example would be Charlie Parker's "Ornithology," which is a newly composed melody written over the chord progression of the standard "How High the Moon." Students composing their own contrafacts are thus able to enter into a perhaps otherwise esoteric world of jazz composition because they need only focus on writing one element of the music: The melody. To supplement their new melodies, students may write simple, repetitive backgrounds or riffs to support solos, which are indicative of the big band jazz tradition. The Count Basie Orchestra, for example, was well known for having many head arrangements in its library, including tunes such as "One O'Clock Jump" and "Splanky."

While specific to the jazz idiom, the example of the "head arrangement" or contrafact approach may serve as a suitable comparison for initial forays into the creative process of any musical tradition. It is not always necessary for compositions to be complicated with thick harmonies, themes, and motifs; in fact, this arguably perpetuates the notion that composition is an act reserved for a knowledgeable and gifted few. Instead, musical learners should come to understand that within *everyone* lies the ability to create music from nothing, and moreover, that creating *simple* music is equally as valuable as creating music in any other form. It is upon these approaches that this chapter bases many of its following suggestions for immersing students in the act of global music creation.

Stifling Creation for Flourishing Performance?

While the tradition of jazz music lends itself to a necessary emphasis on improvisation, music educators would likely agree that the ability for students to spontaneously or meditatively create original music within any tradition is a highly desirable outcome of any music program. However, other school music ensembles beyond the jazz band often face large barriers that preclude such activities from occurring. First, a closer look at the typical school instrumental ensemble reveals that enrollment is simply much greater than in a jazz band, making the work of teaching improvisation far more difficult. Yet, while improvisation and composition indeed tend to be thought of as being individualized activities, this chapter will argue that this need not necessarily be the case.

Further, and as discussed in Chapter 1, the demands of ensemble performance obligations often minimize the opportunity for composition and improvisation during classes and rehearsals, which tend to be process-based activities. As much as music educators may value process-based activities, they also recognize that their music program is "on display" during concerts and presentational events (e.g., football games for the marching band, the school musical). These other responsibilities often make engaging in process-oriented activities difficult, perhaps even causing educators to lament that time spent on teaching improvisation and composition could have been better spent further developing performance skills for a concert. Other music educators might acknowledge the importance of improvisation, but maintain that because "their" ensemble is not one that traditionally utilizes improvisation, teaching such skills is beyond their responsibility.

Yet, the truth of the matter is that the so-called responsibility of teaching composition and improvisation does not lie only within particular musical domains, even if historical conventions might make this appear to be so. Humans are a naturally creative and inventive species, making musical creativity not a learned behavior, but a fundamentally innate one. From birth, children are fascinated with the properties of different sounds and how they are organized, exploring them from a sensory perspective long before understanding how to manipulate them in a purposefully musical manner. Indeed, young children experiment musically through short moments of melodic utterances, rhythmically tapping and banging physical objects and the use of musical toys long before they learn to cognitively produce concrete musical phrases. Yet, in the process of becoming more purposeful musicians, young learners mysteriously seem to forget their exploratory past selves, replacing their inquisitiveness with a focus on idiomatic musical learning. Musical exploration is replaced with learning songs and pieces. This, some may suspect, is the product of musical enculturation in a Western society which traditionally values reproduction over creation. If young students have the opportunity, they may regain an interest in improvisational and compositional musical practices if they join a jazz or rock band, but for many, this ability is believed to be lost forever. Of course, such musical skills are not lost at all, but merely forgotten. No matter how "lost" one's creative musical skills may appear, however, it seems as if it is never too late for someone to begin composing and improvising original music. From playful creations performed in solitude, to the "serious business" of improvisation, the calling lies in the educator to tap into their students' creative flow and encourage the act of spontaneous musical creation once again.

Guiding Principles in Creating World Music

In order to cultivate the most enriching experiences possible, there are a number of matters for teachers to first consider before embarking on creative journeys of global musical styles. First, to reiterate, with whatever musical culture into which the students are being immersed, plentiful listening is key. As discussed, the processes of Attentive, Engaged, and Enactive Listening are essential for building a framework of sound within the musical culture. These listenings should be plentiful enough for students to feel like they have developed a sense of expectations within the conventions of the musical tradition. In other words, students should become comfortable enough with the music that they are able to recognize when musical elements extend beyond what is considered "conventional" or "typical" within the style. When students have established this feeling of expectation within the tradition, their ears have arguably developed a sturdier familiarity of that culture.

Second, utilizing key resources for specific musical practices will greatly inform and supplement these listenings by establishing deeper understandings of the culture— including approaches towards improvisation and composition. *The Global Music Series*, edited by Patricia Shehan Campbell and Bonnie C. Wade offers a breadth of culture-specific ventures into the practices and customs of various musical traditions. Additionally, Huib Schippers's (2010) book *Facing the Music* provides a logical framework for envisioning how particular musical cultures can be conceptualized across a number of continuums, which he refers to as the "Twelve Continuum Transmission Framework." This framework can help teachers pinpoint the "path of least resistance" towards their creative goals. Finally, Ted Solís's (2004) *Performing Ethnomusicology* offers practice-based conversations regarding the performance of global musical cultures within world music ensembles (including the implementation of creativity within these ensembles).

Third, the authors have already offered a rationalization for using Western instruments in global traditions, but here it is expressed again in the interest of reminding the reader to not become overly concerned with matters of authenticity in the course of creating new music within these cultures. Authentic instruments should certainly be used if they can be reasonably obtained—*djembes, congas, sikus, quatros, ouds*, and the like—but close equivalents that bring students as close as possible to the timbral and stylistic nuances of the musical tradition are perfectly acceptable, *provided that* the connection is made to the actual musical recordings (and instruments) that are found within the tradition. Photos, videos, and field recordings can be utilized to great success in these efforts, and resources such as Smithsonian Folkways, the Association for Cultural Equity, and even YouTube can serve as excellent tools in connecting the classroom adaptation back to the original context of the tradition. Just as in the case of performing world music, the absence of authentic instruments from the creative musical experience is no longer an excuse for not providing learning that is tailored to any of the world's musical expressions. In fact, adapting world music styles for Western instruments is ideal in many situations, because they allow students to dive into the practices of an unfamiliar culture without also needing to learn a new set of technical skills to play an unfamiliar instrument.

Fourth, teachers should be reminded that *arranging* is another important form of composition in which fully original musical ideas are not generated insofar as the primary melody may go, but the music takes on a new character by being recontextualized for another ensemble (e.g., symphony orchestra to wind ensemble), another style of music (e.g., classical to jazz), or another stylistic approach (e.g., meter change, chord reharmonizations, change in modality). Not all musical cultures utilize arrangements, at least not in the same way that arrangements are written and performed in the Western tradition. Yet, the technique of arranging may often represent the perfect middle ground between the musical leap from imitation to original composition. Indeed, performing any world music in the context of Western instrumental ensembles will require a degree of musical arranging, and this act is every bit as valid a form of creation as composition and improvisation. Therefore, not every suggestion for creating world music will necessarily involve producing something altogether new, but perhaps simply reorganizing the music in a new and creative manner.

Finally, at this point it should be reiterated that there are some cultures in which improvising is deliberately reserved until after competent understandings of the techniques and procedures of the music have been amply learned. For example, in teaching Thai classical music, significant training is needed before performers are said to be ready to improvise. However, as compellingly as this may be communicated to outsiders, culture bearers in school settings have also been known to allow their pupils to experiment with improvisation at relatively early stages. For example, as David Hughes (2004) reports, a visiting teacher of Thai classical music allowed his students to experiment with improvisation before it would have otherwise been allowed within the culture. Of course, the teacher utilized a different approach than he would have used with his students in Thailand by offering immediate feedback to let students know if their creative ideas were allowable. While reverent to his culture, this teacher allowed for the traditional transmission process to be altered in order to develop meaningful results within the shorter time constraints of a classroom context. To be sure, for teachers who are "outsiders" of these cultures, it is always best to avoid confusion or possible displays of disrespect towards the culture by checking with a culture bearer or other resource (i.e., book, trusted web source, cultural society) to understand if creative activities might be planned in an accelerated fashion in order to maximize the limited experience by instrumental music students with the culture at hand.

Initial Techniques for Creating World Music

Repetition

One of the most accessible entry points into a given musical expression is through the act of repetition. Many traditions utilize repetitive devices which musicians use to seamlessly insert themselves into the music. For example, by engaging in a simple *ostinato* or *groove*, musicians can continually repeat a simple melodic or rhythmic phrase. Take for example, Héctor Lavoe's salsa hit "Mi Gente." Musicians can enter into the groove through the most basic rhythmic device of salsa music, the *clave* (Figure 5.1a). Students can perform the clave pattern on a pair of actual claves, or clap along with it while stepping to the steady beat (an activity which would likely begin during the

Figure 5.1a-e   "Mi Gente" clave, coro, and *moñas*

Enactive Listening phase; see Chapter 3). Once comfortable, students can begin to improvise rhythmic patterns that interlock with the underlying clave. This activity might mimic the role of the conga player (or the timbales player), who improvises over the groove established by the rest of the salsa band.

Melodically speaking, a handful of musicians could perform the *montuno* (a repetitive arpeggiated melody usually played on piano), which is heard most clearly at 0:18 in the recording (Figure 5.1b). (Note that from 0:18 until the start of Lavoe's singing at 0:24, the *montuno* vamps on the E-flat chord only.) In deciding which instruments should be responsible for maintaining the *montuno*, the students are naturally engaging in the decisions of an arranger. Further, students can create their own simple ostinatos (called *moñas*) that echo the *sonero* (vocal improviser) during the *coro* (call-and-response section) of the tune (around 2:08 in the recording, Figure 5.1c). Instead of the two-measure descending line that the winds perform (and is later sung around 2:25), students can compose their own repeating pattern, which is passed around various sections of the group. Students within each instrumental section may even compose their own separate *moñas*, which can be traded in and out over various improvising soloists. Depending on how the composed *moñas* fit together, they may even be layered on top of one another. For example, although not two separate *moñas*, at 3:07, the singers repeat the line in Figure 5.1c while the wind players perform another riff (Figure 5.1d). Additionally, the winds can also learn to play the vocal response "que cante mi gente" on their instruments (perhaps harmonizing them if possible), since this response becomes an iconic part of the song (Figure 5.1e). In sum, utilizing these techniques becomes similar to the approach used in writing a head arrangement for a jazz band: A number of riffs, responses, and backgrounds that are traded in and out organically and in the moment. Importantly reiterated here is that these activities are possible not only in the easily adaptable setting of the jazz band, but in wind band and orchestra settings as well—sites which have perhaps rarely encountered the charge to move beyond the page and create on their own.

Episode 5.1: Salsa in the Classroom (Learning Pathway #1)

Specific Use: Instrumental Ensembles (e.g., band, orchestra, jazz); Grades 4–12

Materials:

- "Mi Gente" by Héctor Lavoe; students' instruments
- Optional: claves, conga(s), cowbell, *güiro*, timbales

Procedure:

Rhythmic Improvisation

1. Ask students to begin by clapping the clave pattern (Figure 5.1a) and stepping to the steady beat.
2. As the class establishes a groove through the clave, ask them to break into small groups (4–5 or full instrumental sections, depending on ensemble size).
3. Encourage students to improvise around the clave groove either (1) solo, with all others maintaining the clave, or (2) collectively, with at least one maintaining the clave.
4. Rotating in small groups, provide an opportunity for each group to practice improvising over the clave using instruments (e.g., claves, congas, cowbell, *güiro*)

Melodic Improvisation

1. Bring students' attention to the I-V chord structure of the song. Have students indicate that they hear the chord changes by pointing either one finger (I chord) or five fingers (V chord). *Note: The chord change oscillates every two measures.*

2. Beginner students may experiment with improvising over the major scale of the key (E-flat concert); More advanced students may pay attention to the chord changes, playing an E-flat major scale over the I chord, and a B-flat mixolydian scale over the V chord.

3. For advanced students: Direct students to listen to the brief trumpet solo (1:18–1:23) as well as Lavoe's improvised singing. Encourage them to first find certain phrases that stand out to them, then locate the notes on their instruments, and finally incorporate them into their improvisations.

4. Extension: Direct students to listen to other salsa songs that might feature their instrument soloing and encourage them to find salient phrases to learn for their own instrument to supplement their improvisations.

Arranging

1. As a class, have students create a "road map" arrangement of "La Gente": How will they begin? Will some sing the melody, or will it be fully instrumental? What instrument(s) will play the *montuno*? Which *moñas* will accompany solos? How will they be layered? How will the arrangement end? Write or project this road map on the board for all to see.

2. Once practiced as a class, have students create their own individual arrangements. Choose a few to perform, and have students choose their favorite arrangement.

Composing

1. If possible, have students transcribe the *moñas* in "La Gente".

2. Have students write their own *moña*, either by ear or by writing it down.

3. Have students teach their *moñas* to the class by ear.

4. Extension: Have the class select their favorite *moñas* and compose new melodies above them.

As one of the Learning Pathways selections, "Mi Gente" is a perfect piece through which instrumental music students can dive into the craft of improvising and composing. Not only does the music sing of Latino pride and solidarity (Latinos being a subculture that is largely represented in many school districts around the United States), but also because its simple I-V chord structure provides plenty of opportunity for improvisation from beginner to advanced levels. By immersing students into the repetitive nature of the song, students have multiple entry points into which they can participate in the music: Composing one of the ostinatos to be played during the *coro* section, improvising during the *coro*, arranging the instrumentation for the piano montuno, and improvising along with the groove of the music (on congas, timbales, or adapted percussion instruments).

In participatory musical traditions, Thomas Turino (2008) uses the term *elaboration* and *core* to distinguish between the two different musical roles in a given musical event. For example, the rhythm section of a salsa band (i.e., conga, claves, cowbell, and *güiro*) provides the core of the ensemble, whereas the *moñas*, *montuno*, and improvised solos would represent the elaboration of the song. Thinking of musical roles in this way allows students to enter into whichever musical role they are able to grasp more easily. The core of many participatory musical traditions is highly repetitive, and thus may be an appropriate place to start for the less-experienced musicians, or those who are unfamiliar or uncomfortable with the musical style. But as student musicians become more comfortable within a particular tradition, they will expectantly begin to branch out into more elaborative musical activities, such as improvising and composing new phrases and melodies.

Call-and-Response

Similar to the idea of performing ostinatos or grooves, student musicians may engage in call-and-response patterns, in which a short phrase is echoed by a specific response. This approach also utilizes core and elaboration roles, with those more comfortable with performing the core of the music typically engaging in the response, while musicians who prefer elaboration roles may initiate various calls. Call-and-response patterns can either include exact re-statements of a phrase, or a unique phrase that is itself repeated continuously. Call-and-response patterns are often vocal in nature, but instrumental call-and-response patterns are also common. For example, with a song like "Mi Gente," many of the repetitive devices used are in fact a form of call-and-response. The *moña* is an instrumental form of call-and-response, and the response "que cante mi gente" to the trumpet solo (1:16) and Héctor Lavoe's improvisation (1:22) is a vocal form of call-and-response.

Another example of call-and-response can be found in Lora Chiorah-Dye and Sukutai's Zimbabwean Shona song "Chemtengure." Lora Chiorah-Dye initiates the call by first singing "chemtengure" twice, which is echoed by the vocalists in blocked harmony. She then expands her call with additional lyrics, but the vocalists' "chemtengure" response is repeated mostly as-is. The song uses a traditional Shona melody, but the lyrics are composed about a vendor name Vajeke who "brought familiar treats like sweet potatoes to children living in boarding schools far from home."[1] Because the song is a traditional melody, perhaps students can engage in a compositional activity in which they maintain the melody of the song, but compose their own unique lyrics by utilizing call-and-response techniques. For example, students can choose a theme such as freedom, peace, solidarity, unity, friendship (or perhaps something more playful), and compose original lyrics according to that theme. Of course, composing lyrics is not an activity that would typically take place in an instrumental ensemble, but this by no means suggests that such an activity would not be fruitful and productive for instrumentalists as well. In fact, creating a strict dichotomy between vocal and instrumental world music is perhaps unnecessary to begin with, as demonstrated in the Teacher Feature later in this chapter.

Episode 5.2: Composing Shona Call-and-Response Songs (Learning Pathway #3)

Specific Use: Instrumental Ensembles (e.g., band, orchestra, jazz); Grades 6–12 (adaptable for 4–5)

Materials:

- "Chemtengure", Lora Chiorah-Dye and Sukutai; students' instruments

Procedure:

1. Remind students about the meaning of "Chemtengure," discussing the nostalgia about the man Vajeke that the song is singing about. In small groups, brainstorm various topics for students to sing about themselves. Have them first choose a theme, and then a phrase that encapsulates that theme (e.g., solidarity: "Anything worth doing is worth doing together").

2. Have students write lyrics for their song in call-and-response form. Suggest that students may write their theme phrase as the response of the call-and-response pattern, making up short calls to accompany it (although they should also be encouraged to try other ideas as well).

3. Optional: With the help of online resources, challenge students to translate their songs into the Shona language.

4. Have students practice reciting the words to their poem (in English or Shona) in a chant-like manner, repeating the call-and-response numerous times. This will begin to create a rhythmic flow, which may eventually become the rhythm of their song.

5. As students begin to develop consistent rhythmic patterns, encourage them to add melodic inflections as well. Challenge them to create a response that repeats the same way every time, and allow them to choose between calls that alternate in melody/rhythm, and calls that maintain the same melody (but with different lyrics).

6. Add instruments. Consider emulating an *mbira* with an arpeggiated ostinato (like in the opening of "Chemtengure") on the piano, marimba, or guitar. Other students may use other percussion instruments to create a groove. Have students decide if there should be an instrumental interlude after a number of call-and-response patterns, and if so, what it should sound like.

7. Ask students to consider: Should the entire song remain sung, or should the melodies be placed on their instruments? Encourage students to create a full composition that uses vocal and instrumental sections within their newly composed song.

8. After rehearsing the song, have students experiment with dancing patterns: Stepping patterns, formations, free style, etc.

9. For the class (or a concert), have each group share and perform their Shona composition.

Finally, in "Sounds of the Surf Overture" by the Thai Piphat Mai Kheng Ensemble, students can similarly engage in melodic call-and-response. At 0:41, for example, the ensemble engages in a short call-and-response technique, called *luk loh luk khad*, in which the *pi* (oboe) and the *ranad ek* (treble xylophone) present the "call," and the *ranad thum* and *khong wong* (melodic gongs) follow with the response.[2] According to the liner notes, the composer intended this call-and-response technique to symbolize surging waves, which build in tempo and intensity until the end (p. 9). After determining the form of the call-and-response phrases (ABCB), students can compose a new call-and-response melody in predetermined form (e.g., ABCB, ABAC, AABA), assigning instruments to play either the call or the response.

Drone

A drone is a relatively simple compositional technique in which one or more pitches are maintained underneath a moving melody. Many world instruments are known for utilizing a drone, such as the hurdy gurdy in Eastern European instrumental music, the Scottish Bagpipe, the Indian *sitar*, and the Chinese *hulusi*. The melody played above the drone can be either pre-composed or completely improvised. For example, the Egyptian piece "Amal Hayate" performed by Umm Kulthum opens with a drone performed on an accordion, which supports the Arabic *maqam kurd* (melodic mode, see Figure 5.2). Whether the opening solo was originally composed or improvised is unknown, but many subsequent versions of the same song can be found utilizing the same solo. While this may suggest that the solo was pre-composed, that may not necessarily be the case; improvised solos are often preserved and performed fully intact with ensuing performances. For example, in the jazz canon, the trumpet and saxophone solos in Glenn Miller's "In the Mood" are often performed exactly the same in ensuing performances, preserving these once-improvised solos in time.

Students can learn the melody to "Amal Hayate" as it was recorded, internalizing it as well as possible through repeated participatory musickings (again, depending on age and skill level, it is best for students to attempt to learn as much of the solo as they can by ear). Afterward, students may choose to compose or improvise a new solo based on the same *maqam kurd*, which is known as the *Phrygian scale* in Western music (in this case, the E-major scale beginning on the third scale degree, G-sharp). By freely improvising, students will begin to embody the sonic character of the *maqam*, feeling the unmistakable character of the half-step between the first and second scale degrees. While soloists take turns improvising over the *maqam*, other members of the ensemble may perform the G-sharp drone in unison or open fifths, adding ornamentations as desired (again, directing themselves to the recording to hear where such ornamentations would likely occur).

It should also be noted that the *maqam kurd* is merely one of many possible *maqams* typically used in Arabic music. While *maqam kurd* uses pitches that can be easily transferred to any instrumentation, many other *maqams* utilize microtones, which may

Figure 5.2   *Maqam kurd,* or G-sharp Phrygian scale

present a challenge for traditional Western instruments. In these instances, it is again important for students to rely on their listening skills to identify exactly how a microtone ought to sound within the context of the given *maqam*. Through Engaged and Enactive Listenings, students will become increasingly familiar with these microtonal nuances, ultimately resulting in an ability to approximate them on their own instruments.[3]

Further, the ability to perform a drone in world music contexts becomes a transferrable skill that develops musical expertise in general. While instrumentalists engage in the process of creating music with drones, they are honing a number of other necessary skills necessary for playing music at a high level within any tradition, such as (1) maintaining a steady tone through staggered breathing and intentional bowings, (2) maintaining a consistent quality of timbre as the drone passes through the ensemble, and (3) keeping the drone well in-tune over time (especially if it is performed as an open-fifth drone).

Hocket

The technique of hocketing involves sharing the presentation of a melody between two or more voices. Many cultures utilize this practice, such as the *imbal* technique in Balinese gamelan music, *rara* street processions in Haiti, and *siku* (panpipe) music in the Andes. For an example of the latter, the song "Tupac Katari" by the Peruvian ensemble *El Sikuri* opens with a hocketed melody shared between two *sikus*. The tones of the *siku* are split across two rows of pipes, requiring alternation between the two rows in order to perform a complete scale. While it is possible for both rows to be performed by a single musician, the tradition of hocketing *siku* melodies is still maintained within *sikuri* ensembles.

The technique of hocketing is one that requires skill and practice, but its rewards are plentiful in performance. Not only does such a technique compel students to engage in intensive intragroup listening skills, but it also demands that they work together to create a melody that sounds smooth and unbroken rather than staggered and jagged. Students might practice the technique through intensive listenings of "Tupac Katari," determining which tones are shared by the *ira* and *arka* parts of the *siku*. Students can practice performing the song as a duet, or further challenge themselves to split the melody by instrumental part (e.g., brass/woodwinds, strings/winds).

Once familiar with the technique, students can compose a new melody, and then split up the melody by two (or more) parts. Students may practice this independent of a particular style to practice the skill, and then attempt to compose and perform a melody that is representative of a particular musical culture (e.g., Andean *sikuri*, Dominican *gaga*).

Episode 5.3: Composing Hocketed Melodies

Specific Use: Instrumental Ensembles (e.g., band, orchestra); Grades 4–12

Materials:

- "Tupac Katari", El Sikuri; students' instruments.

Procedure:

1. As part of the Engaged Listening strand (see Chapter 3), have students learn the melody of the *siku* part by ear. Have them sing along to the melody first (to make sure it's internalized), and then work in sections to place the melody on their instruments.

2. Once the students have learned to play the full melody, have them figure out how the melody would be hocketed between two groups. If necessary, displaying on the board the pitches that each *siku* row plays could assist with this task.

3. Have the students notate the hocketed melody.

4. After notating the melody, have students determine which part would play each pitch, using the *ira* and *arka siku* figure as a guide (see Figure 5.3). For younger students, have them color in the melodies using two different colors to represent which part is played by the *ira*, and which is played by the *arka*. For older students, have them notate two separate parts (with rests reflecting where one part rests and another plays).

5. Have the students perform the melody, hocketing by (1) instrument group, (2) pairs, and (3) mixed pairs (for greater challenge)

   Note: Steps 1–5 are considered engaged and Enactive Listening activities. However, they are listed here to demonstrate the importance of these steps in developing facility in the hocketing technique before engaging in compositional tasks.

6. Encourage students to experiment with various timbral mixtures between the hocketed parts. Have them explore such combinations as brass versus woodwind, high versus low, mixed sections, and so on.

7. Have students compose a new simple melody following a simple form (e.g., AB, AABA, ABAC) within a chosen style (e.g., Andean *siku*, Dominican *gaga*, Haitian *rara*).

8. Ask students to determine how many hocketed parts they would like to include in their composition; have them split the melody by part.

9. Repeat the process outlined in step 4 for the new composition.

10. In small groups, encourage students to repeat the process in step 5 to determine the timbre and blend they are most satisfied with.

11. Share all of the new compositions in class or in a performance.

Figure 5.3 *Arka* and *Ira* tones in Andean *siku* (panpipe) music

Figure 5.4 Melody to "Tulina's Carmona"

Motives

Motives are recurring musical figures that provide some sort of structural or characteristic quality to a larger piece of music. They are utilized to varying degrees in compositions, improvisations, and arrangements in various musical cultures around the world, as well as throughout the Western canon. A motive might be explicitly stated or imbedded within inner voices and harmonies. It might provide the underpinning of an entire piece or may appear sporadically as musical themes are developed and modified.

Take a contemporary Syrian song for example. Kinan Azmeh's "Tulina's Carmona" opens with a melodic phrase (Figure 5.4), which evolves into a melodic motive that is repeated several times throughout the presentation of the main theme. As the melody progresses, the first three notes are subjected to a descending melodic sequence (Figure 5.4, meas. 7, 8, and 9).

Motives can be utilized effectively in early compositional and improvisational activities because they allow students to invent a simple melodic fragment that can be used as a device to be creatively expanded upon, ornamented, and changed altogether. This gives students a sense of structure that frees them up from feeling like every note and phrase they compose or improvise needs to be fully unique and original. Students can begin with a melodic (or rhythmic) motive, and practice improvising and composing new ideas on top of that simpler motive. In effect, the envisioned purposes of global musical repertoires are able to expand and demonstrate extended utility within the aims of music education.

Episode 5.4: Contemporary Syrian Music
(Learning Pathway #2)

Specific Use: Instrumental Ensembles (e.g., band, orchestra); Grades 6–12

Materials:

- "Tulina's Carmona," by Kinan Azmeh; students' instruments

Procedure:

Motivic Composition

1. Provide students (in small groups) with a handout of empty sheet music, with time signatures remained intact (see Figure 5.4).

2. Have groups compose two different motivic phrases in the key of A harmonic minor. Motive #1 should be written in 7/8, and Motive #2 should be written in 3/4.

3. Students should write Motive #1 in measures 1, 4, and 7, and Motive #2 to measures 3 and 6.

4. Instruct students to develop a simple variation of Motive #1. This variation could simply be a transposition of the motive (up or down; step or skip), a changed rhythm, or an inversion or retrograde of the motive, or anything else the students come up with.

5. Students should write this variation in measures 2 and 5.

6. For measures 8, 9, 10, and 11, have students continue to expand upon their variation of Motive #1. By this point, groups should have originally composed music in all 11 measures of the main melody.

7. On their instruments, have students perform their new melody in unison. As a group, encourage students to make alterations to their melody as needed to establish a better melodicism or flow with their composition (as desired).

8. Have groups perform their new compositions for one another during class.

(*Note: This activity has been designed to be highly structured to give students the maximum amount of support with a potentially unfamiliar musical task. If students are either already comfortable with composition, or are looking for an additional challenge, this activity may be altered to be more open ended. In this scenario, students might be free to choose as many motives as they would like and arrange them in whichever manner they chose.*)

Changing Meter

So much of the identity of any piece of music can be tied to its metric organization. Perhaps this is because of the close relationship between music, dance, and movement in so many cultures (including Western Art music, with established ties to European folk and court dance styles). The feeling and groove of any piece of music can be significantly altered by switching between simple and compound meter (i.e., 2/4 to 6/8), by changing between duple and triple meter (i.e., 4/4 to 3/4), or by shifting between symmetrical and asymmetrical beat patterns (i.e., 4/4 to 7/4).

Of course, whether or not it may be deemed *appropriate* to make such metrical changes can sometimes be quite equivocal, depending on the rigidity of the tradition in question. However, with musical examples for which performances or recordings can be found in alternate meters or groupings, new life can be breathed into venerable classics. With folk songs throughout Eastern and Western Europe in particular, contemporary

Figure 5.5 New York City–based music teacher Madolyn Accola (left) leading a professional development session on Balkan dance

alterations are often welcomed by new artists and veterans alike. When it comes to changing the meter of a song, however, a change in the music's intended purpose may take place as well. For example, the Macedonian folk song "Jovano, Jovanke"[4]—well known throughout the Balkan Peninsula—is traditionally associated with the *lesnoto* (or *lesno*) dance rhythm, which is comprised of a $3 + 2 + 2$ asymmetrical beat structure (7/8 meter). This traditional rhythm can be clearly heard in Aleksandar Sarievski's iconic recording of the tune. However, in at least one contemporary version of the folk song from the Czech Republic, the meter has been changed to 4/4. The recording by the Czech women's group Psalteria utilizes four voices in harmony and Renaissance-period instruments in their arrangement. What results is a hauntingly beautiful rendition of the tune, but with its *lesnoto* rhythm removed, the song has arguably been fully removed from the context of a Balkan dance. While many might argue that "Jovano, Jovanke" and the *lesnoto* dance rhythm ought to be inextricable from one another, others throughout the region might contend that giving new life to the folk song is paying respect to the culture in an altogether unique and creative way.

Episode 5.5: Finding Time for Balkan Music

Specific Use: Instrumental Ensembles (e.g., band, orchestra); Grades 4–12

Materials:

- "Jovano, Jovanke," Aleksandar Sarievski; "Jovano, Jovanke," Psalteria; students' instruments

Procedure:

Aleksandar Sarievski Version

1. Starting with the traditional Sarievski version, ask students to find the pulse by lightly clapping or tapping. *Note: this would be considered an Engaged Listening activity.*

2. Ask students to hum the melody or sing it on a neutral syllable. If desired, the teacher may also choose to have students learn to sing the lyrics by posting them on a whiteboard.

3. Standing in a large circle, have the students sing along with the recording while performing the *lesnoto* dance rhythm. *Note: While beyond the space of this book, many resources can be found describing the steps to this dance in detail,[5] as well as many quality videos on YouTube.*

4. Have students find the melody on their instruments, starting at 0:11. If possible, have them locate the parallel harmony on their instruments as well.

Psalteria Version

1. Once students can confidently perform the Sarievski version, play the Psalteria arrangement. Ask them to generally compare how the two versions are similar and different.

2. Ask students to find the pulse of the arrangement as before. Ask them to identify how the pulse feels different from the Sarievski version (Answer: it is in simple/symmetrical meter).

3. Optional: Have students attempt to dance the *lesnoto* rhythm with the Psalteria version, noting the slight awkwardness in the dance steps. Although the steps can be executed in this 4/4 meter, note that the dance no longer represents the *lesnoto* rhythm because it has lost its characteristic $3 + 2 + 2$ metric trait.

4. Have students find the melody (and harmony, if possible) on their instruments, as with the Sarievski version. *Note: this version is in a different key, so students will have to transpose the melody they performed for the Sarievski verison.*

Creating a New Folk Song Arrangement

1. In small groups, using online resources (such as Smithsonian Folkways), have students find another traditional folk song from the Balkan peninsula. Have them bring their selections into class to share.

2. In their groups, have the students conduct steps 1–4 with their newly chosen folk song. If the song does not utilize the *lesnoto* dance rhythm, encourage them to either research what dance it does utilize, or allow them to incorporate their own movement that captures the metric organization of the piece.

3. Ask the students change the meter of the music in some way (like with Psalteria's version), and work together to decide how it will affect the performance of the melody.

4. After students have had sufficient time to re-create their folk song in the new meter, have the class reconvene to perform for each other. On their instruments, have each group perform (1) the folk song as originally written (maintaining the meter), followed by (2) their arrangement of the song in the new meter.

(Note: While this episode was specifically intended to be used for an immersive experience with Balkan music, students can certainly create their own new arrangements of folk songs from other applicable cultures as well (e.g., Italy, Greece, Ireland, England).)

Advanced World Music Creation

The aforementioned techniques for composing and improvising within global musical cultures can become a useful starting point for instrumental musicians engaging in world music activities within their ensembles. However, there is an important distinction between creating music within a world music tradition to simply develop facility and competence within that culture and creating music in an explicit effort to engage meaningfully in the authentic musical pastimes of that culture. The first effort is largely surface level, with reduced focus on authenticity (although always with maximal *integrity*). The second, however, might aim to move students closer to a sense of authentic musical creation within the given tradition (or perhaps a purposeful recontextualization). As discussed in Chapters 1 and 4, the ideal of authenticity is an elusive one, and becoming overly preoccupied with fully authentic musical creation becomes tenuous to the overarching goals of world music pedagogy. However, by maintaining the integrity of a culture, deeper and more advanced forays into improvisation, composition, and arranging can bring students closer to an immersive understanding of the culture at hand.

Because the acts of improvising and composing are new activities for many Western musicians, it is often helpful to loosely follow a progression from familiar-to-unfamiliar musical cultures. Recall the Matrosyska nesting dolls from Chapter 1, in which students arguably learn best if they begin with what is familiar to them, afterwards branching out to musics that are increasingly less familiar. This is the progression that is demonstrated by the Learning Pathways selections (see Appendix 1), as well as the following techniques for more advanced approaches toward creating world music.

Full-Fledged Improvisation

To start with musical culture that would be largely familiar to many students, a New Orleans second line might be a perfect place to start. Musical processionals that are typically led by brass bands, second lines are very closely tied with African American and Creole culture. During a second line, musicians typically perform a traditional song with a simple chord progression, which is further extended through solo improvisation. For example, in the selection "Second Line" by the Hustlers Brass Band,[6] the melody is first presented after a trumpet call, followed by improvised solos following the typical 12-bar blues form. As jazz band directors can already attest, inexperienced students often begin to improvise within this style by playing freely around the well-known blues scale, continually developing their skills until they are capable of improvising over each chord of the progression (in the case of the blues, the I, IV, and V chords). In line with the jazz tradition, students can internalize the trumpet solo performed at 1:08 either by ear or by transcribing it (depending on age and ability), perhaps borrowing various lines or motives into their own improvisations.

Next, students may choose to progress into improvisation with more unfamiliar musical traditions. For this, a salsa may be appropriate, such as Héctor Lavoc's "Mi Gente," because it will be familiar to some students while being relatively unfamiliar to others. Yet, while the playing style might be different from what they are accustomed to, opportunities for improvisation are highly accessible because of the simple I-V chord structure.

Finally, students may emerge into musical styles which represent altogether unfamiliar styles. For example, they may choose to engage more deeply with improvising within an unfamiliar musical idiom, such as within the style of "Sounds of the Surf Overture" or improvising over the *maqam* used in "Amal Hayate."

Full-Fledged Composing and Arranging

As students become more comfortable within a musical culture, they also become more capable of making stylistically intelligent decisions that lead to original compositions and arrangements of world music. The vignette featured at the opening of this chapter demonstrates precisely that musical inclination. Additionally, consider the following potential scenario:

> *After a few days or weeks of Enactive Listening, a middle school student becomes captivated by the beautiful arpeggiated harp melody in the opening of the Peruvian* sikuri *song "Tupac Katari," which inspires her to learn to play it on her flute. Hearing how the timbre transfers delightfully from the harp to the flute, a sudden stream of ideas follow: In her head, she hears a hocketed iteration of the melody from the clarinet section, with the B melody (heard at 0:43) transitioning into the brass section with lush woodwind harmonies underneath.*

Examples of world music selections that have been recontextualized and adapted for other ensembles can be found in similar fashion all over the world. For example, Zimbabwean musician Thomas Mapfumo recorded an arrangement of "Chemtengure," which featured a number of electric instruments. Various arrangements of "Amal Hayate" have also been recorded by several artists throughout the Near East. Students might do well to explore these various arrangements, supplementing their already immersed ears with interpretations by other musicians perhaps within or beyond the given culture. Analyzing how a piece changes from one context to another serves to critically develop an even deeper understanding of the music at hand, which perhaps may transfer into original ideas of the student's own.

For instance, it might be expected that students would begin with arranging music within a musical culture, which may eventually lead to original compositions. These students may have become so fully immersed within a musical tradition that they fully understand the role and function of each instrument in the ensemble, how the melody and harmonies are represented and developed, and what musical conventions define the style—making the task of arranging a natural next step in their creative process. With these skills so well internalized, they may eventually begin to hear original music playing in their heads (such as Debbie in the opening vignette). Along the way, they may continue to learn how to adapt what they hear in their heads for the resources of the ensemble in which they participate.

Teacher Feature: Katie Noonan on Arranging Ewe Music for Elementary Band

Katie Noonan, Elementary Band Director at a Public Elementary School in Long Island, NY

During the summer of 2012, Katie Noonan traveled to the small village of Kopeyia in Ghana, where she studied Ewe dance and drumming at the Dagbe Cultural Institute (www.dagbeinstitute.org). Upon returning home, she decided to share her experiences with her students by arranging some of the music she learned for her 5th-grade concert band. Taking two folk songs she learned while in Kopeyia, Katie taught her students the songs by rote, which they first learned to sing in the Ewe language, and then transferred to their instruments. Katie then chose about 15 students to play the drum part, which she taught by rote (in line with Ghanaian teaching practices). Katie and the students worked together creating the arrangement, deciding to create a medley of the two folk songs: First the drums played, followed by the band singing the folk song in call-and-response fashion, and then performing the folk song on their instruments. For this piece, Katie's typical role as the conductor transformed to that of the master drummer. Where, as the conductor, she might provide cues with hand gestures, her altered role as the master drummer meant that cues would be instead provided by the drumming patterns she would play.

Katie premiered the arrangement at her school concert, taking a moment to explain to the audience the practice of Ewe drumming—including its dependence on non-verbal communication, listening, and group cooperation (especially understanding the function of each of the various sized drums). Parents expressed that they were thrilled with this linking of Ghanaian drumming with a Western ensemble. In fact, one parent came up to Katie after the concert to tell her that she was herself from Ghana, and that she appreciated not only the arrangement, but Katie's explanation of how Ewe drumming functions within Ghanaian culture.

Q: How might you extend this project if you had the opportunity to do so?
A: I would incorporate dancers! There are traditional dances that go with the songs, so it would have been amazing to incorporate dancing into the performance as well. Also, I would have liked to have involved more students than just the band students, but given time restraints, that wasn't possible. Finally, we only performed the piece once during our concert, but it would have been great for the band to have the opportunity to perform the piece elsewhere.

Q: If you didn't have authentic instrumentation (i.e., Ghanaian drums and auxiliary percussion), how would you adapt the performance? Do you think it would be appropriate to use Western instruments?
A: I think it would be absolutely fine to use Western instruments if you didn't have access to traditional drums. It might be a little more difficult to hear the different parts, since Ewe drumming uses different-sized drums, but I don't think anyone would have a problem with adapting the music to fit the instrumentation you have available.

Q: Do you feel like performing Ghanaian music in the concert band setting resulted in a change of authenticity? Was authenticity an important consideration when writing the arrangement?
A: I wanted to preserve some authenticity, but I felt that taking artistic liberties was perfectly acceptable. I remember when I was in Ghana the teachers said, "we hope you go back to your homes and teach everyone this music," and I remember asking, "what if I can't remember the words or the rhythm exactly?" They shrugged and said, "just change it! It changes all the time!"

Q: Can you suggest how you might have students be more involved with the process of arranging the music themselves?
A: Originally, I wrote the arrangement. But after the band played it, some things didn't seem to work, so I asked for feedback from the students. Originally, we weren't going to sing the songs in the arrangement, but then someone suggested, "why don't we sing it and then play it after?" and everyone said, "yes! Absolutely, let's do that!" I also think I originally wrote an accompaniment part for the low brass, and they said, "we want the melody! We don't want to play this part." So, we decided to have everyone play the melody in unison, which was fine, because that's the way they sing it in Ghana anyway.

Q: Did you extend this project into any other discussions about life in Ghana? How did you go about doing this?
A: I gave each student a map of Africa and had them color in where Ghana was, because they had no idea. I would like to extend the project by delving more into

the details of Ghanaian life, but I do remember one important discussion we had about the perseverance of their culture. We talked about how their poverty is so severe—how they sometimes only get one meal a day—but everyone was so pleasant and friendly, and so happy with so little. I think that meant a lot for the students to hear.

A Holistic View of World Music Creation

Such illustrations of organic musical creation represent the height of immersive musicking within a world culture. Over time, students begin to hear global musical traditions not merely as rigidly defined musical conventions within cultures, but as holistic and universal ways of artistically being. As they naturally discover through listening and participating, musical ideas transfer within and between cultures, with creations breaking beyond the margins of a single tradition. When music transcends borders in such a manner, it takes on an exciting new life—a life into which students become privileged to immerse themselves.

Iraqi *oud* player Rahim Alhaj demonstrates this sentiment beautifully in his recording, *Letters from Iraq*. Performing masterfully with a string quartet, the music is decidedly Western in influence, which can be heard not only in the supporting instrumentation, but in the melodies and harmonies as well. Yet, the music stands on its own as an unequivocally intracultural Iraqi-inspired soundscape that venerates the stories and struggles of the war-torn Iraqi people.

Additionally, in a symbolic display of solidarity through music, the Seattle Symphony programmed an ad-hoc concert in response to the United States' 2017 implementation of a travel ban affecting a number of Muslim-majority countries. This concert, entitled *Music Beyond Borders: Voices from the Seven*, demonstrated that perhaps there is more in common between us than differences that divide us. In regards to the event, the Seattle Symphony states:

> As artists and Americans, we are committed to freedom of expression and the
> open exchange of ideas which create an environment of mutual understanding
> and the capacity for empathy. At the Seattle Symphony, we are inspired to add
> our voice in the hopes that we can come together through music.[7]

Featuring music from many of these nations, the pieces performed that evening were often difficult to place cleanly onto a map. An Iranian composer wrote a piece for Indian *santoor* (dulcimer) and Eastern European accordion. A Sudanese musician composed a selection based upon African rhythms for violin, percussion, and piano. The instruments of the Western symphony orchestra joined with the percussive strings of the *oud* played by Rahim Alhaj and participated in the rhythmic grooves and improvisatory melodies of Syrian clarinetist Kinan Azmeh. These compositions represent the pinnacle of musical creation within a so-called world music context. The music maintains the fragments of each culture's identity, but in so doing, creates a new musical identity that serves as a metaphor for the multiplicity and complexity of a transcultural society.

In sum, the act of creating original music is arguably a pursuit of the highest musical degree. To many, it represents the creative pinnacle of artistic human existence. Whether the music becomes extemporaneously created through the act of split-second decision making, or thoughtfully developed through inspiration and experimentation, the opportunity to make music on one's own accord can become among the most emancipating artistic activities in which a human can engage. Moreover, decisions regarding how the music should remain intact or develop into neighboring musical realms become the moments of student learning that manifest themselves into the deepest and purest expressions of musical being.

Notes

1 Seeger, A., N'Diaye, D., & Kertzer, J. (2000). [Liner notes]. *Safarini in transit: Music of African immigrants*, [CD], SFW40457, p. 15
2 Chitrabongs, M. R. C. (1994). [Liner notes]. *Royal court music of Thailand*, Piphat Mai Kheng [CD], SFW404013_101
3 Of course, microtones cannot always be executed on "fixed" tuning instruments such as pianos, marimbas, and some fretted string instruments, but they can be approximated by most other melodic wind and string instruments by bending pitches.
4 Also search "Yovano, Yovanke" for other arrangements of this folk song.
5 For example, see Pittman, A. M., Waller, M. S., & Dark, C. L. (2015). *Dance a while: A handbook for folk, square, contra, and social dance*. Long Grove, IL: Waveland Press.
6 While the selection by Hustlers Brass Band was chosen for this example, hundreds of recorded versions of "Second Line" can be found. During the listening stage of this song, it might be of interest to explore various other recordings and discuss how they are similar or different from one another.
7 www.seattlesymphony.org/beyond-borders/live-stream

References

Campbell, P. S. (2004). *Teaching music globally: Experiencing music, expressing culture*. New York, NY: Oxford University Press.

Hughes, D. W. (2004). "When can we improvise?": The place of creativity in academic world music performance. In T. Solís (Ed.), *Performing ethnomusicology: Teaching and representation in world music ensembles*. Berkeley and Los Angeles, CA: University of California Press.

Kratus, J. (1995). A developmental approach to teaching music improvisation. *International Journal of Music Education*, 26(1), 27–38. doi:10.1177/025576149502600103

Schippers, H. (2010). *Facing the music: Shaping music education from a global perspective*. New York, NY: Oxford University Press.

Small, C. (1998). *Musicking: The meanings of performing and listening*. Middletown, CT: Wesleyan University Press.

Solís, T. (Ed.). (2004). *Performing ethnomusicology: Teaching and representation in world music ensembles*. Berkeley and Los Angeles, CA: University of California Press.

Turino, T. (2008). *Music as social life: The politics of participation*. Chicago, IL: University of Chicago Press.

Wade, B. C. (2009). *Thinking musically. Experiencing music, expressing culture*. New York, NY: Oxford University Press.

Listening Episodes

"Mi Gente," Héctor Lavoe, iTunes/Fania. A Puerto Rican salsa classic, featuring a full salsa band and iconic singer Héctor Lavoe. https://itun.es/us/Nn0aF?i=520308589

"Chemtengure," Lora Chiorah-Dye & Sukutai, Smithsonian Folkways. A traditional Shona melody performed with *mbira*, *hosha* (shaker), and voices. www.folkways.si.edu/ lora-chiorah-dye-and-sukutai/chemtengure/world/music/track/smithsonian

"Sounds of the Surf Overture," Thai Piphat Mai Kheng Ensemble, Smithsonian Folkways. Thai court music composed by His Majesty King Prajadhipok to represent rolling waves. www.folkways.si.edu/piphat-mai-khaeng-ensemble/sounds-of-the-surf-overture/ world/music/track/smithsonian

"Amal Hayate," Umm Kulthum, iTunes. Egyptian popular music from the 1960s using the *maqam kurd*. https://itun.es/us/XYC_2?i=922602705

"Tupac Katari," El Sikuri, iTunes/EFR Records. Peruvian pan pipe *(siku)* music. https:// itun.es/us/83Go-?i=1043992073

"Tulina's Carmona," Kinan Azmeh, iTunes. Contemporary piece in mixed meter by a Syrian clarinetist and composer. https://itun.es/us/iHNdP?i=688814352

"Jovano, Jovanke," Aleksandar Sarievski, iTunes. Traditional Macedonian folk song using the *Lesnoto* dance rhythm (7/8). https://itun.es/us/5LDK3?i=932308418

"Jovano, Jovanke," Psalteria, iTunes. Contemporary arrangement of the Macedonian folk song, with four female voices and Medieval-period instruments. https://itun.es/us/ J2hzp?i=258246559

"Second Line," Hustlers Brass Band, iTunes. New Orleans second line featuring trumpet, trombone, tuba, saxophone, and percussion. https://itun.es/us/sTVXs?i= 315030496

6

Integrating World Music

As the airplane sat on the tarmac, Mr. Gabriel looked out at the distant mountains of Cusco, Peru. He had come here searching for a bit of relaxation and learning after a tough year at Hampton High School. He had spent three weeks in Peruvian highlands with the Qechua Q'eros, learning about their music, food, and culture. Through videos on YouTube and a collection of CDs, he listened to music from the Andes before his voyage, but there was something about hearing it in its original setting that truly changed him. He wondered how he would share this powerful set of travel experiences with his instrumental music students.

In the first week of school that following autumn, he received an email from the group that had coordinated the trip, announcing that a "Peruvian musician is in San Diego to Provide Workshops." Mr. Gabriel was thrilled, as this was the musician with whom he had studied in Peru. He immediately sent an email to the organization to offer his enthusiastic interest in possibilities for development at Hampton High School. A few days later, an email arrived with an approval for an arts integration residency with Jorge.

During the musician's 3-month residency at Hampton High School, Mr. Gabriel's students not only learned to build and play and the handmade sikus that his family had constructed for over 1,000 students in the district, but they also witnessed him perform a Peruvian ritual blessing of the instruments before they were played (Figure 6.1). They came to understand Peruvian dances that illustrated social relationships. They had conversations about the Peruvian hocketing of a melody as a demonstration of the importance of community relationships in the Andes. The Hampton High School students learned through the residency of the Peruvian artist by seeing with their own eyes, and hearing with their own ears, that music functions differently and carries different meanings across cultures. For Mr. Gabriel, his world of concert etiquette and stage deportment completely crashed into this frantic reality of music-as-celebration, music-as-ritual, music-as-life. He began a process of integrating understandings of

Figure 6.1   Peruvian musician performing a blessing on *sikus*

culture in the music he and his students would work on in their everyday rehearsal and
study in the band room (sometimes in collaboration with teachers of other subjects)
and in the performances they offered to the school and community.

As the process of World Music Pedagogy continues to develop ever-deeper layers of
musical and cultural immersion for students, moving beyond intensified listenings
and well into organic reproductions of a tradition's sound, there is a longing that rises
in students of wanting to understand how music fits into the larger picture of society
and culture. The purpose of Integrating World Music is to enrich learners—whether in
band, orchestra, jazz, or other instrumental settings—through a holistic understanding
of the music's vitality and function as it exists within a particular culture. This need is
fulfilled with the support and collaboration of various subjects and disciplines of the
school curriculum, and through the efforts of not only teachers (and students) but also
the administration, parents, and the surrounding community. To be sure, this dimension is not merely a next step in the process—it is integral to the process, wholly, as
a means of knowing music as a reflection of people of a musical culture. Integrating
music into interdisciplinary study can occur not merely *after* all the repeated listenings,
participatory musickings, and full-on performances, but easily within every facet of the
WMP process. Integrating World Music is not the final stage of the WMP approach,
but it is a dimension that can be inserted from the initial exposure to a recording, in the
middle of preparation for a performance, and during "breaks" in the process of creating
music in the style of the studied work. The principles found within this chapter can be

incorporated throughout the process, from beginning-to-end, by music teachers, with agency and involvement of their students, and by teachers across subjects in elementary schools, middle schools, and high schools.

What Is Music Integration?

Put simply, music integration is the process of knowing music through the prism of many disciplines, subjects, and fields. As instrumental music students listen to, perform, and create music of the world's cultures, they have questions about who makes the music, where it is made, for what purposes, and why it is meaningful to players, singers, dancers, and all the community within a village, a neighborhood, or a region of the world. In school curricular development, integration encourages teachers and students to explore cultural understandings by using music as a starting point for knowledge construction, and for knowing people's perspectives on history, culture, politics, religion, and a host of other characteristics that comprise their cultural identities. The concept of integration has been one of the most discussed (and challenged) topics throughout the history of music education in schools. An early conversation on the topic of music integration comes from a conference keynote prepared by former Music Educators National Conference president Lilla Belle Pitts (1937). In her speech, she argued that music education in self-imposed isolation would be removed from being a core component of a broader conception of education and learning. A narrow and isolated approach to music-as-sound (only) would inevitably prevent it from reaching its full meaning or purpose as an innate form of human knowledge construction. Music integration was argued as uniquely positioned to broadly engage students in an interdisciplinary manner through an emphasis on generalized learning before specialized training. Integration in music education was described as essential to serving the specific needs of students, whether they be social, personal, or aesthetic. Importantly, Pitts maintained that the aesthetic influence of music would not lose any of its potency when musical study by students could be instilled with personal and social values. The movement to integrate carried forward, at least by some innovative music teachers in the decades to follow. They recognized that children could learn through a song something of its origin-culture, including the language and the topic of local cultural interest, be it about a culture's vegetation, animals, modes of transportation, or festive occasions of valued calendrical seasons and holidays.

The sentiment of "music, integrated" resonates with current efforts to connect music education to other subjects across the proverbial curricular board, from language arts to social studies, with attention also to integrated studies of music with conceptualizations found in math, science, the various arts, and other subjects as well. Music can be seen not merely as an educational confection but, rather, a distinct mode of learning that can help to deeply engage students across the disciplines. In fact, contemporary interest in integrated teaching and learning is apparent through the United States Department of Education's reauthorization of the Elementary and Secondary Education Act (ESEA) in 2015. This Act has expanded opportunities for schools to use Title I funds (money allocated for curriculum enhancement at underserved schools) to develop integrated learning modules. The goal of initiatives such as music mixed with language arts, or music and social studies projects, is to expand the benefits of arts integration to academic achievement, student attendance, and parent and community engagement. Through the use of federal, state, and local funds, school districts have developed programs with major arts organizations, such as school music programs that partner with the San Diego Opera and the San Diego Unified School District, and the establishment of umbrella organizations in municipal districts to oversee arts integration in schools such as the Chicago Arts Partnership in Education (CAPE). While the scope of programs vary, the majority of in-school and school-community integrations of music with other fields and disciplines have demonstrated measurable gains in achievement[1] while providing enriching educational experiences for the students involved.

Arts integration efforts are visible internationally in schools across the world where teachers find that music can motivate the learning of other subjects. One project initiated in Iceland and working its way across Europe and Asia is the *Biophilia Educational Project*, which provides students with interactive experiences that focus on the integration of music with science (see Teacher Feature: Skúli Gestsson). In this program, students connect natural phenomena to musical features and compositional techniques. For example, one activity that integrates geology and music explores the musical concept of tension and release by comparing it to tectonic plates. Another explores musical forms by using the growth of crystals to demonstrate how songs are constructed. In this module, students float down virtual crystalline corridors acquiring song fragments and sections (e.g., verse, chorus) that they then recombine to create a version that suits their tastes. Students in schools across various Nordic countries where *Biophilia* was implemented have demonstrated measurable gains in interest and achievement in both music and the natural sciences,[2] strong evidence to suggest that mutual enrichment occurs when music is used as a starting point for the exploration of other subjects.

Music Integration in World Music Pedagogy

In World Music Pedagogy, the purpose of integration is twofold: First, to develop activities through the world's musical cultures to enable a "global[3] approach to learning and instruction [that] blurs subjects that have too often been separated by adults who tend to classify, categorize, and compartmentalize their encounters" (Campbell, 2004, p. 224); second, to examine *music-as-culture* in order to gain insight into how the musical practices of diverse groups developed. In many music education settings, an attitude of compartmentalization manifests itself in learning *music-as-music* (see Campbell, 2004, p. 216). Those who view music as a subject that exists solely as musical sound, where the product fits only into an aesthetic silo, typically favor outcomes that emphasize the cultivation of playing techniques as a means to generate highly polished performances. As mentioned before, this model of music-making is long-standing and highly regarded in schools of every sort, and it should continue to be honored as a critical component in the overall educational landscape. On the other hand, in a time of the "world as a village," with countries and cultures increasingly dependent upon understanding one another, it is essential to not only know more of the world's musical expressions but also to understand the people behind the music—including both the musicians and those who value the music within the culture. We affirm that it is a moral imperative to ensure that students engage in studies, including music as it integrates with other understandings, that prepare them for the globalized society in which they will play a part as responsible adult citizens of the world.

When it comes to embracing these changes, however, some teachers may feel that school music is untethered from any sociohistorical baggage and is instead a so-called culturally neutral space where students engage solely with musical expressions to objectively learn how other cultures organize sound. Others simply seek to augment their Spring concert program with something fun and exotic that tips a hat perfunctorily at an underrepresented population at the school. At the same time, there are instrumental music teachers who recognize their roles in both teaching music and teaching *through* music a whole set of understandings, attitudes, and possibilities for truly transformative cultural experiences. Regardless of personal perceptions of incorporating world musical cultures into the classroom, educational realities such as the demographic shifts that have occurred in recent years require all stakeholders to check their heading and correct to follow a course that will ensure the development of cultural awareness.

To accomplish such a shift in trajectory, proponents of World Music Pedagogy advocate for examining *music-as-culture*. This approach enables teachers and students to engage in activities for musical learning that situate music as the entry point for acquiring cultural understandings. Moreover, it allows students to examine and ultimately embody the epistemological processes that cultures go through when constructing musical knowledge. In this way, the overarching goal is to establish a bidirectional process of learning music and other subjects through integrated activities from the perspective of the culture that created the music being performed.

Some teachers of instrumental music may accept that this process is well-intentioned but may feel that it ultimately detracts from the goal of developing student musicianship. We authors posit that these efforts to integrate music into the matrix of subjects for study actually help to expand the very definition of music and complement the musical skill development with musical and cultural understanding. By establishing music as a viable means of acquiring knowledge, integration centers musical experiences as an essential mode of making sense in the world through a multicultural lens. Through the process of Integrating World Music into the curriculum, both teachers and students come to learn about, embody, understand, and apply important aspects of musical traditions to their own musical practices. Ahead are recommendations of ways for music teachers to meaningfully engage in subject integration in their classrooms and on campus. When reading the following suggestions, it is important to understand that the intention is not to pile the entire school curriculum onto the music teacher. Rather, they are to serve as manageable entry points for activities that center music as an integral component of education at large. Furthermore, they allow for the expansion of co-teaching possibilities with colleagues from different departments as well so that the music teacher does not have to go it alone. This is an essential component in moving music education from the periphery to the center of education and learning, by positioning it as a springboard from which holistic learning through music can launch.

Examining Function and Context
Through World Music Pedagogy

An important aspect of approaching music-as-culture is the understanding of the various contexts in which music exists and the functions which it performs. In many cultures, music is thoroughly integrated with daily life and is often connected to certain events or social functions. These functions vary widely in scope and seriousness from the jovial (e.g., birthday celebrations in the United States, drinking songs during Oktoberfest in Germany, mass-singing during a soccer match), to the sacred and strictly ritualized (e.g., Native American naming and honoring ceremonies). The uses of music are as diverse as the musical styles around which they function and operate as an integral part of how people create meaning in their lives.

Understanding these variety of uses allows students to engage not only with the organization of sound, but also with the social practice of music-making as conceptualized by the culture being represented. In its infinite variety, music can embody various ideals of sound production, conceptions of time, formal structures, transmission practices, and values. As many might ardently argue, it is the function, not the sound, that imbues the music with meaning. To tease out deeper understandings of these meanings, Integrating World Music focuses on the interconnectedness of all aspects of a musical practice, not just sound reproduction.

Cultural Prism Model

One successful method that has been used in music classrooms to help students examine the surrounding sociocultural context of music is the *Cultural Prism Model* (Campbell, 2004). This approach utilizes a series of questions to examine how a musical performance can refract other cultural knowledge (see Figure 6.3). A brief illustration of this process comes from an author's previous discussion with an Indonesian music expert which revealed that the shape of the fingers when playing *kecapi* (Indonesian plucked zither) are the same form as the word *allah* in Arabic (Figure 6.2). If viewed

Figure 6.2 Hand position for the *kecapi* from Sumedang, Indonesia (left) and Allah written in Arabic (right)

merely from a technical standpoint for facilitating performance, the deeper sociohistorical meaning of this specific shape of the fingers would be missed. Specific questions from the Cultural Prism Model (see Figure 6.3, Musical Meanings) reveals that the position of the fingers supports the cultural belief of their sacred shape that will bless all musical sounds that emanate from the musical instrument. Viewing the musical practice in this way illustrates how this music was developed and influenced by Islamic culture and religion. The musical sounds are then complemented by an understanding of how specific performance techniques (and finger positions) add cultural meaning to the music. Music teachers can utilize this approach to help connect the students to the deeper meanings of music beyond the sound: To shift their understanding from the *how* to the *why*.

The questions offered in the Cultural Prism Model provide a way in which instrumental music teachers can develop an integrated approach to musical study in their classes through these questions (and their answers) on the origins of the music, the ways in which it continues to be meaningful today, and the meanings of the music to the musicians who make it. This information can be culled and compiled by both students and teachers alike from any resources available including books, liner notes, the Internet, and community or campus culture bearers.

The following examples (Figures 6.4, 6.5, and 6.6) present illustrations of how questions from the Cultural Prism Model can be applied to different musical examples. It should be mentioned here that not all questions necessarily need to be answered, depending on the musical selection in question. Moreover, questions that have not

---

Figure 6.3: Questions for the Cultural Prism Model (Adapted from Campbell, 2004)

Musical Beginnings: *Who created the music? When and where was it created? How old was the creator when the piece was created? What inspired the creation of the piece? Who first performed it? How was it performed: As music with expectations for quiet listening, dancing, marching, or as background to social conversations?*

Musical Continuities: *Who performs it now? What qualifications do performers of the music have? Does it always sound the same, or is there flexibility within the tradition to personally interpret it, vary it, transform it? Are there recordings of the piece? Who teaches it? How is it learned? How do audiences respond to the music? Are there social norms for these responses?*

Musical Meanings: *Are there particular social or cultural themes to the music? What use or function does it fulfill? Do historical and contemporary performances of it demonstrate different meanings? Do particular groups of people, as defined by age, gender, ethnicity, religion, socioeconomic status, nation or religion, identify with this music?*

been covered in the Cultural Prism Model may also emerge. As with all other suggestions presented in this volume, this teaching-learning approach can be applied in a flexible process that will allow tailoring by music teachers to fit the unique educational needs of their students.

The Cultural Prism Model in Action

Figure 6.4: Salsa in the Classroom (Learning Pathway #1)

Materials:

- "Mi Gente," classroom audio/video technology

Musical Beginnings

- This piece was composed by Johnny Pacheco, the band leader of Héctor Lavoe's group. He was also a producer at Fania Records, a label that specialized in promoting salsa music.

Musical Continuities

- This song is performed worldwide in spaces where members of the Latino diaspora are located. Depending on the region, the song can be arranged in a variety of styles including *reggaetón, cumbia,* and even classical guitar.
- This song is considered part of the standard repertoire of salsa music and is taught and learned in a variety of formal, informal, and nonformal education settings.[4]
- Because of its strong link to a specific identity, individuals who perform this song, but do not identify with being part of the Puerto Rican diaspora often change the *coro* (chorus) from "que canta *mi* gente" (let my people sing) to "que canten *su* gente" (let his people sing).

Musical Meanings

- This song is considered to be the unofficial "Nuyorican" national anthem. The term "Nuyorican," a portmanteau of New York and Puerto Rican, refers to individuals of the Puerto Rican diaspora who have settled in New York and reflects Lavoe's own background of having been born in the Puerto Rican city of Ponce.
- Héctor Lavoe's vocal delivery has been considered a marker of identity because it is often shaded with the style of a *pregonero* (singer) in *jíbaro* music.

Figure 6.5: Contemporary Syrian Music
(Learning Pathway # 2)

Materials:

- "Tulina's Carmona," classroom audio/video technology

Musical Beginnings

- "Tulina's Carmona" was composed by Josh Myers, the bassist for Kinan Azmeh's group *Kinan Azmeh's City Band*, circa 2010. This group, based out of New York City, is comprised of four core musicians: Kinan Azmeh (clarinet), Josh Myers (bass), Kyle Sanna (guitar), John Hadfield (percussion). They perform contemporary fusion music that blends elements of classical, jazz, and Syrian traditional music. This particular piece was inspired by several influences including Turkish *taqsim* (improvisatory introduction), Indian *ragas* (melodic modes), Syrian rhythms, and Afro-Caribbean *tumbao* (bass rhythm). Although this piece is notated, the final version was developed through musical negotiation that occurred through rehearsals (Myers, personal communication, October 11, 2017).

Musical Continuities

- This piece is a contemporary composition specific to this group and is not performed widely.
- Although this piece is notated with a specific form, there are several ways that it can be arranged.

Musical Meanings

- According to composer Josh Myers, this piece was inspired by a cousin of his moving to a different part of the world. He wanted to capture the feeling of being out of place and adapting to a new environment. This sentiment could connect to discussions about refugee populations, particularly from Syria.
- Musically, the contemporary Syrian music that Kinan Azmeh's City Band performs could also represent transculturalism in the 21st century. Instruments used in traditional Syrian settings include the *qanun* (zither), *kamancheh* (fiddle), *derbakki* (goblet drum), *daf* (frame drum), and *ney* (end-blown flute). In this group, the sounds have been adapted to accommodate an ensemble that typically consists of clarinet, guitar (nylon and steel string), electric and upright bass, *cajón*, and various other percussion instruments.

Figure 6.6: Zimbabwean Shona for Band (Learning Pathway #3)

Materials:

- "Chemutengure," classroom audio/video technology

Musical Beginnings

- This piece was composed by Lora Chiorah-Dye who immigrated to the United States from Zimbabwe in the 1970s. After her arrival, she began teaching her children Zimbabwean marimba and eventually founded Sukutai Marimba and Dance Ensemble.

- "Chemutengure" was arranged for *mbira* (percussion instrument with tuned metal tongues), guitar, and vocals. It is based on the *Shona* melody she recalled hearing when she was a child in Zimbabwe. She was inspired to arrange the song after moving to the United States in an effort to honor a vendor named Vajeke who she knew in her youth. This vendor would travel to the British boarding schools where the students were living to bring them familiar treats such as sweet potatoes. Since these boarding schools were so far away from their homes, the children often lacked access to familiar foods.

Musical Continuities

- This piece is performed widely and is considered part of the standard repertoire of *Shona mbira* music. Various arrangements of this piece are used in a variety of performance settings internationally including staged concerts, community gatherings, and children's education.

- Several recordings of this piece exist including a version performed by Zimbabwean music legend Thomas Mapfumo, the founder of *chimurenga* music. *Chimurenga* was a style of music that was used to create solidarity during the Zimbabwe revolution.

Musical Meanings

- *Shona* songs are based on proverbs or stories and typically contain multiple interpretations. In "Chemutengure," the song references wagon wheels and a wagon driver which refer to the ox-cart; the first vehicle used by Europeans in Zimbabwe. The word *chemutengure* is also believed to be an onomatopoeic reference to the sound the ox-cart wheels make as it travels down the unpaved roads. This song is said to have marked the "coming of the West," referring to British colonialism in Zimbabwe. This connects to Chiorah-Dye's memory of boarding schools that she attended in her youth. These sites, often established in rural areas by British missionaries, were a key component in assimilating Zimbabwean youth during the colonial era.

- In Shona culture, there is a high importance placed on connection to ancestral spirits (*mweya*) and *mbira* music is believed to be a useful tool in communicating with them.

Subject-to-Subject Integration

When engaging in integrative activities through music, it is important for instrumental music teachers to understand that each subject—from music to science, history, American literature, and French—is the result of a developed system of thinking, and that each subject maintains its own set of disciplinary questions, methods, and lenses with which to view the world. Although subjects maintain their conceptual distinctness, they are not necessarily as separated as they are often perceived to be. Human knowledge is constructed through the interaction of overlapping domains of knowledge and each educational experience can be viewed from a variety of perspectives. For example, the length of a typical pop song (approximately 3 minutes and 30 seconds) can be viewed in the musical domain as a compositional convention that emerged at a particular point in history. However, when viewed through a historical and technological lens, it becomes apparent that this length was not a musical decision after all, but rather the size of the recording medium (the 45 RPM, 7-inch vinyl record single) which dictated the limits for recording at the time. This illustrates the integration of combining music and technology studies in historical perspective, and it develops a holistic understanding of how specific sociocultural factors that shape musical trajectories.

When developing integrative activities, it might seem that certain subjects (e.g., geography, social sciences) lend themselves more easily to their integration with music studies than others (e.g., mathematics, physics). Reflecting conventions in "siloed" educational settings, this perspective perpetuates the perception that some subjects are further removed from cultural and creative matters than others. This leads to the belief that some disciplines (e.g., music and math) are mutually exclusive and are not possible to integrate. Advocates for WMP seek to challenge this belief and espouse the understanding that music, as a profound distillation of all aspects of culture, can be used to help acquire knowledge in various others subject areas. The following sections provide considerations for developing integrated activities in an assortment of subjects.

The Visual Arts

Since music and the visual arts are inherently creative in nature, they are a natural starting point for integration with one another. Several of the world's musical cultures are deeply connected to the visual arts. In Indonesia, the tradition of *wayang kulit* (shadow puppetry) features intricately carved and painted leather figures that depict characters from important traditional stories. Additionally, musical instruments from around the world also provide examples of the importance of musical instruments as visually artistic objects. For example, the Burmese *saung gauk* is often constructed with ornate decorations, gold leaf, and rare deer skin. Other instruments such as the Japanese *koto*, the *sitar* and *sarod* of India, the *kora* of Mali, and the *oud* that is performed in Egypt, Turkey, Iran, Iraq, and elsewhere in the Near East are also examples of the artistic detail with which instruments are constructed. Integration activities that examine the elaborate decoration of musical instruments and associated artifacts from the world's musical cultures can be developed as a way for students to acquire an understanding of how art is used to honor these traditions.

While the previous examples illustrate how visual arts can enhance the beauty of instruments, it can also serve a functional, process-oriented purpose as well. In Learning Pathway #2 (Episode 6.1), Kinan Azmeh has partnered with a visual artist Kevork Mourad to present a series of live performances for Syrian children in refugee camps in Jordan.

This project pairs the performance of a clarinet composition with the live-painting of an image depicting a scene from Syria. The children are then asked to discuss the feelings that were invoked during this process. Similar activities can be developed through partnerships with music and art teachers. For example, a themed concert that focuses on the music of Africa can feature a live-painting of a natural scene from the Serengeti or even traditional fabric patterns. As with all aspects of the WMP process, the music selected and outcomes desired will guide the development of these projects.

Episode 6.1: Contemporary Syrian Music (Learning Pathway #2)

Materials:

• "Tulina's Carmona,"[5] classroom audio/video technology, selected resources

Geography: Syria is a country in the Middle East that is bordered by Turkey (north), Iraq (east), Jordan (south), Israel (southwest), Lebanon (west). It also has a coastline that provides access to the Mediterranean Sea.

Sample discussion question:

• *In this region, similar instruments are found in different cultures. How do you think proximity of these countries contributed to this? Can you find any examples in your country or culture?*

History: Syria's history dates all the way back to the Paleolithic era. As a part of the fertile crescent, this area was influenced by several cultures including the Persians, Greek, Roman, Arabic, Turkish, and French. In modern history, Syria acquired recognition as an independent country in 1944, but has been ruled by the Ba'ath party for several decades.

Sample discussion question:

• *Syria has a long history of interacting with several different cultures in the region. How do you think that this has influenced the development of their music? Can you find any examples of influence from different cultures in terms of instruments? Tuning systems? Scales and modes?*

Social Sciences: In recent years, Syria has been in the international spotlight due mainly to the civil war that has raged across the country since 2011. The ensuing refugee crisis that has resulted from this conflict has led to the displacement of 11.6 million individuals across the globe.[6] This dispersion of Syrians has also led to xenophobic sentiment in several countries including the United States which, through Executive Order 13769 signed by President Donald Trump, sought to ban the entry of individuals from predominantly Muslim countries, including Syria.

Sample discussion question:

- *The song "Tulina's Carmona" is an example of transnationalism because of the variety of instruments as well as the ethnic and musical perspectives that have coalesced to inspire its creation. What are the broader implications for arts and culture when certain populations are (1) re-located to different countries as refugees, and (2) restricted from entering a country based on the region they originate? Find one example of how music organizations have responded to events such as the Syrian refugee crisis.*

Laboratory Sciences and Mathematics: One instrument in Syrian music (the *qanun*) is a zither that is tuned using several musical bridges. This could lead into a lesson on the musical ratios of Pythagoras and his tuning system. After constructing their own guitar string monochord (single stringed instrument) students could calculate the frequencies of different intervals. This could lead to a discussion of how the tuning systems of the West (equal temperament) and microtonal music of the Middle East differ according to these mathematical principles.

Sample discussion questions:

- *Why do you think different cultures have different tuning systems? How does this influence instrument construction?*

World Languages: The official language spoken in Syria is Arabic. However, due to its geographical location there are several other languages are spoken as well including Kurdish, Armenian, Aramaic, Circassian, French, and English.

   As an activity, learn the definition of the following Arabic music terms: *maqam* (scales), *waslat* (song cycle), *taqsim* (improvised introduction to a song), *oud* (lute), *nay*, *qanun*.

Sample discussion questions:

- *Several of these instruments have traveled to other cultures including Western Europe. Can you find examples of any of these instruments? Has the name changed? Is it similar? What evidence do you have?*

Geography

Since World Music Pedagogy focuses on utilizing the world's musical cultures to achieve its goals, geography provides several opportunities for integration with music. A fundamental understanding of WMP is that world musical cultures are associated with particular locations (even though many instruments and students are also globalized and performed in places far from their origin cultures). The scope of the musical selections that are used can vary from regional examples (e.g., Latin America, The Middle East, West Africa), to countries (e.g., China, Egypt, Mexico), and even specific cities (e.g., second line from New Orleans, salsa in New York, *landó* from El Carmen, Peru, *flamenco* from Granada). Examining the geography of where a culture's music originated helps to acquire a better sense of questions such as where cultures settle, how environments influence societies, and how the distribution of cultures within a certain area influences surrounding groups. This information can lead to deeper musical understandings such as why certain scales and tuning systems are used, why instruments are constructed from specific materials, whether the musical practice is participatory or not, and why certain timbres are favored.

When delving further into Learning Pathway #1 (Episode 6.2), an understanding of the geography of Puerto Rico can illuminate ways in which certain musical features emerged in this musical culture. For example, the proximity of Puerto Rico to the United States could be examined as a possible influence on decisions to colonize the island. This colonization led to cultural exchange and, eventually, migration of Puerto Ricans to New York. In the ethnic enclaves that these immigrants established, musical influences (i.e., jazz, *jíbaro*, Cuban son) fused and eventually gave birth to salsa music.

Episode 6.2: Salsa in the Classroom
(Learning Pathway #1)

Selection: "Mi Gente"

Materials:

- "Mi Gente," classroom audio/video technology, selected resources

Geography: Puerto Rico is an archipelago in the Caribbean Sea that is part of the Greater Antilles. Locate it on a map and discuss what possible relationships might have developed with the United States or other countries based on proximity.

Sample discussion question:

- *How do you think the proximity of Puerto Rico to the United States influenced its relationship? Why?*

Social Sciences: The Caribbean islands before European colonization were home to several indigenous groups including the Arawaks, Caribs, Siboneys, and Tainos. After the arrival of Christopher Columbus, the islands in the region were quickly, and violently, transformed into colonies for Spain. This colonization endured until the Spanish-American War that resulted in the transfer of several colonies from Spanish to U.S. control. As a result of this, Puerto Rico is currently considered to be an unincorporated territory of the United States.

Puerto Rican culture is comprised of several different streams including Indigenous (Arawak, Taino), African (Ashanti, Mandinga, Wolof, Bantu-Kongo, Yoruba, Ewe, Ashante, Fon, Ibo), and European (Spanish). This is present in several aspects of culture including religion and music. For example, the three main instruments in *jíbaro* music, the *güiro*, *tres*, and *bongo* represent the three main cultural influences: Indigenous, Spanish, and African, respectively. As individuals in an unincorporated U.S. territory, Puerto Ricans were able to move freely within the country and settled strong communities in East Coast cities, particularly New York. As Puerto Rican individuals settled into new communities, interactions between musicians, especially jazz players, transformed the musical landscape of within the region and, eventually, the country. These collaborations led the emergence of salsa, hip-hop, and other popular styles of music.

Sample discussion question:

- *As with the Immigration and Naturalization Act of 1965, how do you think the relationship of Puerto Rico as a territory of the United States influenced the dissemination of Puerto Rican arts and culture in the United States?*

Sample discussion question:

- *Why do you think musical collaborations often occur when individuals move to different countries (re: jazz in New Orleans via Congo square; conjunto music in Texas via Monterrey, Mexico; bluegrass music in Appalachia via England)? Can you think of any other contemporary examples? What implications does this have for current conceptualizations of music education?*

World Languages: Spanish is the primary language used in this song. The following translation of key lyrics of the song could be provided to the students:

Mi gente ¡Ustedes! | My people!
Lo más grande de este mundo | They are the best in the world
Siempre me hacen sentir | They always make me feel
Un orgullo profundo | So proud
Los llamé ¡vengan conmigo! | If I call to them "come with me!"
No me preguntaron dónde | They won't ask where.
Orgullo tengo de ustedes | I am so proud
Que canta mi gente | Oh, how my people sing!

Following a reading of these lyrics, the students could discuss how this connects to this song being considered the unofficial national anthem of Nuyoricans. Next, the students could discuss how music helps to shape their own identities and connect them to a broader community.

Sample discussion question:

- How do the lyrics provide evidence that this song is deeply tied to identity? Can you think of any other songs that might function in a similar way in a different cultural group?

Social Sciences

Questions in the social sciences come from a variety of fields such as history, sociology, anthropology, and political science. Situating culture in sociohistorical context allows for an examination of how societal developments influence the emergence of specific musical practices. As the featured song "Chemutengure" in Learning Pathway #3 (Episode 6.3) was arranged to honor a food vendor working in a British school in Zimbabwe, there is a connection of the colonial history of the West in Zimbabwe and elsewhere on the African continent. The piece can also be examined for its reappropriation by *chimurenga* (roughly translates to *struggle music* in a reference to its revolutionary undertones) musician Thomas Mapfumo (see Figure 6.6). During the Zimbabwe revolution, and well after, Mapfumo's music was popular and used in helping to forge strong solidarity for all those seeking to oust the British colonists. This could be used as a powerful example of how context influences a piece of music's meaning and function.

Episode 6.3: Zimbabwe Shona for Band
(Learning Pathway #3)

Materials:

- "Chemtengure," classroom audio/video technology, selected resources

Geography: Zimbabwe is a landlocked region that is located in the southwestern region of Africa. It is bordered by five countries: Mozambique (east), South Africa (south), Botswana (west), Zambia (north).

Sample discussion question:

- *Do you think the bordering countries influenced cultures in Zimbabwe? Why or Why not? What are some possible reasons for your answer?*

Social Sciences: Zimbabwe has a history that begins circa 800 CE. Throughout its early existence, the Shona kingdom and several smaller groups utilized the strategic position near the Indian Ocean to trade with several groups from the Middle East including the Persians, Indians, and Arabs. Interaction with European powers came early with the arrival of the Portuguese circa 1500 CE and culminated with the British colonial which spanned from 1888 to 1980. During this time, the country's name was changed to Rhodesia and several changes occurred through the cultural imposition of British colonials. In the 1970s a civil war broke out which eventually led to Zimbabwean independence in 1980. Immigration to the United States of individuals from African countries was heavily influenced by the Immigration and Naturalization Act of 1965, also known as the Hart-Celler Act. In response to the civil rights movement of the 1960s, this Act allowed for the entrance from several previously restricted regions such as Africa, Asia, and Latin America.

Sample discussion question:

- *How does colonialism and transnationalism influence musical practices? How can Chemtengure be seen as an example of this? Please provide an example from your own life.*

- *Could Lora Chiorah-Dye's arrival from Zimbabwe to the United States in the 1970s be related to the Hart-Celler Act? How did these immigration policies influence the development of arts and culture in the United States (re: the development of cultural groups like the Sukutai Marimba and Dance Ensemble). Are there any modern examples of this phenomenon?*

World Languages: The lyrics of this song are in Shona and could be used in two ways, (1) introduce students to the language through pronunciation and translation, and (2) use the lyrics to explore the theme of British colonialism in Zimbabwe. In a version of Chemutengure that was recorded by Dumisani Maraire and Ephat Mujure, the following lyrics are sung:

(1:03) *chava chemutengure vhiri rengoro* | (Is it a traditional transport made of wood?)

This is repeated several times until the repeated chorus section.

(3:25) *uno tambira mari?* | (How much is your pay?)

After a translation of these lyrics are presented, the students can discuss how a connection to British colonialism can be inferred.

Sample discussion question:

- *It is widely understood that lyrics in Zimbabwean music typically have multiple meanings. What are some possible meanings that could be inferred from "Chemutengure?"*

Laboratory Sciences and Mathematics: Students could view the construction of the *mbira* as a culturally specific technology. To begin, they could examine the wooden body of the instrument and question how it was cut, with what tools, and from what materials. The students could then examine the timbre of the tongues and question why they might sound the way that they do. This could then lead to a conversation about the overtone series and how the presence of different frequencies influences the timbre.

Sample discussion question:

- *How do you think the materials of the instrument affect the timbre?*

Another integrated activity in the social sciences could be inspired by the featured example "Tulina's Carmona" in Learning Pathway #2 (Episode 6.1). Musically, this song was composed with several influences including Syrian, Indian, and Puerto Rican elements, representing the truly transnational nature of music in the 21st century. Discussions that explore globalization and other sociocultural factors that lead to mass movements of people, as in the case of asylum-seekers from the Near East and Africa to Europe, can help to enlighten the subsequent effect that this process has on musical practices.

World Languages

Singing is a powerful tool used by all musical cultures of the world in their musical expressions. It can convey dual meanings both emotionally and semantically as well as bond members of diasporic communities through the common identity found in a shared language. This provides many opportunities for music teachers to venture into the realm of world languages for integrative inspiration. Since language is the medium for poetry, lyrical content can be mined for meaning and insights when developing these activities. A project focused on translating lyrics can help students to acquire a deeper understanding of the meaning and emotional content of a song. This translation practice can help to inform the feelings that the performers wish to invoke in their audiences.

Another way that integration might be accomplished between music and world languages is through a process of seeking out idiomatic expressions, specific words, and phrases in the language of a song that might help provide insight into deeper cultural meaning contained within the song. In Learning Pathway #1 (Episode 6.2) the song "Mi Gente," what is considered by many to be the unofficial *Nuyorican* national anthem, features Héctor Lavoe artfully weaves certain English phrases into his soloistic vocal exchange with the *coro* (chorus) that repeats "que cante mi gente." During the song (2:48) he sings the Spanish phrase *"Ese es un morro!"* which is promptly answered by the English phrase *"I see you tomorrow."* To emphasize this difference, he also sings the words to a variation on a melody that is borrowed from the Westminster Abbey chime theme, the ubiquitous tune that plays on most bell tower clocks at the top of the hour. This musical moment masterfully foregrounds the blended ethnic identity of diasporic Puerto Ricans in New York (as well as their attunement to the world, including London!).

Lastly, examining music through a world language lens could also reveal how certain accents and styles of singing are also tied to specific cultural identities. Sticking with the example of "Mi Gente," Lavoe's voice was considered to be an accurate representation of the Nuyorican identity because it had elements of both a *jíbaro* (inhabitants of the mountain regions of Puerto Rico) and New York sonority.

Laboratory Sciences and Mathematics

Exploring the world's musical cultures for connections to mathematics and the sciences might at first seem like a daunting task. However, the manipulation of musical sounds and instrument construction could be viewed as culturally specific technologies. For example, many of the world's musical instruments are constructed using specific methods and materials. Additionally, tuning systems on these instruments reflect specific and systematic understandings of mathematical ratios even if they are not conceptualized as such. Using "Chemutengure" (Episode 6.3) as an example, an activity that focuses on the *mbira* could be developed to explore how the instrument is constructed and why it might have its particular timbre. The goal here is to try to understand how the technology to construct this particular instrument might have emerged in this culture. Another possible integration activity can be found in Learning Pathways #2 (Episode 6.1) with the exploration of tuning systems in music from the Near East.

Music Integration in Daily Life: Developing Ethnomusicological Perspectives

In recent years, there have been increased efforts for the fields of music education and ethnomusicology to engage in dialogue about overlapping interests. Issues of how music is learned, once perceived to be the province of teachers in schools, have been increasingly examined by ethnomusicologists since the late 1960s (Rice, 2003). Likewise, the responsibility of exploring music as culture was believed to lie only with ethnomusicologists, but teachers are now discovering the importance of knowing music for its cultural meaning and values which thus inspires the examination of ways to pair musical experience and study with various other subjects. By instilling students with a sense of how to examine music through an ethnomusicological lens, they will develop an understanding of how music reflects the behaviors and values of people in culture.

The following sections provide possible topics and experiences that can guide students in their exploration of how music is integrated into different aspects of their lives. These suggestions launch other means for acquiring deeper understandings of the mechanisms that shape musical taste and that connect music to other aspects of culture.

Music and Transnationalism

Currently, the world is undergoing an unprecedented spike in access to global information through the use of smart phones, social media, and other technologies. This trend, compounded with a parallel growth in personal music consumption and creation, has led to questions as to how the world's musical cultures are being influenced by these information technologies. Anyone, in nearly any place in the globe, can explore any musical culture. One pertinent example of this phenomenon can be found through the global reach of "Despacito" by Luis Fonsi and Daddy Yankee. This song draws influences from both modern (*reggaetón*, electronic music) and traditional styles (*bomba*), and has exposed over four billion listeners (at the time of this writing) to Puerto Rican culture through music. Furthermore, groups of musicians throughout the world have "covered" this song within their own musical practices and languages (i.e., Indonesian gamelan, the *Kimeru* language in the Kenyan highlands), tuning themselves evocatively into facets of Puerto Rican popular music and culture.

As modern consumers of music, students have a unique vantage point with which to examine the mechanisms that lead to the dispersion of cultural expressions from around the world. A carefully planned lesson can provide enriching opportunities for students to develop both a global and local understanding of their how they are positioned within, contribute to, and influence a global music ecology. Approaching these issues from this perspective will help students to understand transnational music exchange as a dynamic and bidirectional process that requires a knowledge of both local *and* global contexts. This also provides justification for the importance of being informed about, and developing a sensitivity for, diverse cultures.

Figure 6.7: Music, Globalization, and Transnationalism

To acquire a better understanding of how their musical tastes are influenced by global influences students should begin by examining their own consumption of arts. The following questions provide a systematic way for students to evaluate their listening choices.

1. From which country does this music come?
2. What are the names of the artists? Where do they live now? How did they get there?
3. Where did they first hear about this music? Friends? Internet?
4. Are the lyrics sung in the local language? If not, which language? Is it blended?
5. Are there any unfamiliar musical elements in the piece (e.g., instruments, meter, timbre, scales)?
6. What are the current social-political conditions in the origin country of the music? Are these themes present in the lyrics?
7. What is the most appealing part about this music?
8. What is one thing that might be interesting to learn about this music?

Exploring Music of the Diaspora: The Global Turned Local

Of course, in addition to the increased movement of music through digital media, there is also an increased movement of immigrants around the globe. These groups establish new communities wherever they settle and, as mentioned in Chapter 4, bring along their cultural knowledge to these new settings (including clothing, cuisine, musical practices, and so on). As they settle into their new communities, their children are inevitably enrolled in local schools. It is here in these educational settings that students undergo the often-painful process of assimilation when they are exposed to environments that are unfamiliar, uncomfortable, and sometimes hostile. For teachers, early and often musical engagement becomes a crucial component of these students' success, and can also be a way that they develop the necessary social capital to successfully incorporate into their new campuses and communities.

For these populations, music integration provides a desirable medium to accomplish this goal because it provides these students with opportunities to use music as a starting point with which to develop deeper relationships with peers. One method involves teachers recruiting these students (or their families) as culture bearers, if they so desire to represent their musical culture. In one example, a school counselor and music teacher provided an opportunity for a family of Guatemalan students to continue their musical tradition on campus (Mena, 2017). This group had arrived in the United States already possessing profound knowledge of Guatemalan marimba music but did not have access to resources to continue performing it. Seeing this as an opportunity to connect them to campus culture, the school counselor and music teacher teamed up to help the students put on a performance where they were able to share their music, aspects of their culture, and details of their journey to the United

States with an audience of teachers and peers. Through a musical performance the students were able to situate their experience within a broader sociocultural context and provide a first-hand knowledge of their culture.

In another example, a high school near a major refugee resettlement center in San Diego has the highest concentration of immigrant and refugee students in the district. In an effort to create a space where teachers, the student body, and the public could learn about the various groups represented on campus a group of teachers (English, music, art) developed an integrated arts event called the "Big Celebration." During this event members of various ethnic groups on campus created a presentation or performance that featured poetry, music, dance, language, and traditional dress. As a requirement for their English Language Learner classes the students would be required to begin each performance with background information on their culture as well as curate an exhibit that featured artifacts from their culture. The goal of this event was to provide a cross-section of cultural expressions to educate audiences with the purpose of dispelling any fears or assumptions that they might have about these groups.

While this might seem like an insurmountable undertaking, it is not necessary for music teachers to initially set out to accomplish such large goals. Small actions such as conversations with students, visits to ethnic communities, and even participation in a small volunteer opportunity can help teachers to develop a level of comfort that can perhaps lead to repeated visits and sustained engagement. These small actions lead to subtle shifts in attitudinal trajectories which can ultimately result in great changes to personal perceptions. The following questions (Figure 6.8) can help music teachers to organize their information when approaching culture bearers for possible collaborations.

Figure 6.8: Developing an Understanding of Music of the Diaspora

In this activity, students (and teachers) can seek out culture bearers on campus (e.g., students, staff) or individuals in the community to examine which musical traditions are represented. Here is a list of suggested questions to ask culture bearers about their musical traditions.

1. How did the culture bearer come to the country? Were they born here? Are they an immigrant? Refugee?
2. How did the culture bearer learn the music? What was the level of formality?
3. Is there notation associated with this musical culture?
4. What are some of the ways that the culture bearer has been involved with music? Composer? Performer?
5. Is this music central to any community events or ceremonies?
6. Where is this music typically performed? Are there any restriction of where it is performed?
7. Is this music popular in the country where it originated?
8. Is this music available on YouTube? iTunes? Streaming services?

Music and Identity: Integration and Acculturation

As most school populations undergo major changes to their demographics, and as global cultures become local, the issue of cultural representation in the curriculum must also be examined. Often, formal (i.e., textbook) and implicit (i.e., classroom) information presented in learning environments omits key contributions of ethnic minority groups to the social fabric of a particular locale. Students seeing themselves represented as members of a valued group can be helpful in envisioning pathways to success. In one example from 2009, teachers, students, and community members fought (albeit unsuccessfully) to keep an ethnic studies program in the Tucson Unified School District curriculum in response to the historical erasure of Mexican Americans in this region. This program was initially established because teachers complained that when Mexican American history was included in mainstream curriculum the information was often incongruent with historical accounts and ignored the valuable contributions of this population. At-risk Mexican American students who were enrolled in the program had measurable gains in achievement which they attributed to feeling valued, safe, capable, and represented. Conversely, tension created by a lack of cultural representation can prove detrimental and often leads to students disengaging with the learning process. Projects focused on music integration can be powerful tools for underrepresented students to counter these effects.

For example, students who come from rich musical traditions and choose to participate in large ensembles might find that the techniques and learning process that they excel in one tradition might not be valued in the other. The activities outlined in the WMP process can be used to connect with these students through the exploration of their own musical heritage. As illustrated in the earlier examples, centering their musical culture as a key component in the curriculum can introduce insights that demonstrate the important cultural contributions of these students and situate them as integral components of the social fabric of their adopted communities.

Experiences such as these can both enriching and empowering for students, but it is important for instrumental music teachers to involve the students themselves in this decision-making process. Providing students with opportunities to include their unique perspective into the musical culture being performed will increase the likeliness that they feel comfortable with it being represented. A prime example of unintended conflict can be found in the case of a teacher in Chicago who developed a mariachi program to connect with her Latino students. This teacher had noticed a recent increase of Mexican immigrants to the area that the school served, and she wanted to provide a culturally relevant space for these students to explore music. Being a middle-class White woman, her credibility to teach this musical style was eventually called into question by one of her students. After reflecting on the performance of "La Raspa," the student shared the sentiment that she had perceived it to be just "one big Mexican stereotype" (Abril, 2009). Although the teacher's intentions were clearly grounded in genuine concern and care for these students, the implementation eventually left some feeling tokenized and essentialized (see Chapter 1). The students wanted to perform music that they valued, but they were left performing music that someone else felt represented their lived experiences. By including students in conversations about which cultures should be represented and how to approach musical experiences and activities, instrumental music teachers will more likely avoid the pitfalls of misrepresentation.

Teacher Feature: Skúli Gestsson on Integrating Music and Science Through *Biophilia*

Skúli Gestsson, Musician and Music Teacher, Iceland

He worked on the curriculum for the Biophilia Educational Project, which was implemented in the Nordic countries. He has also co-authored textbooks for elementary music in Iceland and had a successful career with his pop-rock band Dikta.

Q: What is the Biophilia Educational Project *and how did it begin?*
A: The project was originally developed by Icelandic artist Björk in cooperation with the University of Iceland and the City of Reykjavík. The idea behind Björk's 2011 album Biophilia was to use music in a way to explore the natural sciences, and vice versa. To accomplish this, a series of ten interactive "songapps" were created with various activities exploring concepts in natural sciences. In Reykjavík, an accompanying curriculum aimed at 10–12 year olds was built around the app album by a team of music teachers and scientists. After it was completed, it was implemented in several schools around Iceland. Those who chose to participate were provided with a flight case full of iPads, instruments, and teaching guides. After a successful run in Iceland it was then picked up as a part of the Icelandic presidency in the Nordic Council of Ministers in 2014 and subsequently implemented in eight Nordic countries.

Q: Could you please explain more about why music and natural science integration was so important in your work?
A: This idea was ingrained in her album of the same name, Biophilia. When she was writing the album she was fascinated with science wanted to be able to develop a project where she could use the touchscreen as a musical interface to explore science. This resulted in the songs themselves being about ten different elements in the natural sciences. There was also a lot of discussion around how to incorporate interdisciplinary teaching around that time, with questions about how music could be used to look at other subjects. Since I had already done that kind of work I was brought on board to

help develop the program. The thing that excited me the most about Biophilia was the chance to approach music from the sciences, not just the other way around. Instead of music playing the role of "hey, let's make this subject more exciting by adding music" here we were actually looking at musicology, musical cultures and composition, from a scientific angle.

Q: What are some the benefits that you have seen from these integrative activities?
A: If you go to the Biophilia website (www.biophiliaeducational.org) you can view the results from an official project evaluation. One exciting finding was that teachers were, in general, pleased with the project. This is exciting because, well, as anybody who has ever worked in education reform understands, teacher buy-in can be a little difficult at times. The benefits for the students were also remarkable. They demonstrated a deeper understanding of concepts in music and science—with increased interest in both—and was also found to promote creative learning strategies with teachers and students alike.

Q: What were some of the challenges in developing integrative activities?
A: The biggest challenge was finding a way to bring the project into the school while accommodating their rigid schedules. Since this project emphasizes the importance of two teachers co-teaching music and natural sciences in the same space, finding time to plan for activities was a challenge. Adding to this difficulty was that fact that the teachers had to find a way to structure their curriculum so that they would be able to teach two groups of students at the same time. To be successful these efforts relied on the understanding and support from administrators; something we were very much grateful for.

Q: In one of the activities there are several scales that are derived from various musical cultures around the world. What was the reasoning behind adding these into the program?
A: Björk's ideas behind the project were to break out of traditional Eurocentric ways of thinking about musicology: To break up traditional classical instruments and make new ones. For example, the "Biophilia character" in the app that she originally created was wearing a dress with a harp around her waist and wearing a wig that was inspired by nebula photos from the Hubble telescope (photo: www.bjork.fr/IMG/jpg/bjork-2011-inez-vinoodh-biophilia-cover-sans-illustration.jpg). She has described this character as her version of a music teacher. After viewing the photo it is easy to see how this image challenges the archetypal image of what most people think of when they hear the words "music teacher." For Björk it was important to have music education break out of traditional Western modes, both musically and in thinking. To do this she set song in various modes from around the world to bring a fresh perspective into this sonic space.

Q: You also perform rímur *(traditional Icelandic music). How would you approach subject integration using this genre of music?*
A: The first thing that I would do is develop an activity that is based on the Icelandic language. The reason for this is that since rímur are inherently in Icelandic, this provides an opportunity to explore how the rhythm and flow of the language inform each other. Another activity that I would develop is a historical lesson that traces the

development of rímur and the ancient concepts contained in them. For me, it's a window into our past, as an isolated and poor agricultural society, a population of proud descendants of Vikings, living on and off an unforgiving volcanic island in the North Atlantic. I think it is important for our youth to understand this.

Q: What advice would you give music teachers who are considering developing integrative and interdisciplinary activities for their students?
A: I would tell them to do it! The rewards outweigh the initial discomfort of developing the activities . . . by far. Students are more engaged, they are making deeper connects with the materials, and, most of all, they are having fun. Be sure to plan though. Some music teachers might have expertise in other fields but they are the exception. Because of this, you are going to need to recruit a teacher from another subject to help plan. That is one reason why we emphasize co-teaching.

Note: There is a 90-minute documentary about the development of this project that includes a live performance: www.biophiliathefilm.com/

Integration in WMP as Essential to Global Learning

This chapter has demonstrated the ways in which music integration and the WMP process can help teachers to develop projects that place music at the center of knowledge production in culture. Outside of the benefits that modern efforts to integrate music have demonstrated, there are multiple ways in which this will be useful to students. In terms of critical thinking, practicing the skills to examine music holistically will help students to develop their capacity for examining complex issues from multiple perspectives. The globalized nature of the world in the 21st century simply requires this. Additionally, growing an understanding of the diversity of cultural expressions and perspectives will enable students to approach collaborative endeavors with sensitivity towards the various ways in which individuals from different cultures interact socially. Music is not merely an ancillary activity that is used only to entertain but an essential expression of humanness that enlightens both listeners and performers through exposure to a unique articulation of how one group has made sense of the world around them.

Notes

1 ArtsEdSearch is a clearinghouse of studies on the benefits of international arts integration efforts.
2 Report available on the Biophilia website.
3 A dual meaning of this word can be inferred: (1) referring to a worldwide approach, and (2) referring to the comprehensive nature of integrated curriculum.
4 The convention for distinguishing these three settings is explored in K. Veblen's (2012) chapter "Adult music learning in formal, nonformal, and informal context," in G. McPherson and G. F. Welch's (Eds.) *The Oxford Handbook of Music Education* (Vol. 2). In this chapter, *formal* refers to learning in a school setting, *informal* refers to being self-taught, and *nonformal* refers to systematic learning that occurs outside of the classroom.

5 Information gathered from a personal interview with composer Josh Myers, October 11, 2017.
6 Amnesty International. Retrieved from www.amnesty.org.nz/syria-worst-humanitarian-crisis-our-time.

References

Abril, C. (2009). Responding to culture in the instrumental music programme: A teacher's journey. *Music Education Research, 11*, 77–91. doi:10.1080/14613800802699176

Campbell, P. S. (2004). *Teaching music globally: Experiencing music, expressing culture.* New York, NY: Oxford University Press.

Mena, C. (2017). Music teachers reimagining musical focus, function, and performance, for newcomer students. *Journal of Folklore and Education, 4*, 105–111.

Pitts, L. (1937). Music education, isolated or integrated. *Music Educators Journal, 24*(1), 33–73. doi:10.2307/3385492

Rice, T. (2003). The ethnomusicology of music learning and teaching. *College Music Symposium, 43*, 65–85.

Selected Resources

Salsa in the Classroom (Learning Pathway #1)

Moore, R. (2010). *Music in the Hispanic Caribbean: Experiencing music, expressing culture* (Global Music Series). New York, NY: Oxford University Press.

Waxer, L. (2013). *Situating salsa: Global markets and local meanings in latin popular music.* Florence, IT: Taylor and Francis.

LISTENING LINKS

American Sabor. www.abericansabor.org

"La Loma del Tamarindo," Ecos de Borinquen, Smithsonian Folkways. www.folkways.si.edu/ecos-de-borinquen/la-loma-del-tamarindo-the-tamarind-hill/latin-world/music/track/smithsonian

"Mi Gente," Héctor Lavoe, iTunes/Fania. https://itun.es/us/Nn0aF?i=520308589

Contemporary Syrian Music (Learning Pathway #2)

Neville, M. & Rogers, C. (producers), Neville, M. (director). (2015) *The Music of strangers: Yo-Yo Ma and the silk road ensemble* [Motion picture]. United States: Tremolo Productions.

Rasmussen, A. K. (2009). The Arab world. In *Worlds of music: An introduction to the music of the world's peoples* (5th ed., pp. 473–532). Belmont, CA: Schirmer Cengage Learning.

LISTENING LINKS

"Tulina's Carmona," Kinan Azmeh, iTunes. Contemporary piece in mixed meter by a Syrian clarinetist and composer. https://itun.es/us/iHNdP?i=688814352

"Music Beyond Borders: Voices from the Seven," performance by the Seattle Symphony (www.seattlesymphony.org/beyond-borders/live-stream)

Zimbabwean Shona for Band (Learning Pathway #3)

Jones, C. (1992). *Making music: Musical instruments of Zimbabwe past and present.* Harare, ZW: Academic Books.

Locke, D. (2009). Africa/Ewe, Mande, Dagbamba, Shona, BaAka. In *Worlds of music: An introduction to the music of the world's peoples* (5th ed., pp. 83–143). Belmont, CA: Schirmer Cengage Learning.

Listening Episodes

"Chemtengure," Lora Chiorah-Dye & Sukutai, Smithsonian Folkways. www.folkways.si.edu/lora-chiorah-dye-and-sukutai/chemtengure/world/music/track/smithsonian

"Chemutengure," Dumisani Maraire & Ephat Mujuru, iTunes/The Orchard. https://itunes.apple.com/us/album/chemutengure/id279282211?i=279282355

"Chemutengure," Thomas Mapfumo, iTunes/Thomas Mapfumo. https://itunes.apple.com/us/album/chemutengure/id204323917?i=204323955

"Nyoka Musango," Thomas Mapfumo, iTunes/Thomas Mapfumo. https://itun.es/us/OxT86?i=988993395

7

Surmountable Challenges and Worthy Outcomes

"Check it out, Mr. Solie!" A 7th grader enthusiastically turns up the volume on her iPod. "I told my neighbor about the Chinese music you shared with us last week, and she told me about how she used to hear her parents sing that music when she was young. She shared these recordings with me, too—you've gotta check 'em out."

***

Mrs. Davis puts her baton away after a long, arduous rehearsal of the orchestra's festival music. Many students begin packing up their instruments, but a few continue playing on their own into the lunch break, trying to finally master the most difficult passages of the compositions. But also being skilled at "picking up" tunes by ear, many of the band members stray from the page and begin playing music that was shared with them earlier in the term. A percussionist begins to perform an asymmetrical 7/8 rhythm on his snare drum. Two tuba players sing atop their lungs "Jovanoooo," and several classmates respond "Jovankeeee!" Trombones and tenor saxophones join in, soon providing an accompaniment over which others improvise. Mrs. Davis smiles as a number of flute and clarinet players place their instruments on their chairs, clasp hands, and begin dancing around the room in pairs.

***

One-by-one, Mr. Gabriel thanks his students' parents for their support following what seemed by all accounts to be a very successful concert. The parents, in turn, express their gratitude for the extraordinary music they heard. "I loved your arrangement of 'Mi Gente,'" one parent says. "I felt I was there in San Juan!" Mr. Gabriel quietly demurred, feeling that the praise was exaggerated. The performance was satisfactory but was far from authentic, he thought. Just then, another parent—himself a Puerto

*Rican native—echoed the earlier sentiment he had overheard. "Yo tambien [me too],"
he said as he put his hand over his heart. "Y gracias, señor [and thank you, sir]."*

Just How Realistic (or How Radical) Is All of This?

Throughout this volume, we have outlined an approach to a musical education that
embraces music from the entire world as potential repertoire. Here, the term "repertoire" is used in a very general sense, recognizing that many of the world's musical
practices exist as living traditions, with melodies and tunes that may or may not be
found in notated fashion. Many cultures (although not all) have hallmark songs or
"pieces" of music that are readily distinguishable as belonging to a particular people
and to a specific musical tradition. More frequently, however, there are characteristic
instruments and timbres, particular forms and musical gestures, and accompanying
dances and other functional attributes of the music that are the most important musical features of a given culture. In the real music classrooms featured, and in the future
classrooms imagined within these pages, both the music itself and the context from
which it comes are examined, performed, and celebrated by students, not as discrete
units of study (i.e., "knowing about" versus "knowing how," or music appreciation
versus music performance) but as inseparable features of understanding, as fully as
possible, various human musical cultures.

And to what end, particularly for students in a band or orchestra class? A rich
array of musical treasures already awaits those who learn and teach the Western-
focused classical, contemporary, jazz and popular and repertoires that are common
in schools. An enormous diversity of styles certainly exists within each of those
genres, and each have a unique and special history to be learned as well. Mastering
a musical instrument, gaining fluency in music reading, and sharpening ensemble
performance skills are challenges that can assume the entirety of a student's musical
career, whether during the school years alone or throughout his or her lifetime.

But for as many rewards that exist within the Western musical canon, still more
await for those who venture beyond. Analogies to learning world languages might
be fruitful here in expanding the musical cultures that instrumental students can
experience and understand: Being able to identify the geographic origin of a particular
foreign language one hears might represent one very basic level of understanding,
and recognizing a few words or phrases in that language might be another. But being
able to speak the language and carry conversations in it—or further, visiting the
once-foreign land, making friends there, and fully immersing oneself in the culture—
represent new ways of thinking for the formerly monolingual student. He or she
learns ideas and concepts that are idiomatic to that new culture—ones which cannot
quite be translated to another language without losing something of its essence.

In short, learning a new musical culture can help one to become "bi-musical" (a
term coined by ethnomusicologist Mantle Hood in 1960), much as learning a new
language renders one as bilingual. Doing so affords us a new perspective on our
"native" musical practices, and on our very notion of musicianship itself. Perhaps,
bi-musicality is a stepping stone to multimusicality, knowing multiple musical cultures
by listening and comprehending their sound and cultural meanings, and expressing
multiple musical styles in performance and in new compositions and improvisations.

We recognize that virtually every element of music-making and musical organization—pitch and rhythm, timbre and color, notation and tradition, leaders and followers, uses and functions—are arranged in particular ways that reflect something of the people to whom the music belongs. More and more, it seems inadequate to know music of other cultures only through the filter of the media, or only as mere melodies, which are arranged and repackaged as published, ready-made works for a school band or orchestra. We become leery of musical exoticism. Yes, we are fascinated by the unique sounds of "far-away lands," but we do not want to keep this music at arm's length—because indeed, those whose music this is are now closer to us than ever before. Often, they are our neighbors, or our students' parents, or our students themselves. Or, they may still be a continent away, but are nevertheless people with whom we wish to form a sense of kinship through knowing their music and their culture more thoroughly. A global perspective demands that we go deeper into each music inasmuch as we can by listening to it in its native form, performing it on whatever instruments we have available to us, improvising and composing in a similar fashion, meeting with culture bearers, and so on.

Toward an Expansive Ensemble Culture

Admittedly, such efforts to globalize the secondary band or orchestra experience may seem radical at first. The accouterments of the school ensemble experience, evident throughout the rehearsal room, seem to speak to an already-existing school ensemble culture (Morrison, 2001) that would make no room for novel approaches: Concert tuxedos and marching band uniforms, a library of sheet music, *Funky Winkerbean* and *Tone Deaf Comics* posters, instruments and tuners calibrated to the Western tonal system, even the chairs and stands arranged in a semi-circle around the conductor—all of this suggests that school bands or orchestras ought to look and behave in a certain way. Even stronger factors mitigating against such curricular innovations are the voices and expectations from many stakeholders in the broader educational and music education communities. Parents imagine for their children a particular kind of ensemble experience, perhaps modeled on their own activities from years earlier. Administrators expect that concerts look and sound a certain way, in a manner that upholds the traditions and expectations of the school. Perhaps most powerful are district-wide and statewide contests and festivals in which ensembles are expected to participate, and the honors that accrue to the teachers and schools who succeed in them. The motivation to earn a "Superior" rating, or to earn an invitation to perform at a state or national festival of some kind, can seem overwhelming to many ensemble directors, and can preclude attention to other priorities. And, the gatekeepers and power structures within those organizations are usually quite rigorous in their expectations, demanding full-time adherence from participants. It can be difficult for a forward-thinking instrumental music teacher to find allies or even to remain motivated in these efforts.

But the globally minded teacher can take inspiration from recalling that so many of the very structures that exist today within the school band and orchestra realms are products of innovations and risk-taking from earlier generations. Individuals and organizations took advantage of opportunities that presented themselves, often taking just small steps in new directions—honoring the familiar while innovating in part. Granted, societal forces within and around education encouraged particular practices and sustained their growth; still, the development of what is now considered to be the norms of ensemble instruction came primarily from within the profession—from individual band and orchestra teachers. The very existence of bands, for instance, as a popular means of student musical involvement came in large part from former military bandsmen who saw teaching opportunities in a growing number of schools following the First World War. Band teachers and instrument manufacturers organized interscholastic tournaments and contests, which helped standardize instrumentation for school ensembles. William Revelli's extraordinary success as a small-town band director in Hobart, Indiana, and later as the chair of the Wind Instrument Department at the University of Michigan, inspired generations of future instrumental music programs and their teachers. Later, the scholastic wind ensemble (or "orchestral winds") tradition, with limited or flexible instrumentation and with a pursuit of original compositions written expressly for that medium, was initiated at the Eastman School of Music by Frederick Fennell, and was promulgated at the high school level by Frank Battisti in Ithaca, New York. Similar strides were also made by leaders of school orchestras: A successful performance by Joseph Maddy's Richmond (Indiana) High School Orchestra at a national school administrators' conference in 1922 led to a subsequent performance in 1927 of the National High School Orchestra, also led by Maddy, which in turn inspired superintendents to bring music programs to their school districts all over the country. With ensembles firmly established in American schools by the mid-20th century, music teachers in selected schools welcomed composers in their rehearsal rooms as part of the Ford Foundation's "Young Composers Project," beginning in 1959, to help modernize the repertoire of school band and orchestra (and choral) ensembles; in 1963, this became the Contemporary Music Project, under the auspices of the Music Educators National Conference (MENC, now NAfME). The Comprehensive Musicianship movement followed in the 1970s, which in turn arguably laid the foundation for the National Standards for Arts Education of 1994 (and, more recently, the National Core Arts Standards of 2014)—documents which even now guide and inform music curricula in both K–12 and higher education.[1]

Such events show that music programs in schools are not static entities, and that the very structure and content of seemingly tradition-laden ensembles can indeed be reshaped and moved in new directions, all while still serving the ever-present socialization needs of the young people who join school bands and orchestras, and the functional needs of school communities who still look to these ensembles to perform at various events. Being the large entities that they are, with heavy investments in Western-specified instruments and literature, bands and orchestras might not be as intrinsically nimble and responsive to calls for cultural inclusivity as are other genres of school music. General music programs seem to have been taken the forefront in this regard: A half-century ago, just a year after the Tanglewood Symposium whereby MENC called for greater representation of "non-Western musics" in school curricula, Barbara Reeder Lundquist led a group of 300 junior high school musicians in a concert of African drumming and song at the 1968 MENC national in-service conference in Seattle. Since then, many best-selling general music texts for use in elementary school classrooms have been replete with songs gathered from around the world and presented with an ever-keener sense of cultural context. Choirs, too, are somewhat naturally given to exploring the music of various cultures (notwithstanding concerns of authenticity, comparable to those instrumental programs face), with foreign pronunciations often being the most salient challenge for young choristers. Nowadays, it is not uncommon for the world-minded school choir teacher to select a concert program which features songs in a half-dozen or more different languages. With due regard to the inherent challenges for instrumental music programs, it would seem "high time" for band and orchestra teachers to follow suit by exploring the possibilities through which the broadest possible spectrum of the world's musical cultures can be meaningfully experienced by their students.

The Bigger Picture: Where to Begin?

The manner in which each teacher might best design and implement a World Music Pedagogy program will inevitably be unique to their own school and district and will certainly be informed by individual strengths and interests. Opportunities that might exist today could be different in future years, particularly as the demographics of a given community change over time. Some teachers might find it safest to pick and choose from among the strategies and ideas offered in this volume, seeing what works best at first and then expanding to other activities in a more-or-less organic fashion. Still, the tide of the "status quo" in the world of instrumental music instruction is very strong, and tepid WMP efforts might be easily overwhelmed by traditional expectations for school ensembles.

Thus, for most programs, it is probably best for teachers to plan for a deliberate and systematic approach to World Music Pedagogy. Per the spirit we have proffered, we advise activities that are woven throughout the school year, rather than ones that are relegated to a token "multicultural" season (or single session). As indicated in Chapters 1 and 2 (and elsewhere), the choice of which particular cultures to study at first may be best informed by the cultures that are already represented in the school community, but are not yet reflected in the instrumental music program. Or, a teacher may elect to begin with another musical culture, perhaps drawn solely from personal interest and/or from the stated interests of his or her students. Regardless of the starting point, the impetus of these pursuits is not defined by locality, but rather by a desire to help students understand music as a global phenomenon with a pan-human palette of expressive possibilities, with each musical activity—whether listening, performing, or creating—serving as a gateway to cultural understanding.

But such opportunities notwithstanding, a new teacher in (for example) a mid-sized middle school with an already-established instrumental music program might elect to present one "other" musical culture, or genre, or single selection each month, chosen primarily as listening material and pursued alongside whatever regular rehearsal activities that would normally take place. Attentive and/or Engaged Listening activities could comprise a regular part of class instruction, and each given culture could be revisited in future years in a somewhat "spiral" format, affording students both a breadth of musical experiences from throughout the world and a certain depth of familiarity of the music from each of them. Alternatively, a more in-depth approach (and one which might be more idiomatic to the natural "rhythms" of the life of a school ensemble program) would be to select a single "other" culture for each concert cycle. Teachers might begin with already-published ensemble literature that incorporates melodies, sounds, or themes from a given culture, then plan to use that as a springboard to explore a wide variety of source material. After having listened to recordings of those melodies in more authentic form (and to other music from that same place-of-origin), and after having engaged with that musical culture in a myriad of other ways, students can return to the published literature with a richer understanding of that music and with a thirst for future experiences that more closely approximate the sounds and the lives of the people who made it. Concerts, otherwise presented as usual, could be supplemented with features that showcase students' unique cultural experiences, ranging from brief explanations from the stage or student-written program notes, to special performances of the culture's music offered in more of an "unarranged" fashion.

Suitable next steps for such a program could also take several forms, still while building upon the basic elements of listening and performing. "Visits in" and "visits out" should be arranged—that is, opportunities for culture bearers (drawn from the local community, where possible) to come to the school and share their music, along with opportunities for students to travel to places where a given musical tradition is practiced and sustained, so that they can witness such music-making in in an authentic local context. All of this can be done as separate class activities, or in conjunction with ensemble literature being prepared for performance. As resources allow, a teacher may seek to add a new, culturally specific ensemble as an elective option among the school's instrumental music offerings, perhaps even for academic credit. Purchasing and/or otherwise acquiring suitable instruments may be challenging, but this could be facilitated by building partnerships with cultural organizations in the community.

Teaching, Alone and With Others

A longer-term goal might be to influence fellow music teachers in the school district towards crafting a district-wide World Music Pedagogy curriculum. Doing so necessitates discussion from all parties involved and will inevitably require some give and take in a manner that balances the autonomy of each individual teacher's school music program with the demands of a shared vision for the community. Having school and district administrative personnel "on board" with the need for culturally responsive pedagogy and a globally inclusive curriculum certainly helps, particularly if such support is actualized in tangible form, such as by providing for dedicated in-service days for curriculum development or through inviting like-minded music teachers to serve on hiring committees. Because school music curricula are most often imparted through programs and not through disparate classes—that is, because students usually have the same music teacher throughout their elementary school years, and then have the same instrumental or vocal music teacher throughout their early secondary school years, in a multi-year enrollment—music teachers who coordinate their efforts have the opportunity to craft particularly powerful experiences for their students. Moreover, given that music is considered a "special" subject matter (with only one music teacher per building, in many cases), music teachers are seen as the sole music experts for a school or district and are often given more curricular autonomy than are grade level teachers or teachers of other subject matters. Music teachers who wish to capitalize on the advantages of a coordinated curriculum would do well to take advantage of this opportunity.

Students who have already had deep and varied encounters with music of many cultures through a WMP-inspired or multiculturally oriented elementary music program will be well-equipped to build upon these experiences as they enter secondary school instrumental programs. Such prior learning may have taken the form of singing and dancing in primarily one "other" musical tradition, in which case the secondary program can build upon this by expanding the listening opportunities within that tradition, and by offering new composing, improvising, and performing experiences, now with instruments. Perhaps even better (and more common) is when students come from elementary school programs that afforded them experiences from many different cultures. To them, no music is entirely "foreign," and the attitudes that they have developed since the very beginning of their formal musical education render them particularly receptive to new musical engagements. In these cases, the secondary school music teacher may be able to capitalize on their already-suitable dispositions when selecting new listening activities, and may be able to take greater advantage of their more extensive knowledge base and their emerging intellectual maturity. Instrumental performance opportunities might now be drawn from several different cultures, or might focus more deeply on a limited number of selected musical traditions.

Teachers in a "WMP district" ought also to have a vision of the student who completes their K–12 school experience in their music program—a vision of the graduate at graduation, or the "grad at grad." Doing so does not come naturally: Being ensemble leaders, music teachers are more inclined to craft a vision of just what our own *programs* look like, all the while remaining comfortable that students will pick and choose what they wish from among what we offer, and that they will decide for themselves their level of involvement. Fair enough; given that music study is usually an entirely elective experience for students (beyond a compulsory credit or two of "fine arts" usually required for graduation), envisioning programs alone may seem most prudent. It is also true that the National Core Arts Standards (and by extension, any state or district that have modeled their own standards accordingly) offers its own vision of sorts. But the NCAS documents are arguably curriculum-free and would thus allow for any number of musical activities—culturally inclusive or otherwise—to qualify as evidence of having "achieved the standards."

With intercultural competencies in mind, WMP teachers will wish to be more specific regarding their musical expectations for students, yet also maintain an eye for a diversity of types and levels of involvement. Such an approach necessitates allowing for a certain degree of student freedom, and correspondingly, it demands that teachers and programs offer a breadth of viable opportunities for students to explore their own musical interests. Some young musicians may elect to play music of two (or more) different cultures on their primary instrument (say, a trumpet player who can play both classical literature and mariachi, both with fluency), and others may strive to play both a Western instrument (such as a violin) and a broadly similar non-Western instrument—say, a *kamancheh* (Persian [Iranian] bowed instrument)—in idiomatic fashion. Still others may engage in typical band and orchestra activities as per usual, while also delving deeply into other music of other cultures via reading, listening, visiting, improvising, and/or composing. The authors steer clear of advocating a particular set of fully realized WMP expectations for students—such matters are ideally decided by local educators who know their own communities best—except to say that at the heart of any such curricular guidelines is an expansive sense of inclusivity regarding what it means to be musically educated.

Building and Rebuilding in Communities Large and Small

Particular challenges and opportunities for WMP will be present in every different setting, reflecting the people and communities in which they are situated, and the innovation-minded teacher will need to adapt his or her own goals and objectives for a culturally inclusive music program accordingly, in a manner suitable for their local community. Rural districts, for example, may only have a single music teacher for all its students, and may have limited funds for the purchase of instruments (much less a budget for students to be able make a "visit out" to a cultural center). Long-time residents who may have seen the area population slowly dissipate over the years may pine for the return of a strong, small town marching band as the pride of its community, and they may not at first see the value of devoting scarce resources to having their children learning "foreign" musical cultures. Teachers must be always savvy in these situations and must be willing to build programs not just around ideas, but rather around relationships with students, parents, teachers, and townspeople. "Solo" music teachers can capitalize on their autonomy in crafting a K–12 curriculum, and on being the primary spokesperson for music programs in their community. (If immigrant communities are nearby, a music teacher would be wise to develop relationships there as much as possible—expressing curiosity about their music, and seeking performing and listening opportunities, accordingly.)

Alternatively, a new teacher hired as an assistant band or orchestra director in a very large school with a well-established instrumental music program will encounter a different set of challenges. There may likely already exist particular expectations for achievement, and certain markers for success (e.g., "superior" contest ratings, "sweepstakes" at festival) may seem to leave little room for curricular innovations. As is always the case when hired as a new colleague (and especially when at the beginning a teaching career), one must tread professional relationships carefully, being mindful of others whose tenure and authority in curricular matters may take precedence, and always remaining respectful of the ways of "musical being" that has been honed and developed in a particular school's music program. Modest WMP efforts, pursued regularly and with good will, may yield greater results over the long term than initiatives to overhaul a well-established curriculum. One should also not underestimate one's own power to influence others through informal, casual interactions—say, by expressing enthusiasm for a particular *Smithsonian Folkways* recording, or by practicing one's own skill at music-making in another tradition. Consistently modeling attitudes (and the corresponding behaviors) of inclusion and curiosity can serve as an extremely strong model for both students and colleagues alike.

Other circumstances will present any number of possible scenarios for WMP in an instrumental music program. A teacher opening a brand-new school as part of its inaugural faculty may have a special opportunity to define the musical expectations for the school community. The purchasing of instruments as part of the initial capital outlay (say, a full set of mariachi instruments or steel drums, in addition to school-owned tubas, string basses, etc.), and possibly even the designing of rehearsal and performance spaces, could prepare the students for success in multiple musical cultures, and could serve as a strong signal to others regarding the inclusiveness of the music curriculum. Or, in another setting, a new teacher hired to rehabilitate a music program in need of rebuilding can use the opportunity to redefine the terms of success, both for individuals and for ensembles. If other music programs in the district or in the area are already perceived to be more competitive in some fashion (say, on the marching field or on the concert stage), new WMP ensembles could become a mark of distinction for the school and could become a much-needed point of pride for teachers and parents alike. Still another situation might be a school—maybe in an urban setting— which might already have a strong jazz program, or an established popular music pedagogy program, perhaps in addition to traditionally configured school band and orchestra ensembles. Here, WMP efforts could represent a move towards "tri-musicality" (i.e., traditional school ensembles *and* jazz or popular music *and* robust ensemble experiences in still another musical culture) and even greater musical diversity for the school—not only in the independent musical pursuits of individual students, but as a valued part of the established teaching program of the music faculty.

Thinking Globally, Acting Locally

Even more visionary WMP efforts include ones aimed at challenging the very scope and culture of school music programs throughout the profession, starting at the local level. Many interscholastic structures (e.g., regional honor bands, regional band festivals, All-State bands and orchestras, solo and ensemble competitions) have long provided incentives for students to excel at particular kinds of music-making within Western art music genres, broadly speaking. These have, in turn, also served to inform teachers, administrators, and parents regarding what types of music are valued, and which ones will be rewarded when performed well. Public recognition is indeed a powerful motivator for nearly everyone within a school community, and the professional accolades that accrue to the band or orchestra teacher for success within defined boundaries are often especially demanding of our attention. Eschewing such norms, even partially, is difficult when so many colleagues and mentors within the school music profession expect new teachers to join in pursuit of a particular type of "standard of excellence."

Still, it is right for the conscientious, broad-minded, ambitious school music teacher to question these structures (or "deconstruct" them, as said in academic jargon), and to imagine and even create new ones (thus perhaps "disrupting" common band and orchestra practices, to coin a term from the business world). *Why not* insist upon a new category of performance at a regional or state solo and ensemble festival, so as to allow a skilled *guqin* (Chinese string instrument) player, or a *conjunto* accordionist, a *krar* (Ethiopian lyre), or an accomplished gamelan orchestra to share in the accolades that would otherwise be reserved to their Western art music-playing classmates? *Why not* bring to the next district band or orchestra festival a teacher-and-student-made arrangement of, say, "Taqsim Maqam Lami" (with whatever adjustments made for suitable ensemble performance) as a demonstration of the kinds of musical learnings that can happen in an instrumental music program? Following suit, it would seem entirely fitting (if not morally imperative) to ask one's representatives in the state music educators association why the strong mariachi programs already flourishing in some schools are not represented as featured ensembles at the annual or bi-annual conference.[2] Many similar projects could be attempted as well, hopefully pursued with a spirit of cooperation rather than subversion. Examples include forming one's own interscholastic "WMP festival," or (in cases where such resources permit) pursuing ensemble travel opportunities to locations *other* than the high-profile national or international "destination" locations often encouraged by various tour companies, opting instead for unmediated experiences that immerse students in native cultures and their music-making practices, with ample opportunities for cultural exchanges between the student musicians and those whom they are visiting.

Teacher Feature: Mario Yuzo Nieto on Teaching Music from West Africa

Mario Yuzo Nieto, Music Teacher at the Highline Academy in Denver, CO

He specializes in music from Guinea, Mali, Burkina Faso, Cote d'Ivoire, Senegal, and Ghana. He previously taught at the SOAR Charter School, also in Denver, and has taught private percussion, guitar, piano, and saxophone lessons to middle school and high school students.

Born in Denver and a former "band kid" from East High School, Nieto first came to learn other musical traditions through his performance experiences with jazz, ska, and punk. He grew up listening to music by popular artists such as Linda Ronstadt and Paul Simon, who themselves both explored music of other cultures in their recordings. Later, inspired by a West African dance class he took in college, Nieto traveled to Guinea to learn more about music of the Kissi, Fula, and Mandinka peoples.

Q: How do you generally go about teaching a complex piece of music from another culture to your secondary school instrumental music students?
A: I'll teach the drumming component orally, in a somewhat Orff-like approach, using words to approximate the rhythms. Then I'll teach the lyrics in the specific language, and I'll teach the meaning of the lyrics and the meaning of the song as a whole. Finally,

I'll teach the dance, which I think is important: In a lot of cultures, the word for "dance" is the same as the word for "music"; they're not construed as separate things. Through this approach I've been able to get kids as young as second grade to play complex polyrhythmic songs, like "Djaa," quite successfully.

In terms of culturally responsive pedagogy, one practice that I've been very proud of doing—and I think this can be manifested in a lot of different ways—is that I try to identify the cultures of the students who are in my class, and I make sure they are represented in my listening units. This requires me to be willing to deal with the unknown: If I am not familiar with one of those cultures, I try to talk to families about music they enjoy and music they value, both traditional and modern. Then, I will focus on one type of music at a time in my class, perhaps starting with traditional ranchero music from Mexico, then moving to something more modern. It's phenomenal to see the students' responses. I have this Bosnian student, and to see her face when that music got played, and her classmates' reactions, too . . . to see them really engaging with that music was an extremely powerful experience for everyone.

Then, after having listened to music from around the world (including the music from Guinea and Mali that I share with them), they get to choose as a class which selection they most enjoyed—this gives them a sense of ownership—and then we rehearse and perform that piece.

Q: Do you generally teach the music first, and then integrate an understanding of its cultural context, or the reverse? Or do you approach this simultaneously?
A: A little bit of both, and it also depends on the developmental age of the students. For my youngest students, I will generally focus more exclusively on the music itself. For older students, I might offer a little bit of cultural background on a piece when I first introduce it, but then I will quickly turn to learning the rhythms. I will offer more context about the piece—its meaning, its usage—as we continue to rehearse it, especially as we add vocals and dancing. Finally, as we near our performance, I will have the students "reconstruct" all those meanings I have given them. This prepares them to serve as "announcers" who will explain the music to the audience.

Q: How can an instrumental music teacher best learn to bring music of other cultures to their school bands or orchestras?
A: First, try to find ways to engage your instrument with music of even just one other culture, and really envelop yourself in it. Strive for extremely acute, active listening, and really try to pinpoint the fine details of how they play, in terms of techniques and scales and modes. Be patient and try to "play the tradition" as best you can. Then, as an educator, I think the best thing to do is to meet with families and talk to people of this culture—ideally with musicians, but really with anyone who can provide insight into what's important and meaningful to them. You might make mistakes when teaching the music, but you can go to others for help. The process of teaching actually helps you gain cultural and musical understanding.

Also, I feel that representing both traditional and contemporary music is important, because young people can really engage with those cultures when they can make a connection to something contemporary. So, if I'm presenting Korean music, I'm bringing out "Gangnam Style" in addition to Gugak. Later, I might play some Japanese ska-punk and then teach some Taiko rhythms.

Q: In your teaching, are there elements of wanting to imbue in your students a sense of respect for various world perspectives, and a sense of being open to new experiences? Are there larger, attitudinal qualities that underlie your work?
A: One of the thing that always comes of this is students developing a higher level of empathy for other cultures and for each other. As a person of color myself, I remember that as a student, I really didn't "connect" with my education, especially in subjects like history and social studies (at least until I was in college, when I first encountered ethnic studies). Now, a big driving force in my teaching is seeing the narrative of people who have a shared experience of oppression represented as a central part of my music curriculum. This engages kids of all backgrounds in a way that no other experience can match—they can "see themselves" in this music.

Pursued diligently, these efforts may indeed capture the attention of numerous other instrumental teachers, and these perspectives and practices may spread widely such that the very notion of what it means to have experienced an instrumental music education program in a secondary school will broaden so as to include a broad spectrum of musical experiences drawn from throughout the world. As described throughout this book, this is already seen in many nascent and flourishing secondary school programs, scattered throughout the United States and beyond, with ensembles of every type and stripe making all sorts of music. The teachers leading these groups often freely traverse among mainstream school music offerings and other culturally specific musical practices, even to the point that the other traditions are no longer seen as "alternative" modes of music-making, but rather as equal experiences among an ever-increasing range of viable options for students' deep musical involvement.[3]

A movement is afoot—one which will come to fruition by the work of those teachers and future teachers reading this volume, and by the students whose lives they affect by the music and experiences that are afforded to them. Ironically, school instrumental music programs in the early-to-mid-21st century could be fashioned and refashioned through efforts somewhat similar to those pursued by "giant" composers of Western music a century earlier: Bartók, Grainger, Vaughan Williams, and others, all voraciously curious about the native music of their own respective peoples (and in some cases of neighboring nations as well), went "to the field" to collect folk songs and traditional instrumental tunes, then brought them back to incorporate what they heard as source material for their own compositions. Since then, generations of musicians and music listeners have admired and lionized their work. Relatively few, however, have *imitated* their efforts per se. Yet perhaps the next generation of students will pursue music of "the other" with similar inquisitiveness, not for purposes of appropriation, but rather to honor and understand these cultures, and to delight in the sonic wonders that a truly global musical education provides.

Notes

1   This is a necessarily brief and selective overview of many events in the history of music programs in America. For more, see Battisti (2002), Cipolla and Hunsberger (1994), Humphreys (1994), and Mark and Gary (2007), from which information in this paragraph was drawn.

2 Admittedly, some such groups may pursue similar recognition via other events that are unaffiliated with regional- or state-level interscholastic organizations. This seems to be changing. For example, as of this writing, the University Interscholastic League (UIL) in Texas is now piloting its State Mariachi Festival. Previously, similar events had been hosted locally in communities throughout south Texas.
3 Higher education has taken notice, too, with an expanded variety of culturally diverse programs in both academic and applied music studies, as seen in the proliferation of bluegrass programs in several colleges and universities, and in the revisions of the music concentration curriculum at Harvard and the music history sequence at Vanderbilt.

References

Battisti, F. L. (2002). *The winds of change: The evolution of the contemporary American wind band/ensemble and its conductor*. Galesville, MD: Meredith Music Publications.

Cipolla, F. J., & Hunsberger, D. (Eds.). (1994). *The wind ensemble and its repertoire: Essays on the fortieth anniversary of the Eastman Wind Ensemble*. Rochester, NY: University of Rochester Press.

Hood, M. (1960). The challenge of "bi-musicality". *Ethnomusicology, 4*(2), 55–59. doi:10.2307/924263

Humphreys, J. T. (1994). Instrumental music in American education: In service of many masters. *Journal of Band Research, 30*(2), 39–70.

Mark, M. L., & Gary, C. L. (2007). *A history of American music education* (3rd ed.). Lanham, MD: Rowman & Littlefield Education.

Morrison, S. J. (2001). The school ensemble: A culture of our own. *Music Educators Journal, 88*(2), 24–28. doi:10.2307/3399738.

Appendix 1
Learning Pathways

The following three Learning Pathways represent a beginning-to-end manifestation of the five dimensions of the World Music Pedagogy approach. Together, they constitute the pedagogical episodes on three musical works that were featured across the chapters and are conveniently located here so that the flow between dimensions can be recognized, and one continuing pathway of learning the music and its cultural purposes can be clearly delineated. These progressive WMP episodes may be parceled out over many class sessions, repeated in part, or varied and extended in order that students can orient themselves to the nuances of new musical expressions. Alternatively, they can be economically pressed into a single session, as necessary. The intent of the Learning Pathways is to map how teaching and learning proceeds over the course of the World Music Pedagogy, where listening, participatory musicking, performance, creating, and integrating experiences open students to the many splendors of a musical culture.

Learning Pathway #1

Puerto Rican Salsa: "Mi Gente" by Héctor Lavoe

Attentive Listening

Specific Use: Instrumental ensembles (e.g., band, orchestra, jazz); Grades 4–12

Materials:

- "Mi Gente," Héctor Lavoe (Puerto Rico/Caribbean)

Procedure:

1. Ask in advance: "Where is this from, and how can you tell?"

   This is a good "standard" opening question to initiate nearly any Attentive Listening experience. For "Mi Gente," many students will likely recognize the Spanish language, and/or they may identify the rhythm section of the ensemble as playing Caribbean music of some kind.

2. Play track (beginning to about 0:30, at the beginning of the first verse).

3. Ask, "What 'Western' components are there here? And, what is distinctly Afro-Caribbean?"

   Here, we are starting with what's "familiar," before proceeding to what's "different." The reverse order could be employed as well. The two questions could be asked and answered simultaneously, or in sequence. Western components include most instruments (piano, bass, brass, etc.), the instrumentation (salsa band which is derivative of jazz bands), and the general tonalities (note the pedal dominant throughout the introduction); Afro-Caribbean components include percussion instruments such as bongos, congas, and timbales. *Güiro* and especially claves are common in this style, but are not heard on this recording. (The clave rhythm is implied and felt by the players, even if not heard.)

4. Play track (same segment).

5. Ask, "What is adventuresome about this music? More precisely, what grabs your attention, what 'sticks out'? What seems to 'break the rules'?" Note the non-chord tone in the piano, and the characteristically "edgier" brass.

6. Play track.

7. Ask, "What do you think the soloist (Héctor Lavoe) is shouting at the very beginning of the tune?" The teacher can ask non-Spanish speaking students to listen carefully to the tone of the exclamation, and to the cackle-like laughter. Like much of Salsa music, the singer is asserting himself and expressing his own pride and masculinity: "¡Cuidado que por ahí vienen los anormales!" [Roughly, "Watch out . . . here comes a crazy person!"]

Then, for added imagery, in a mix of Spanish and English "y con a straight-jacket!" ["And with a straightjacket!"] This "sets up" the main text of the song. "Oigan, mi gente, lo más grande este mundo, siempre me hacentir un orgullo profundo." ["Listen, my people, the greatest of this world, I always feel a deep pride."]

Engaged Listening

Materials:

- "Mi Gente" by Héctor Lavoe; students' instruments
- Optional: claves, cowbell, conga (or substitutes)

Procedure, "Qué cante mi gente" response:

1. "Listen for the repeated response to Héctor Lavoe's solo (*coro*), which repeats every four beats. Hum this response every time you hear it."

2. Play track, approximately 1:14–2:08.

3. "The words are 'qué cante mi gente.'" [display the words on a whiteboard]. Let's sing this response every time you hear it."

4. Play track.

5. "The melody you hear starts on the pitch *fa* [concert A-flat], with an upbeat on *low sol* [concert B-flat]. Find the first two pitches, and then try to figure out the rest of the response on your instrument." *(Note: The notation can be seen in Figure 3.1. However, it is a powerful exercise for students to attempt to work out the melody by ear, even if Puerto Rican salsa is now a largely notation-based tradition in practice.)*

6. Allow students to find this melodic phrase on their instruments, independently or in small groups.

7. "Now I will play the recording, and you should play this response on your instrument every time you hear it."

8. Play track and repeat as necessary.

9. *If students are ready for an additional challenge:* "As you can hear, the singers are performing this response in harmony. If you can, try to listen to one of the harmonic lines, which are sung in mostly parallel harmony with the melody." *Teachers might need to provide the starting pitches for each of the inner voices from top to bottom: re [concert F], ti [concert D], and la [concert C].*

10. Play track and repeat as necessary.

11. "Now, let's try to sing one of the inner voices with the words". *The teacher may need to simultaneously play the desired inner voice on a piano to reinforce the pitches. With parallel harmonies such as this, it can be difficult to hear the movement of each line, and a piano can be a useful tool for bringing out these voices.*

12. Play track and repeat as necessary.

13. Repeat steps 6–8 so that students can place each part on their instruments (independently or in groups).

14. *After each of the inner voices have been isolated, have the students put all four voices together. The teacher may choose to assign each part to an instrumental section, or students may be given the opportunity to choose their desired part on their own.*

15. Play track and repeat as necessary.

Figure 3.1 "Que cante mi gente" response in harmony

Enactive Listening

Materials:

- "Mi Gente" by Héctor Lavoe; students' instruments
- Optional: claves, cowbell, conga (or substitutes)

Procedure:

1. "While the [choose instrument] section continues to perform the "que cante mi gente" response, everyone else should perform the *montuno* part." [Each of these layered components (i.e., montuno, bassline, clave) should be approached through their own Engaged Listening activities like the exercise outlined previously.]

2. Play track, starting at 1:14 (until about 2:08, or as necessary).

3. "Let's do that again, and this time let's perform the bassline all together."

4. Play track.

5. "Now let's add in the percussion, one by one." *Layer in each of the percussion parts: congas, clave, and cowbell.*

6. Play track.

7. "Now let's put it all together to perform the *coro* section in its entirety: the response, the *montuno*, the bassline, and the percussion. At some point, I will fade the recording out. Please continue playing even after the music has been turned off."

8. Play track and repeat, eventually fading out the recording while students are performing.

Creating World Music

Materials:

- "Mi Gente" by Héctor Lavoe; students' instruments
- Optional: claves, conga(s), cowbell, *güiro*, timbales

Procedure:

Rhythmic Improvisation

1. Ask students to begin by clapping the clave pattern (Figure 5.1a) and stepping to the steady beat.

2. As the class establishes a groove through the clave, ask them to break into small groups (4–5 or full instrumental sections, depending on ensemble size).

3. Encourage students to improvise around the clave groove either (1) solo, with all others maintaining the clave, or (2) collectively, with at least one maintaining the clave.

4. Rotating in small groups, provide an opportunity for each group to practice improvising over the clave using instruments (e.g., claves, congas, cowbell, *güiro*)

Melodic Improvisation

1. Bring students' attention to the I-V chord structure of the song. Have students indicate that they hear the chord changes by pointing either one finger (I chord) or five fingers (V chord). *Note: The chord change oscillates every two measures.*

2. Beginner students may experiment with improvising over the major scale of the key (E-flat concert); More advanced students may pay attention to the chord changes, playing an E-flat major scale over the I chord, and a B-flat mixolydian scale over the V chord.

3. For advanced students: Direct students to listen to the brief trumpet solo (1:18–1:23) as well as Lavoe's improvised singing. Encourage them to first find certain phrases that stand out to them, then locate the notes on their instruments, and finally incorporate them into their improvisations.

4. Extension: Direct students to listen to other salsa songs that might feature their instrument soloing and encourage them to find salient phrases to learn for their own instrument to supplement their improvisations.

Arranging

1. As a class, have students create a "road map" arrangement of "La Gente": How will they begin? Will some sing the melody, or will it be fully instrumental? What instrument(s) will play the *montuno*? Which *moñas* will accompany solos? How will they be layered? How will the arrangement end? Write or project this road map on the board for all to see.

2. Once practiced as a class, have students create their own individual arrangements. Choose a few to perform, and have students choose their favorite arrangement.

Composing

1. If possible, have students transcribe the *moñas* in "La Gente."

2. Have students write their own *moña*, either by ear or by writing it down.

3. Have students teach their *moñas* to the class by ear.

4. Extension: Have the class select their favorite *moñas* and compose new melodies above them.

Integrating World Music

Materials:

- "Mi Gente," classroom audio/video technology

Musical Beginnings

- This piece was composed by Johnny Pacheco, the band leader of Héctor Lavoe's group. He was also a producer at Fania Records, a label that specialized in promoting salsa music.

Musical Continuities

- This song is performed worldwide in spaces where members of the Latino diaspora are located. Depending on the region, the song can be arranged in a variety of styles including *eggaetón*, *cumbia*, and even classical guitar.
- This song is considered part of the standard repertoire of salsa music and is taught and learned in a variety of formal, informal, and nonformal education settings.
- Because of its strong link to a specific identity, individuals who perform this song, but do not identify with being part of the Puerto Rican diaspora often change the *coro* (chorus) from "que canta *mi* gente" (let my people sing) to "que canten *su* gente" (let his people sing).

Musical Meanings

- This song is considered to be the unofficial "Nuyorican" national anthem. The term "Nuyorican," a combination of New York and Puerto Rican, refers to individuals of the Puerto Rican diaspora who have settled in New York and reflects Lavoe's own background of having been born in the Puerto Rican city of Ponce.
- Héctor Lavoe's vocal delivery has been considered a marker of identity because it is often shaded with the style of a *pregonero* (singer) in *jíbaro* music.

Learning Pathway #2

Contemporary Syrian Music:
"Tulina's Carmona" by Kinan Azmeh

Attentive Listening

Specific Use: Instrumental ensembles (e.g., band, orchestra, jazz); Grades 4–12

Materials:

- "Tulina's Carmona," Kinan Azmeh (Syria)

Procedure:

The teacher will need to gauge the students' ability to entertain divergent questions while remaining focused on the listening tasks. At times, more direct, convergent questioning may be prudent.

1. Ask in advance: "What kind of music is this?" (Or: "What part of the world is this music from? Is this traditional or modern music?")
2. Play track (beginning to 0:35; first three statements of melody).
3. Play track again, still temporarily withholding the identity of performers. *(Not disclosing the performers' names forces a more direct, focused, and imaginative listening of the music itself, unbiased by cues or clues.)*
4. Encourage students to imagine possible styles and places-of-origin. Possible answers might include jazz, Arabic music, fusion; modern music with traditional flavors. Klezmer is proximous (i.e., not accurate as a place-of-origin for this music, but geographically nearby and possibly related and/or influential on this style).
5. Play track again (same segment).
6. Ask, "What cultural influences do you hear? What cues from the music suggest those cultures?" *Encourage students to use musical vocabulary. Percussion, syncopation, and instrumental texture (clarinet with rhythm section) suggest jazz; modal scalar passages suggest Arabic music; clarinet colorings (e.g., growl, bended notes) might suggest klezmer; guitar stylings may suggest Spanish influences.*
7. Ask, "What aspects of their performance are virtuosic?" Obvious answers include "fast notes" (or more precisely, accurate execution of rapid passages).
8. Play track again and repeatedly.
9. Encourage students to hear both individual and ensemble characteristics. For both percussion and clarinet especially, note the wide range of instrumental colors, and the rapid and dramatic changes in dynamics for expressive effect. Note the precision in the harmonized lines between clarinet and guitar.

10. Discuss and ask: "The clarinet soloist is the composer of the piece and the leader of this group; his name is Kinan Azmeh. How is his clarinet playing similar to and different than the kind of playing our clarinet players normally do?" Similarities include precise intonation, breath support and tonal control; differences may include pitch bending, tonal colors, stop-tongue articulation (which is more common in jazz stylings).

Engaged Listening

Materials:

- "Tulina's Carmona," by Kinan Azmeh; students' instruments

Procedure, rhythmic structure:

1. "Can you tap the beat along with the recording?"
2. Play track (0:00–0:59; melody begins at 0:11).
3. "Are all of the beats even, or do some appear to be longer than others?"
4. Play track. (Answer: The third beat is longer than the others; i.e., *short-short-long*)
5. Place this pattern on the board and have students chant "one-two, one-two, one-two-three" with the music to feel the pattern. "What time signature might we call this?" (Answer: 7/8)
6. Play track and repeat as necessary.
7. "Does the 7/8 pattern hold throughout the entire melody, or does it seem to change? If you hear it change, can you raise your hand whenever you hear it do so?"
8. Play track and observe students' responses
9. Write the changes in time signature on the board for students to see which measures are 7/8, which are 9/8 or 13/8, and which are 2/4. "Now let's clap and say the rhythmic pattern of the melody" along with the recording:

   ‖: 1–2, 1–2, 1–2–3 | 1–2, 1–2, 1–2, 1–2–3 | 1 + 2 + |
   | 1–2, 1–2, 1–2–3 | 1–2, 1–2, 1–2, 1–2–3 | 1 + 2 + |
   | 1–2, 1–2, 1–2–3 | 1–2, 1–2, 1–2–3 | 1–2, 1–2, 1–2–3 |
   | 1–2, 1–2, 1–2, 1–2, 1–2, 1–2–3 :‖

10. Play track; repeat as necessary.

Procedure, melody:

11. "Does it sound like the opening of the melody ascends by steps or skips? While you're thinking about it, can you sing along with the melody on a neutral syllable?"

12. Play track. (Answer: they ascend by step).
13. "The melody is written in concert a-minor. On your instruments, see if you can find at least the first six pitches of the melody (which repeats in the fourth and fifth measure) on your instruments." *Allow students adequate time to find these notes, reminding them that they are in fact ascending by skip. When students are able to play it, ask them to help a neighbor if he or she is struggling.*
14. Play track; allow students to play quietly along with recording to check their pitches.
15. Repeat steps 3–4 for each part of the melody until they are able to play the melody in its entirety.

Enactive Listening

Materials:

- "Tulina's Carmona," by Kinan Azmeh; students' instruments

Procedure:

1. "What sorts of expressive characteristics is Kinan Azmeh giving to the melody when he plays it on the clarinet?"
2. Play track. (Answer: He sometimes "falls" quickly off of the top note of the melody; he "growls" at the end of the second repetition of the melody.)
3. "Let's try to sing the melody along with the recording, trying to perform all of the falls and growls that Kinan Azmeh performs.
4. Play track and repeat as necessary.
5. "Now let's try to add these expressive techniques and ornamentations to our performance on our instruments."
6. Play track and repeat as necessary. Continually compare students' performances to the recording.

Creating World Music

Materials:

- "Tulina's Carmona," by Kinan Azmeh; students' instruments

Procedure:

Motivic Composition

1. Provide students (in small groups) with a handout of empty sheet music, with time signatures remained intact (see Figure 5.4).

2. Have groups compose two different motivic phrases in the key of A harmonic minor. Motive #1 should be written in 7/8, and Motive #2 should be written in 3/4.

3. Students should write Motive #1 in measures 1, 4, and 7, and Motive #2 to measures 3 and 6.

4. Instruct students to develop a simple variation of Motive #1. This variation could simply be a transposition of the motive (up or down; step or skip), a changed rhythm, or an inversion or retrograde of the motive, or anything else the students come up with.

5. Students should write this variation in measures 2 and 5.

6. For measures 8, 9, 10, and 11, have students continue to expand upon their variation of Motive #1. By this point, groups should have originally composed music in all 11 measures of the main melody.

7. On their instruments, have students perform their new melody in unison. As a group, encourage students to make alterations to their melody as needed to establish a better melodicism or flow with their composition (as desired).

8. Have groups perform their new compositions for one another during class.

(*Note: This activity has been designed to be highly-structured, to give students the maximum amount of support with a potentially unfamiliar musical task. If students are either already comfortable with composition, or are looking for an additional challenge, this activity may be altered to be more open ended. In this scenario, students might be free to choose as many motives as they would like and arrange them in whichever manner they chose.*)

Integrating World Music

Materials:

- "Tulina's Carmona," classroom audio/video technology

Musical Beginnings

- "Tulina's Carmona" was composed by Josh Myers, the bassist for Kinan Azmeh's group *Kinan Azmeh's City Band*, circa 2010. This group, based out of New York City, is comprised of four core musicians: Kinan Azmeh (clarinet), Josh Myers (bass), Kyle Sanna (guitar), John Hadfield (percussion). They perform contemporary fusion music that blends elements of classical, jazz, and Syrian traditional music. This particular piece was inspired by several influences including Turkish *taqsim* (improvisatory introduction), Indian *ragas* (melodic modes), Syrian rhythms, and Afro-Caribbean *tumbao* (bass rhythm). Although this piece is notated, the final version was developed through musical negotiation that occurred through rehearsals (Myers, personal communication, October 11, 2017).

Musical Continuities

- This piece is a contemporary composition specific to this group and is not performed widely.
- Although this piece is notated with a specific form, there are several ways that it can be arranged.

Musical Meanings

- According to composer Josh Myers, this piece was inspired by a cousin of his moving to a different part of the world. He wanted to capture the feeling of being out of place and adapting to a new environment. This sentiment could connect to discussions about refugee populations, particularly from Syria.
- Musically, the contemporary Syrian music that Kinan Azmeh's City Band performs could also represent transculturalism in the 21st century. Instruments used in traditional Syrian settings include the *qanun* (zither), *kamancheh* (fiddle), *derbakki* (goblet drum), *daf* (frame drum), and *ney* (end-blown flute). In this group, the sounds have been adapted to accommodate an ensemble that typically consists of clarinet, guitar (nylon and steel string), electric and upright bass, *cajón*, and various other percussion instruments.

Learning Pathway #3

Zimbabwean Shona for Band:
"Chemtengure" by Lora Chiorah-Dye and Sukutai

Attentive Listening

Specific Use: Instrumental ensembles (e.g., band, orchestra, jazz); Grades 4–12

Materials:

- "Chemtengure," Lora Chiorah-Dye and Sukutai (Zimbabwe)

Procedure:

1. Ask students and discuss: "Do you remember any particular song you sang (or one you heard sung to you) in your very early childhood? How long ago? What were the songs about? Did only certain people sing them? Did you sing them, and did others sing with you? If asked, could you play the song on an instrument now? (Or, is it so personal that you might not even want others to play it?) Were they folk songs of sorts, or were they melodies from a favorite television show, or were they originally created songs? Have they ever been notated? Were they passed orally from an earlier generation?" (Consider asking students to ask their own parents/guardians these questions, and ask if they would consider sharing their findings in class.) *Such a discussion could constitute a lesson unto itself, and/or could "contextualize" the more technical aspects of the music that they will hear in this recording.*

2. Play track (first 30 seconds).

3. Ask, "Where is this from, and how do you know?" Students may recognize this as generally "African." With added listening experiences drawn from throughout that continent, students can be led to trace the origin of this music more specifically as Zimbabwean. (Note again that this was actually recorded in Seattle in 1996.) The *mbira* (sometimes Anglicized as "thumb piano") is native to south-central Africa, particularly the Democratic Republic of Congo, and Zimbabwe. Note also the various timbres and tessituras of the *mbiras* heard. Listen to the ring of the metal and the resonance of the wood, and the "rattle" that accompanies the performance of each note.

4. Play track again (same segment).

5. Listen and feel: Allow the layers of sound to "wash over" them. Later, more focused listening on the polyrhythms will reveal the complexity of the music.

6. Play track again (same segment).

7. Ask, "How many layers of rhythms do you hear?" *For now, encourage only a verbal response. If the class proceeds to Enactive/Engaged Listening stages with this particular selection, students may attempt to notate three layers of rhythm.* What else contributes to the "wash" of sound in the music? Note the alternating thumbs in the *mbira* performance, creating a multi-voice effect. The off-pulse accents (perhaps more felt than heard) also contribute to an expansive sense of time.

Figure 2.2 Layers of sound within the opening of "Chemtengure" (approx. 0:09–0:10)

8. Play track again (same segment).

9. Note the general call-and-response pattern. Ask and imagine: "How were the responses likely learned by the performers?" Note the "counterpoint" between high and low voices in the responses. Singers may have already known a general sense of harmonization for this style, which they then adapted specifically for this song, improvising at key points. It is unlikely that particular harmonies were ever notated.

Engaged Listening

Materials:

- "Chemtengure," Lora Chiorah-Dye and Sukutai; students' instruments

Procedure:

1. "As you listen to the piece, focus on one instrument or voice for as long as you can (it is helpful to understand that the melodic fragments are varied). Try to focus on its most basic structure."

2. Play track (first 30 seconds), repeat 2–3 times as needed for students to adequately hear the part they have chosen.

3. "Let's listen again, and this time, try to sing the part that you have been focusing on. Remember, it may be different from what your neighbor has been listening to."

4. Play track.

5. "Can someone share the part they were listening to by singing it?" Allow students to demonstrate their part. "Can you raise your hand if you were focusing on the same part?" Afterwards, try to have the students identify which instrument or voices are performing each of the parts of focus.

6. "Let's listen again, and this time, try to figure out the part you have chosen on your instrument. Be sure to play softly so that we can still hear the recording."

7. Play track, repeat as needed for students to become comfortable performing their parts. *The teacher might need to facilitate this by briefly rehearsing each of the elements that the students are performing one by one.*

8. "Now, try to perform a different part on your instrument—one that you weren't focusing on before."

9. Play track and repeat.

(*Note: Encourage students to focus on the three major melodic parts of the song: the mbira accompaniment, the call (from Lora Chiorah-Dye), and the response (from the choir). This activity could be considered complete when the students are able to identify and perform each part of the song's texture. The Enactive Listening exercise that follows will focus specifically on translating the mbira part to the band.*)

Enactive Listening

Materials:

*   "Chemtengure," Lora Chiorah-Dye and Sukutai; students' instruments

Procedure:

1. "Now we are going to focus on performing just the *mbira* part alone. Like the piano, it is played with two hands—typically the thumbs. In fact, that's why the *mbira* is also known as the "thumb piano." During the opening, there is an interlocking melody played by the two thumbs. Try to sing along with this part once you have it."

2. Play track, 0:00–0:04.

3. "Now let's do the same for the lower part that comes in afterwards. Try to sing along with this part once you have it."

4. Play track, 0:04–0:08.

5. "Now let's try to figure these two parts out on your instruments." Give the students ample time to complete this task, either by working in groups or individually. If students appear to struggle, partial notation may be provided, but the authors reiterate the importance of learning through aural transmission during this process.

6. "Now, with our instruments, let's split these two parts in half. Half of the ensemble will play the main melodic part (the first part), and the other half will play the countermelody (the second part)."

7. Play recording. *The teacher can decide how to facilitate this, from pre-assigning parts, to having students come up with the instrumentation themselves.*

8. "Now let's play along to the recording to see how well our parts fit." Have the students play along with the recording to check their execution of the style.

9. Play track, repeat as needed.

10. "Now that we are comfortable with the *mbira* part, let's try to perform it on our own. We are also going to record it so that we can compare it to the recording and check our stylistic accuracy."

    (Note: Recording and comparing to the original is another technique for engaging students in a critical examination of their performance. This can be used in conjunction with, or instead of, fading the recording in and out.)

11. "Now let's compare our recording to the example. Do we sound like an *mbira*? Why or why not? What are some ways that we can improve our performance to sound more like the ensemble in the recording? Is it ever really possible to obtain the 'true' sound of the *mbira*? Why or why not?" Have the students listen to their performance and compare it to the example. Have them discuss ways to improve and rehearse in their own groups.

12. Repeat this process until students are satisfied with their performance.

(Note: The focus of this lesson should be to acquire an understanding of how to reproduce the sound of the mbira. *Since the mbira is a plucked instrument, it has a percussive attack that gives way to a mellow buzzing sound. The students should consider how they might use their instruments to create this sound. Additionally, the piece lends itself to an exploration of compositional techniques used in Zimbabwean* mbira *music, such as repetition and variation. By focusing on the repetition and variation of these musical concepts, the students can focus*

on how their parts fit rhythmically with others, and can work towards creating a cohesive polyrhythmic texture.)

Figure 3.4   Notation of *mbira* part to "Chemtengure"

Creating World Music

Materials:

* "Chemtengure," Lora Chiorah-Dye and Sukutai; students' instruments

Procedure:

1. Remind students about the meaning of "Chemtengure", discussing the nostalgia about the man Vajeke that the song is singing about. In small groups, brainstorm various topics for students to sing about themselves. Have them first choose a theme, and then a phrase that encapsulates that theme (e.g., solidarity: "anything worth doing is worth doing together").

2. Have students write lyrics for their song in call-and-response form. Suggest that students may write their theme phrase as the response of the call-and-response pattern, making up short calls to accompany it (although they should also be encouraged to try other ideas as well).

3. Optional: With the help of online resources, challenge students to translate their songs into the Shona language.

4. Have students practice reciting the words to their poem (in English or Shona) in a chant-like manner, repeating the call-and-response numerous times. This will begin to create a rhythmic flow, which may eventually become the rhythm of their song.

5. As students begin to develop consistent rhythmic patterns, encourage them to add melodic inflections as well. Challenge them to create a response that repeats the same way every time, and allow them to choose between calls that alternate in melody/rhythm, and calls that maintain the same melody (but with different lyrics).

6. Add instruments. Consider emulating an *mbira* with an arpeggiated ostinato (like in the opening of "Chemtengure") on the piano, marimba, or guitar. Other students may use other percussion instruments to create a groove. Have students decide if there should be an instrumental interlude after a number of call-and-response patterns, and if so, what it should sound like.

7. Ask students to consider: Should the entire song remain sung, or should the melodies be placed on their instruments? Encourage students to create a full composition that uses vocal and instrumental sections within their newly composed song.

8. After rehearsing the song, have students experiment with dancing patterns: stepping patterns, formations, free style, etc.

9. For the class (or a concert), have each group share and perform their Shona composition.

Integrating World Music

Materials:

- "Chemutengure," classroom audio/video technology

Musical Beginnings

- This piece was composed by Lora Chiorah-Dye who immigrated to the United States from Zimbabwe in the 1970s. After her arrival, she began teaching her children Zimbabwean marimba and eventually founded Sukutai Marimba and Dance Ensemble.

- "Chemutengure" was arranged for *mbira* (percussion instrument with tuned metal tongues), guitar, and vocals. It is based on the *Shona* melody she recalled hearing when she was a child in Zimbabwe. She was inspired to arrange the song after moving to the United States in an effort to honor a vendor named Vajeke who she knew in her youth. This vendor would travel to the British boarding schools where the students were living to bring them familiar treats such as sweet potatoes. Since these boarding schools were so far away from their homes, the children often lacked access to familiar foods.

Musical Continuities

* This piece is performed widely and is considered part of the standard repertoire of *Shona mbira* music. Various arrangements of this piece are used in a variety of performance settings internationally including staged concerts, community gatherings, and children's education.

* Several recordings of this piece exist including a version performed by Zimbabwean music legend Thomas Mapfumo, the founder of *chimurenga* music. *Chimurenga* was a style of music that was used to create solidarity during the Zimbabwe revolution.

Musical Meanings

* *Shona* songs are based on proverbs or stories and typically contain multiple interpretations. In "Chemutengure," the song references wagon wheels and a wagon driver which refer to the ox-cart; the first vehicle used by Europeans in Zimbabwe. The word *chemutengure* is also believed to be an onomatopoeic reference to the sound the ox-cart wheels make as it travels down the unpaved roads. This song is said to have marked the "coming of the West," referring to British colonialism in Zimbabwe. This connects to Chiorah-Dye's memory of boarding schools that she attended in her youth. These sites, often established in rural areas by British missionaries, were a key component in assimilating Zimbabwean youth during the colonial era.

* In Shona culture, there is a high importance placed on connection to ancestral spirits (*mweya*) and *mbira* music is believed to be a useful tool in communicating with them.

Appendix 2

References and Resources

This list provides important resources and references relevant to teaching and learning world music cultures. Included are readings regarding the need for global approaches to music education, strategies to culturally relevant and responsive music teaching, and discussions of matters of social justice. Additionally, this list supplies notable Internet resources for locating recordings, films, and discussions that support the application of World Music Pedagogy in instrumental music education.

Music Education and Ethnomusicology

Allsup, R. E. (2016). *Remixing the classroom: Toward an open philosophy of music education.* Bloomington, IN: Indiana University Press.

Campbell, P. S. (2004). *Teaching music globally: Experiencing music, expressing culture.* New York, NY: Oxford University Press.

Campbell, P. S., McCullough-Brabson, E., & Tucker, J. C. (1994). *Roots & branches: A legacy of multicultural music for children* (Vol. 2). Wauwatosa, WI: World Music Press.

DeLorenzo, L. C. (Ed.). (2015). *Giving voice to democracy in music education: Diversity and social justice in the classroom* (Vol. 2). New York, NY: Routledge.

Fitzpatrick-Harnish, K. (2015). *Urban music education: A practical guide for teachers.* New York, NY: Oxford University Press.

Lind, V. R., & McKoy, C. (2016). *Culturally responsive teaching in music education: Fromunderstanding to application.* New York, NY: Routledge.

Morrison, S. J. (2001). The school ensemble: A culture of our own. *Music Educators Journal, 88*(2), 24–28. http://doi.org/10.2307/3399738.

Nettl, B. (1995). *Heartland excursions: Ethnomusicological reflections on schools of music* Champaign, IL: University of Illinois Press.

Nettl, B. (2015). *The study of ethnomusicology: Thirty-three discussions* (3rd ed.). Urbana, Chicago, & Springfield, IL: University of Illinois Press.

Pittman, A. M., Waller, M. S., & Dark, C. L. (2015). *Dance a while: A handbook for folk, square, contra, and social dance.* Long Grove, IL: Waveland Press.

Reimer, B. (Ed.). (2002). *World musics and music education: Facing the issues.* Reston, VA: MENC.

Rice, T. (2013). *Ethnomusicology: A very short introduction.* New York, NY: Oxford University Press.

Sarath, E. W., Myers, D. E., & Campbell, P. S. (2017). *Redefining music studies in an age of change: Creativity, diversity, and integration.* New York, NY: Routledge.

Schippers, H. (2010). *Facing the music: Shaping music education from a global perspective.* New York, NY: Oxford University Press.

Small, C. (1998). *Musicking: The meanings of performing and listening.* Middletown, CT: Wesleyan University Press.

Sturman, J. (2015). *The course of Mexican music.* New York, NY: Routledge.

Titon, J. T., Cooley, T. J., Locke, D., Rasmussen, A. K., Reck, D. B., Scales, C. A., Schechter, J. M., Stock, J. P. J., & Sutton, R. A. (2017). *Worlds of music: An introduction to the music of the world's peoples* (6th ed.). Boston, MA: Cengage Learning.

Turino, T. (2008). *Music as social life: The politics of participation.* Chicago, IL: University of Chicago Press.

Wade, B. (2009). *Thinking musically: Experiencing music, expressing culture.* New York, NY: Oxford University Press.

Education and Social Justice

Freire, P. (1970/2010). *Pedagogy of the oppressed.* New York, NY: Continuum.

hooks, b. (1994). *Teaching to transgress: Education as the practice of freedom.* New York, NY: Routledge.

Ladson-Billings, G. (2006). From the achievement gap to the education debt: Understanding achievement in US schools. *Educational Researcher, 35*(7), 3–12. doi:10.3102/0013189X035007003

Valenzuela, A. (2010). *Subtractive schooling: US–Mexican youth and the politics of caring.* Albany, NY: SUNY Press.

Films and DVDs

Barber, R. (Producer & Director), & Lambertson, A. (Director). (2013). *The whole gritty city* [Motion picture]. USA.

Neville, M. (Producer & Director). (2015). *The music of strangers* [Motion picture]. USA: Participant Media.

O'Connell, C. (Producer & Director). (2013). *Sousa on the rez: Marching to the beat of a different drum* [Motion picture]. USA: American Public Telecommunications.

Websites

The Association for Cultural Equity. www.associationforculturalequity.com.

The Mayday Group: Action, Criticism, & Theory for Music Education. http://act.mayday group.org.

Smithsonian Folkways Recordings. www.folkways.si.edu.

Wind Band Literature: A Conductor's Perspective by Andy Pease. http://windbandliterature. org.

Index